PRODUCE & PROMOTE YOUR
Music Video

by Greg Forest

HAL•LEONARD®

Hal Leonard Books
An Imprint of Hal Leonard Corporation
New York

Copyright © 2007 by Greg Forest

Published in 2007 by Hal Leonard Books
An Imprint of Hal Leonard Corporation
19 West 21st Street, New York, NY 10010

Produced in association with Mike Lawson, Lawson Music Media, Inc.

Printed in the United States of America

Cover and book interior design by Stephen Ramirez
Cover photo by Chris McClarney
Cover art direction by John Williams/Sound Art Management, Nashville, TN
Edited by Patrick Runkle

Library of Congress Cataloging-in-Publication Data is available upon request.

ISBN 978-1-4234-2727-8

www.halleonard.com

Dedicated to Cindy Terry and Bobby Rector

Giving credit where credit is due could fill a whole book but just to skim the top of my thank you list:

Thanks to the great folks at Hal Leonard Publishing, Mike Lawson of Lawson Music Media, Stan Morris & Melody Corner Music, Wegner Media Productions, Studio Gazelle, Alex Abravanel and Music Office Europe, Turk, Bill Flenniken, Dalis Allen and the Kerrville Folk Festival, Jay Adams and Roadhouse, Jason Strange, Ronnie Leatherman, Blake Olsen, Gaby & David, Tony Young, Ron & Linda Fujiu, Mojo Mickey Lees, Kristian Fjellstad & Duluth, Linda Bullard, Joe Mann, Suzanne Freeman, Hill Country Happenings, Wes & Victoria Hamil, Budreaux Galoote, Desiree Hitchcock, Arlin Williams and Greg Phillips, Louis Real, Jennifer King, David Sumners, Casey Monahan at the Texas Music Office, Louise Meyers at the National Folk Alliance, SXSW and all the video crews over the years that have given so much on locations sometimes less than optimal.

CONTENTS

Contents

Introduction

In recent years, the public image of the musician and recording artist has changed. Once just a pretty face on an album cover with a catchy tune, musicians are now one-stop multimedia commodities. The promotional tools available to the average musician have become more plentiful, cheaper, and much easier to access and use.

With the rise of the Internet as the primary medium for the distribution of new music from unknown artists, the playing field has leveled somewhat from the old brick-and-mortar days of the major record companies. Bands with marketable material, a rabid fan club, and a kick-butt website have sold, in many cases, more units at a higher return than many of their major-label counterparts. The deal is sweetened by having complete artistic control over the creative process. This wasn't possible a few years ago; the only real outlet for new music was radio and cable TV, and the majors had all that airtime locked up. Only a few 3 a.m. "local talent hour" shows were available to showcase new artists.

The Internet and the MP3 boom of the late 90s changed the way that the consumer auditions new music, much to the dismay of the Luddite record labels that have been decrying the ability of consumers and fans to duplicate music without the industry's help. I remember when the RIAA was up in arms over a new technology that was sure to "bury" and "bankrupt" the industry. That innovation was the cassette tape. It came as little surprise that they freaked out over

Napster and the MP3 revolution. I suspect that one of these days, the record companies will figure out that they can still make a ton of money and not make records. As many people have noticed, digital delivery over broadband is the future, and the days of large-scale mechanical reproduction of music are likely drawing to a close. In fifty years, a CD may be just as quaint as an 8-track tape.

Times change. Perhaps I am a bit late in making the announcement, but it's now the 21st Century. Cassette tapes, high-tech CDs with photocopied band bios, and even nicely ripped MP3 files just aren't enough for today's savvy music consumers and venue bookers. Good promotional materials reflect a good business plan; with the latest widely-available technology, now the little guy with big ideas can have a turn at bat.

Keep in mind also that many consumers don't just buy music for the audio content. They want artists who are cool. They want to know what the artist looks like, what s/he wears and whether or not the front person is a hottie. No medium to date can deliver these goods better than video or film. For the budding artist, there is no place better to get your message out to the world than the Internet via an artist website, YouTube, Google Video, MySpace and the other myriad of "Web 2.0" sites.

The internet and streaming video are propelling us into the industry's future; every month, it seems that a new and exciting technology pops up, making the online experience even more immersive and entertaining for the music consumer. It is our job as artists and producers to share our vision and embrace this technology with open arms. You don't have to become a computer nerd, but rather you need understand that technology is just another tool; musicians should try to be as experienced in using it as possible. Failing that, befriend a computer geek who can handle the tech for you!

In 1993, my record company was planning the release of two albums for a new artist and we were looking to expand our traditional promotions with a live concert video. With the best prosumer cameras, switchers, and a bit of nice lighting, we shot our first multi-camera live concert. In the years since, we have videotaped over 150 artists performing in various venues and concept videos. In every case we were working on a small, sometimes nonexistent budget. Along the way we learned a thing or two about budget video and film production.

This book and accompanying DVD are targeted not at video professionals, but instead at musicians and bands looking to get more exposure through the medium. Any video professional will tell you that HD is the only way to go right now, and I am not going to argue the point. However, professional video production can be expensive, and this book is targeted at the do-it-yourself musicians who have access to a decent digital video camera or two and want to try their hand at being the next YouTube rage without breaking the bank. You don't need HD for that. The videos accompanying this book and DVD were shot with consumer models readily available at most electronics discount stores. I will unabashedly say that this is a discount-store production.

We are going to walk step-by-step through two projects in the course of this book: a multiple-camera live concert video, and a one-camera lip-sync "concept" video. Both of the methods have their strengths and weaknesses, but by the end of this book you will be up to speed on how to get a music video project planned, produced, and promoted. I am going to have to share a few technical details with you, primarily to help you plan your attack and give you some background, but for the most part I will be using layman's terms and equipment commonly found on new computers and available at consumer outlets. Although we will drill down slightly on basic concepts, I am trying not to get into a great deal of technical nitpicking. I hope you walk away with a handle of the basic skills that make music video so much fun to produce.

I am writing with the assumption that the reader has a bit of experience with computers already. You should already know how to open and save a file, scan, crop and photo-correct an image. These are tasks you have probably already performed dozens of times so I am not going to touch on many of the basic operations of computing.

I need to say up front that I am a Windows user. I find Windows hardware and software to be a cheaper solution for the budget-minded media creator. Many of my friends use Macs to accomplish the same tasks, and they are great machines. Keep in mind that most of the actual video techniques I will be covering in this book—even the ones related to video editing—are applicable to both platforms. First, this is because Adobe Premiere, the program I use on the PC, is also available for Macs. Second, even if you want to use a different editing program, it is my experience that most if not all of the programs have essentially identical feature sets. Consult your manual if I am referring to a feature or technique that you can't easily locate. You will see that a screenshot of an edit in Final Cut doesn't look much different from a similar screen in Avid, Premiere, Edius, or Vegas. In all NLE systems, the timeline is the focal point of the project.

As I said, for the nitty-gritty editing examples in this book, I will be using images from Adobe Premiere. It's the most common video editing software on both the Mac and PC platform, and is the most common software bundled with video hardware—particularly high-end breakout boxes. Keep in mind that the last thing a music fan cares about is the software platform his new CD or DVD was developed on.

Planning, executing, and editing a music video are just the start. Once your masterpiece is complete and you are all dressed up, where do you go? Thanks to Internet technology, there are now many outlets for your product unheard of as little as ten years ago. Who would have imagined that 55 million people daily (at last count) would log on to YouTube and watch matchbox-sized videos of everything from the latest post-punk band to Aunt Hazel's cat in the bathtub? Bands have carved out some pretty good turf and made some pretty decent money for themselves not by using part of the Internet, but by using *all* of it: a websites, e-commerce sites, email lists, MP3 sites, video streaming sites, bulletin boards, and all the other low-cost or no-cost promotional vehicles just waiting out there to be exploited. You have to do more than phone in a website and a video to make fame knock at your door. Like any worthy endeavor, it takes hard work to make it happen, but the payoff can be quite gratifying at the finish line. With a good music video, you can now look as cool as you sound!

You may notice on occasion I repeat a point. That means it is an important point. As an example, saving your project frequently is a good idea and I will be nagging you to do so constantly.

Throughout the book, you will also see numerous technical tips as sidebars; be sure to read them as they contain some vital information. There is also great info in the appendices, so don't miss them! And of course, the DVD contains the fruits of our labor as well as forms, motion backgrounds and menus, trial software, and more tips and tricks.

Like all "how to" authors, I'm going to try to be everything to everyone. Please wish me luck!

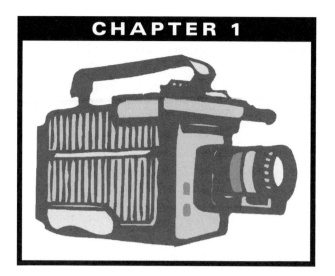

CHAPTER 1

The Emergence of Digital Video

If you buy a new computer today, regardless of whether it has a Microsoft Windows or Macintosh OS, it will in all probability be ready to rock with digital video. New computers have FireWire and USB ports to make video capture possible, and the operating systems now come with basic video-editing software that will burn a DVD of your family vacation pretty easily. I'm here to tell you it is not such a big leap from a family vacation video to your band's music video. I hope it's a big leap in terms of quality, but technically the basic principles are the same.

If you have spent any time on the Internet lately, you will find that most of the popular sites are now incorporating multimedia interactivity. In fact, a high level of interactivity is the hallmark of "Web 2.0" design. Music, user-created pages, and video blogs are commonplace. YouTube, MySpace, Facebook, and Google Video are four of the most popular web destinations, and for good reason. Much of the user-created content is very entertaining. Artists with no outlet for their creative talents now have a big pipe to millions of viewers—an outlet that didn't exist just a few years ago. At the time of this writing, there are dozens of well-designed sites offering a platform for online videos, and the number is growing almost daily. There is a list of current video sharing sites in Appendix B.

You may also have noticed while visiting these sites that there is a lot of pretty bad video out there. Most of the videos posted on

YouTube, for example, have very few views by site visitors. That is because most of the site visitors either don't know about it or don't like what they see. The video quality of the clips can also be awful. There are reasons that some videos on the web look better than others, and we will be looking into the process of delivering the best size and bitrate with your uploads a bit later.

Concept of the Three T's

What would you like to hear first, the good news or the bad news? The *bad news* is that a good music video takes a bit of **time**, **talent**, and **technology** to pull off. And money doesn't hurt either. The *good news* is that it is cheaper now than ever before to accomplish professional results, and the price is still dropping. Very few people look at shooting a vacation on a digital camera, dumping it into their computer, and burning a DVD as rocket science. On the other hand, for the commercial purposes of an aspiring artist, you want something more compelling visually than little Johnny getting birthday cake all over his face. But, as in many art forms, there is more than one way to skin a cat. Let's take a look at the most common and widely used digital video platforms.

HD is coming on strong. Perhaps I should correct myself; the industry is pushing it hard and its ascension to becoming the new standard is assured. Although you can find reasonably-priced HDTVs at Wal-Mart these days, at the time of this writing true HD content is still rare and there are platform battles being fought on delivery methods (BluRay vs. HD-DVD for example) that have yet to be resolved.

We looked at upgrading our video unit to HD and decided to wait for a few years while the technology advances to the point of affordability. For us to make the move to HD, we would need HD cameras, HD editing equipment, and triple the hard-drive space we now have. Also, we'd need HD monitors and DVD burners that can reproduce HD information. All of these items are readily available but are still priced out of the boundaries of the typical musician or consumer budget. Hence, we will be focusing on SD, or Standard Definition, video in this book. The dimensions of the screen are 720 pixels wide by 480 pixels high.

What Is Digital Video?

I am asked what the big deal about digital video is. People notice that although the tapes have gotten smaller, I am still sticking a video tape or disc in a camera, and recording and playing back on what looks like the same little camcorder. What's so new and different about that over a 15-year-old VHS or 8mm camcorder? The answer is "quite a bit, thank you," and all the news is good.

In days gone by, when you wanted to edit a video you didn't have many choices. Generally, you had to have a number of expensive video tape decks synchronized together so that an expensive video controller could queue up the rolls and make the transitions from one shot to the other. Then you previewed the decks to find your next shot and punched in the time code. The decks would fast-forward or rewind to the insert point, and then the controller would roll the scene change or transition and record the output to a master deck. This is known as linear editing. You start at the beginning and create one sequential scene at a time proceeding to the end. The process was time-consuming, expensive, and often infuriating. If you made a mistake at the beginning, you had to do the whole thing over again.

Most of this editing was being done with 3/4'' Beta decks, which were not cheap. An editing suite with three video decks, monitors, and a controller could rent for $75 an hour or more in 1980s dollars. You could save a bit of time if you owned a deck and could preview all the tapes and note where the in and out points of every shot were. Then you would create an EDL (Edit Decision List) that would script what would happen with the decks in the editing suite. Trust me, no one misses that era of video editing!

Enter the digital revolution and Non-Linear Editing (NLE). Under the new protocols, you capture the video clips from the camera or tape over a digital input (FireWire, iLink, 1394, USB) directly into the computer. After all the clips are loaded, you can cut and paste and move from one clip or scene to another instantly. The time saved just by not having to rewind and queue the tape decks is enormous; it's similar to the digital revolution in the audio arena.

With the price of consumer computers and video equipment starting to fall rapidly in the late 90s, the manufacturers of video equipment found a hungry market in the consumer sector. Software products started appearing by a number of developers and vendors such as Apple, Adobe, Digidesign, Pinnacle, Canopus, and others. By now, digital video editing has fully reached the masses. Let's take a look at the process from the concept in your mind to the video on the web and DVD.

PRIMARY FORMATS

When looking at digital video cameras, there are lots of choices out there: cameras that use the MiniDV format, cameras with DVD recorders built in, and now cameras that record direct to hard drives or large chunks of flash memory.

I prefer the MiniDV format. The camera tapes are small and easy to carry around and the picture quality, depending on chip number and size, is the best available. When you capture from a MiniDV tape, unless you have told your software otherwise, you are capturing essentially uncompressed video that will give you the greatest clarity, color depth, and widest range of choices in the editing and delivery process.

A note about *really* cheap video cameras: There are still analog cameras out there in formats that are becoming less popular each month: VHS-C, Hi-8, and Digital 8. These formats are much cheaper than the other formats, but that's because the formats are dying and the manufacturers are unloading old technology. I haven't seen a new camera model manufactured in these formats for a while now. Another primary reason why these cameras and technology are going away is that you can't export the video directly out of the camera into your computer; it must go through a conversion stage. The signal looks ok when the camera is plugged into your TV, but to get this video into your computer you will need some kind of breakout box and with an analog-to-digital circuit in it. You will lose quality in the conversion, and analog video also has telltale fuzziness that will detract from the professionalism of your project.

CODECS AND COMPRESSION

Try to steer clear of any format that compresses the video information in order to make more room on the recording media. The new video cameras with a built-in DVD or MiniDVD recorder might look handy for popping the disc out of the camera directly into your DVD player, but they are no help if you want to do any serious editing. The problem is that when recording directly to a DVD, the digital information is being compressed on the fly with a hardware converter in the camera. DVDs by definition use fairly strong MPEG-2 video compression, and that compression strips a great deal of the raw video information from the files. When you download into your editor, you will be working with files that have already been compressed, leaving you with the equivalent of very little video image quality to spare. At the end of the project, you will probably have to compress your video into another format—back into MPEG-2 for DVDs, MPEG-4, MOV, WMV for web deployment, or any other of the myriad video compression schemes out there. Because you will generally need to re-compress, at the beginning of the project you want the largest uncompressed files you can handle as the picture quality will be far superior to a compressed file. In other words, you won't be compressing the compression.

A special concern for music video is that double and triple compression can wreak havoc on your audio track. A common symptom of this is found on the web in audio or video files that sound like they are being played through a phase, chorus, or flange effect. Each generation of compression yields a funkier sounding and looking video. For more information on codecs, see the glossary or many of the web resources listed in the back of the book.

TIP

Regardless of what any manufacturer says, video compression causes image quality degradation. It creates what is known as a "lossy" image. The more you compress it, the more quality you are losing.

That being said, there are some types of high-quality compression that are OK for certain purposes, particularly when dealing with proprietary codecs. These codecs are usually tied to a particular piece of hardware or software, usually for the "real time" preview feature. As an example, if you buy a Pinnacle breakout box, you may be capturing your video in their proprietary codec, which is completely different from the Canopus video codec. This is not necessarily a bad thing as long as there is only one video editor on the project and the files aren't going to be shared with collaborators. Somewhere in your editing software, you should find the option to capture uncompressed video. To make things simple and transportable I capture, edit and deliver the master edit in the MSDV format if working for a Windows client and QuickTime if the client is on the Mac platform.

We had a large editing project ahead of us a few years back and decided to break it up into smaller components and farm out some of the editing to other editors. Our first speed bump was discovering that the other editors couldn't read our captured files because their editing box didn't have the video codec that we used while grabbing the clips. The time to re-render the clips into a standard and transportable format took more time than it was worth. We quickly learned a valuable lesson in video editing collaboration: Use standard video codecs such as MSDV or QuickTime, or make sure that all the editors can read the codec when capturing or editing your clips. A word to the wise: do it before you start editing and get everybody on the same page in advance.

Let's take a look at some hardware and software, so that you and I are on the same page before we start our video project!

CHAPTER 2

Hardware Considerations

When asked what gear I would use for a "dream" video shoot, I reply that I would prefer a stadium full of rabid fans and high-paid hottie models using a dozen IMAX 3D cameras—a few of them mounted on blimps or helicopters. This would make a very cool video for around a zillion dollars. With fantasy aside, the question is: Can I get the job done with my current camera and computer, or am I going to have to upgrade?

Again, there is some good news and bad news regarding editing video on computers. The bad news is that video editing requires tremendous processing and hard drive resources. The good news is that the price of computing and disk storage has dropped considerably, and the prices are continuing to fall. You will be paying a fraction of what such equipment would have set you back just a few years ago. (Trust me, I know . . . I paid for it back then!) Let's walk through a quick overview of what you should be looking for when buying video hardware and software.

The Computer

There is a general rule of thumb when buying and building a computer: More is better. The more RAM (Random Access Memory), the more CPU (Central Processing Unit) speed, and the more drive space you can pack into your editing box, the better. It is a fact proven by thousands of video professionals that you can never have too much processing or computer power. Let's take a look at each component of your computer and see how it adds up as a video production box.

THE PROCESSOR

Digital video editing, particularly creating effects and renders, is a very mathematical function and therefore extremely processor-intensive. Processor speed is always increasing and doubles every few years. Prices of older processors drop accordingly and there are numerous processors that can handle video editing. With PCs, you have a choice in terms of what processor you want; we will discuss that in more depth later in this chapter. With Macs, you are generally limited to two or three choices based on the currently-available configurations from the company.

THE MOTHERBOARD

There are many different flavors of motherboards out there but here are a few tips on what to look for and what to avoid in a video editing computer:

You will look for a board that supports onboard FireWire (1394) and USB 2.0. There are different flavors of FireWire and USB and you want the most recent. At the time of this writing FireWire-400 and USB 2.0 are the standards on new motherboards. Both have enough muscle for reliable video capture and playback.

Another important factor influencing the overall performance of your computer is the Front Side Bus (FSB) speed; a higher speed is better, of course. Motherboards in the 800 MHz range for a FSB are common. Avoid any motherboard that uses part of the system memory to power the video display. This is usually called "shared video RAM" and is found on many low-end desktop and notebook computers. It pulls down the performance of your computer considerably because the installed video card doesn't have enough RAM to do the job and has to borrow memory from the system RAM. The video card should have its own memory and shouldn't draw on the computer for display resources.

In motherboards—as in anything else—you get what you pay for. You will never regret the money you spend on a quality motherboard.

RAM MEMORY

If your motherboard is the hotrod engine, your RAM memory is the high-octane fuel. Like a good motherboard, you will want as much fast RAM as possible. Currently a 1 GB stick of DDR2 800 MHz RAM will run you about $50-75. Regarding RAM, again, more is better. The minimum amount you will need for video editing is 2 GB; I recommend 4 GB. You can upgrade from there to higher-speed RAM, registered RAM, dual-channel RAM, and other enhancements if you can afford it.

THE DISPLAY CARD

Oddly enough, the display card on an SD video editing computer doesn't have to be the absolute top-of-the-line model, so don't spend a fortune. Of course, better is always better, but keep in mind that you are only displaying at video resolution, which is 92 dpi in print resolution terms. You can get a great video card with 256 MB of onboard RAM for around $50 on the cyber streets of Internet vendors. Good graphics cards that drive two monitors and reach higher resolutions start at around $250 and the sky is the limit.

A great way to judge a video card is to see if it stands up to the recommendations of the latest video games. Go to any store that sells the latest computer games, pick out the most popular, and read the recommended specifications on the side of the box. In almost all cases, the recommended video display will exceed what is necessary for video editing. In terms of the computer display, the game developers are usually a couple steps ahead of the rest of the market; they try to create the most realistic and immersive gaming experience possible for the user. This puts them at the cutting—and sometimes bleeding—edge of video display development. If you are using a PC, your video card should support the latest version of a Microsoft technology called DirectX (the new cards are at version 10) and should also be compatible with the latest shaders and overlay specifications.

Another recent development in video cards is the PCIe (or PCI Express) bus. This is the "slot" on most new motherboards where you will install the video card, and you can now install two video cards on the same high-speed bus. This allows you to have one monitor for your workspace and another for your preview output, which is an important consideration. The video cards in this format are also considerably faster than standard PCI or AGP video. The performance and video quality of an entry-level PCIe card approaches that of the best standard AGP card.

TIP

Another old (as if anything is really that old in digital video) videographer's trick is to use your digital camera or deck as a preview video feed. While you are editing, you will probably have the FireWire or USB cable plugged into your computer. Most cameras and decks, when in VCR mode, will give you a preview on the camera's LCD. If you plug your analog outputs into your camera/deck you can use the composite signal from the camera to feed any TV or monitor that will accept a composite output. Instant preview output!

WINDOWS XP/VISTA

Digital video is very processor-intensive. You will need muscle to process your effects, transitions, real-time video previews and other software features. For Windows XP/Vista users, I recommend at least an Intel Pentium 4 processor running at 2.4 Gigahertz or an AMD 2400+ series processor minimum. Every small bit of processing muscle will come in handy while editing, so get the fastest processor you can afford; it is a great investment in time saving.

I have one video editing computer that runs reliably but is really somewhat of a dinosaur; it's a lowly Pentium 3 running at 550 MHz. Yes, it's a snail-paced box, but still in use at our facility for the purpose of video capture. It is sufficient for editing, but the render times for outputting transitions and effects are horrific compared to a new box.

Another of my primary editing boxes isn't that much of a screamer: a Pentium 4 running at 3 GHz with 2 GB of RAM. Another computer in daily use is a box running the AMD Athlon 3800 processor with 2 GB of memory. Both of these boxes are adequate for video editing, and the render times are short when necessary. I have no problem editing four streams of video in real time on either of these boxes.

MACINTOSH

All of the newer Macs are sufficient for editing video; in fact I believe Apple's top-down integrated computers make it a bit easier to get started in video editing than their PC counterparts. I haven't tried editing on the Macs the size of a paperback novel, but if the specs are there I'm sure they will do the job. All of the primary video editing applications are available on the Mac platform. Apple was a pioneer in video editing, and its early lead in the field is still reflected in the company's software products and those of its third-party developers and partners. One of the original markets for Macs was graphic design; these origins are reflected in software that has had longer to evolve than the Windows counterpart. It is probably an underlying reason that Mac users are so loyal; they have grown and evolved along with the platform. Later on in this chapter, Mac user Elliot M. Smith will open his box for you.

THE VIDEO DRIVE

I can't emphasize enough the necessity of huge and fast hard drives in your editing system and the importance of using your editing drives for nothing but video editing. The first thing you will need while putting together your video screamer is a dedicated video drive. The processing requirements of digital video make a dedicated video drive a must-have item in your toolkit. Uncompressed DV video files are the most desirable, but are also complete hogs when it comes to drive space. You might see your 40 GB hard drive in a different light when you discover that uncompressed video files can eat up hard drive space at the rate of 10 MB a second or more. One hour of raw video will take about 13 GB. If you are shooting with four cameras, multiply that by four, factor in temporary cache files, and the master movie you are going to render after the edit is finished, and you can see that drive space can disappear very quickly. For high definition, the file sizes are much, much larger.

TIP

When looking for a hard drive, a main benchmark to look for is the "sustained" data throughput. Most hard drives spend their lives winking now and then for quick trip to the drive platter. In video editing, however, the read/write head is literally "pedal to the metal" at all times when accessing video streams.

For Windows users, forget about using the FAT32 drive format for editing video. A FAT32 drive has a file size limit of 4 GB, which will severely constrain you. A 4 GB file is huge when it is created in Microsoft Word, but is a wimpy punk in the video world. Most recent computers use drives formatted with the NTFS system. You can check the format of your drives using "system tools" in the "accessories" menu from your start button.

Even if your primary or system drive is huge (150+ GB), it is a bad idea to edit video using the same drive that the operating system and your other programs reside on. As you go about your merry way editing video, in the background your software is making complex calculations to the files and creating temporary files on the system drive. This can really slow down performance when editing, and if something bad goes bump in the night you may lose more than just your video files; you could conceivably trash your system hard drive too.

You should be looking for a drive that is in the 200-300 GB range, one that spins at 7200 rpm or faster, with at least 8 MB of cache memory. You will see very inexpensive drives that spin at 5400 rpm, but we have discovered hiccups and ugly artifacts in some of these slower drives while we are editing. If you have a newer computer, install SATA drives over ATA. I have my video editing drive set up in the BIOS as the slave to the system drive IDE master, and both on the primary bus channel. All aspects of the drive I/O are on the same IDE bus and channel. Read your manuals and/or do some quick googling on your system to figure out how to set up your drives this way.

Video pros commonly use SCSI drives in a RAID array with discs spinning at 10,000 rpm. In a perfect world, a screaming fast SCSI array is top dog, but you can produce broadcast quality video using considerably less. My version of a "poor man's RAID" is just to buy another large external drive and copy my whole drive to the other drive after the end of each editing session. It takes a while, but I have two complete copies of the project at any given time; should one drive fail, it is easy to continue work on the project from the surviving drive. It's not as good as RAID, but it gives you a bit more flexibility in drive usage.

Drives suitable for video are dropping in price every day, and one of the most popular products out there are the external FireWire and USB 2.0 hard drives. At a local discount store here in my small town, I can get a 200 GB hard drive in a USB 2.0 enclosure for about $85. The portability alone makes this a great option. If you want to move the files to another computer, just unplug the USB drive from one computer and plug it into another. For just another five bucks I found a drive enclosure that supported both USB and FireWire. This is also a great way to edit on a notebook computer that may not have a drive large enough for video or the ability to add another internal drive.

CAPTURE CARDS

If you are going to be using any analog input (VHS, VHS-C, 8mm) you will not have the luxury of a straight digital download from your video camera via FireWire or USB. To get these analog signals into digital format, you will need a capture card or breakout box. Make sure you get a capture card that will capture uncompressed video in DV format at 720x480 resolution. Most of these boxes will have s-video and composite inputs (red and white for audio and yellow for video) so you can hook up your older format cameras and decks to the capture card. The video information is usually transferred from the breakout box through USB or FireWire cable.

MONITORS

Again, bigger is better. The larger the screen real estate, the more of your editing environment you can see. This is why multiple-monitor systems are becoming so popular; you can have your editing software display on one screen and your output preview on another. At the time of this writing, the old-fashioned analog monitors (CRT) are, surprisingly, a better value for preview output because they deliver much greater detail and resolution than LCD or plasma displays. This is rapidly changing, as the new generation of LCD and plasma displays is looking pretty good. If your editing box has the capability of outputting HD of one flavor or the other, the new large LCD TVs can make a decent monitor and are available at any consumer electronics store. Although most of these LCD monitors do not function as true HD monitors, they can be much more pleasant to look at than a funky 17" display.

The Video Camera

If you are shopping for a video camera, whether new or perhaps a used eBay pearl, do your research first on the web. If you find you have interest in a given camera, google the brand and model number; not far down the list, you will find customer ratings of the product. See what the people who bought the camera think, and what they like and dislike about the product. This is a great way to shorten the list of prospective cameras.

There are dozens of manufacturers and hundreds of video cameras at the consumer level available on the market today. As the focus of this book is budget video, I will be looking at cameras that cost less than $1,000. I won't be A/B testing all the brands, but I will share with you an overview of features that you should look for and avoid. One great way to shop for cameras is to buy a few issues of the current video magazines; some of them list all the features and prices of new cameras, and many of these magazines have online content as well. Following is a discussion of the features to look for in a good camera.

LARGEST CCD CHIP POSSIBLE
The CCD array in the hardware part of the camera is the eye of the device. In essence, the larger the CCD chip, the better and clearer the video image. Chip sizes for sub-$1,000 cameras can be as small as 1/6th of an inch and as large as 1/3rd of an inch. The next step up is the 3-chip camera, but you won't find one of these for under $1,000 new.

FIREWIRE/USB 2.0 INPUT AND OUTPUT
Digital video production isn't much fun if you can't get the clips into your computer in an uncompressed format. Either of these formats will capture video from a camera and give you control over the camera or deck from inside most software. I prefer FireWire because the pro-level cameras and decks use this instead of USB.

MANUAL FOCUS AND EXPOSURE SETTINGS

Manual focus can be important while shooting a subject in a medium or close shot and the subject is moving in and out of frame. The auto focus is looking at the center of the screen or a certain number of "focus points" to set the focus for you. If the subject moves far enough out of the center of the frame, the camera focuses on the background. When the subject re-enters the frame enough to warrant the auto focus to shift back, you will have a few seconds of worthless focus adjustment frames. If you are using the manual focus, the focus stays the same and when the performer re-enters the scene, she is in focus.

If the camera doesn't have access to manual settings of exposure, the next best thing is to have multiple exposure settings similar to the ones found on digital cameras. Look for sunlight, low light, backlight, and high-speed exposure times. These settings don't give you the control manual settings do, but will put you much closer to a lighting match for the environment you are shooting in.

TAPE-BASED OR DIRECT-TO-DISC RECORDING

The old adage of "garbage in, garbage out" was never more appropriate than in digital recording. The goal is to record uncompressed video at SDV or standard definition. The MiniDV format records directly from the CCD to the tape with essentially no compression. (To make things slightly more confusing, DV is itself a compression codec, but it is a fixed format with high quality, and is essentially transparent to the end user.)

MiniDV tapes are inexpensive and as durable as other media. You can also archive your finished masterpiece back to tape when your editing is finished and lose no resolution in the process. And, every copy made this way remains "first generation" with no loss of information. New cameras that record from CCD direct to a hard drive are now common; if you are considering one, check the specifications to be sure you are getting uncompressed frames to the hard drive. The obvious advantage to this method is that if you are on the same codec page with your computer, you can edit the video directly from the camera hard drive; no video capture is really necessary. If the camera has a DVD recorder in it, you are probably not getting uncompressed data onto the DVD. Check the user manual before you buy!

LENS AND LONGEST RANGE OF OPTICAL ZOOM

Not all lenses are created equal, and in my experience the lenses on a camera brand I am unfamiliar with are not as good as the old pro and consumer standbys like Sony, Canon, JVC and the other major Japanese manufacturers. I have a preference for Canon lenses in general, but have many friends that love the Sony, JVC and other lenses. Optical zoom is a handy feature and can get you a good image at medium range. A 10X optical zoom is a good range of focal length and more than that might become a problem, especially on handheld shots. Digital zoom is another thing entirely and is addressed below.

STEADY SHOT OR IMAGE STABILIZATION

The best way to get a steady shot is a tripod, but some of the smaller and less expensive cameras have decent image stabilization that is good enough to help some long zooms. Not a primary feature, but very handy.

STILL PHOTOS

Keep in mind that standard DV resolution is 720x480 pixels. If the camera takes stills, you want them to be at that size or larger. I recommend a minimum resolution of 3 megapixels for video stills, which will give you a lot more to work with in editing those stills.

REMOTE CONTROL

Not an essential feature, but handy if you are both the shooter and the talent. (You could also consider walking back and forth to the camera as exercise for your health regimen.)

HIGH CAPACITY/LONG LIFE BATTERY

Check the estimated battery life when buying a camera. Look for lithium ion batteries that don't have the battery "memory" problem that plagued early digital video cameras, whereby the batteries would have difficulty holding a full charge. A spare long-life battery is also highly recommended.

GOOD ERGONOMIC LAYOUT

Good ergonomics are not just for aesthetic appeal. The ease of inserting tapes and accessing important buttons are key considerations. I also like a camera with a bit of heft as it will be generally easier to hold steady than an ultra lightweight camera.

A PAPER OWNER'S MANUAL

In an effort to cut costs, many manufacturers are delivering the owner's manual in Adobe Acrobat format. This could require you to spend your paper and ink to print out a copy. This is not necessarily a bad thing, but having the manual in hand out of the box is much more convenient.

Essentially Worthless Video Camera Features

DIGITAL ZOOM

If you have ever seen a 100X zoom digital image you will know why this feature is next to worthless. Images are extremely pixilated and mushy. The higher the zoom, the more mush appears. Conceivably you may want an extremely jerky and pixilated image for your video, but it isn't likely to be on your short list of tricks.

IN-CAMERA EDITING

Most consumer-level cameras will allow you some form of internal editing—at least straight cuts, but the process is slow and cumbersome and the results less than optimal. Editing 200 straight cuts inside a camera for a music video is not likely to happen.

LOW LIGHT /NIGHT SHOOTING

This is another image-degrading feature that might be appropriate for a short special effect. Some cameras have infrared lights on them to illuminate in complete darkness, but the image quality is low. The greenish tint to a clip shot with this feature can be converted to black and white to improve it somewhat, but unless you are looking for a specific night-vision look, you will not be using this feature often.

Online Deals

I have found the best prices for new and used video gear are generally to be found online. Good used accessories, video, lighting and production gear can be found on eBay. I bought a small Panasonic refurbished MiniDV camera on eBay not long ago for $100 and it's a dandy little camera. If nothing else I can use it for a backup or a capture deck and save the head life on my more expensive Canon GL-1. A refurbished or demo model will usually come with some kind of guarantee/warranty if you are buying from a large and respected vendor.

One thing to look for when buying a used camera is not so much how old the camera is but how many hours are on the record and playback head. The camera may be only six months old but may have been spending all that time fast forwarding, rewinding and recording. Check the buyer's return policy and read the item description carefully. I avoid camera and deck descriptions like, "I'm not a video geek but I turned it on and the picture looks great." Check the feedback from other buyers before even thinking of parting with your hard-earned bucks. Stay away from sellers that have no feedback.

When looking for lighting, check to make sure the light you just bought has a bulb and if not, whether bulbs are available. I found a great deal ($5) on a Bescor light complete with barn doors only to find that bulbs are next to impossible to find.

Real Rigs: Elliot M. Smith on Macs

HARDWARE

I use a 15" MacBook Pro, 2.33 GHz dual core, 2 GB of RAM, 256mb ATI video card. This is no longer Apple's top-of-the-line laptop, but as laptops go it is still high end. It's overkill for basic editing, but that's the kind of power needed to run many of the higher-end third-party apps in Final Cut Studio 2, not just Final Cut Pro itself, which can run on less. Another reason I need this setup is because I do motion graphics in After Effects, which is far more processor intensive than editing. Detailed specs on the latest MacBook Pros are available at *www.apple.com/macbookpro/specs.html.*

This is my first laptop. I bought it because I needed a laptop and it let me transfer over from a Windows XP environment as it can run XP natively through Boot Camp. Laptops aren't the first thing people think of for video editing, but dual-core processors and the ability to hold more RAM are changing this. I met an editor in New York who was editing for a low-budget TV show on a PowerBook, MacBook's predecessor, so those are capable as well, however they use PowerPC chips made by IBM/Motorola and can't run Boot Camp, so no XP or Vista. I've completed my migration from Windows, so I no longer need Boot Camp myself.

For drives, I have an ESATA (External Serial ATA) card made by Firmtek that fits in the express/34 card slot (*www.barefeats.com/hard83.html*). It allows me to use external drives with the ESATA connection. This allows me better-than-internal-drive data transfer rates from an external drive. It's faster than FireWire-400 or -800, although I've been considering getting a FireWire-800 drive as it's good to use multiple disks; some editors use one drive for storing files, one for temp files/scratch, and one for writing the finished video file. I feel that having two ESATA drives would be just as good, but that FireWire-800 will be more widespread since Apple is really pushing it, and that can help with working with different people. With FireWire-800 you don't' have to buy the Express/34 card, which is pricey. I've tried three drives with a borrowed FireWire-800 drive and it worked pretty well. Three are best, two are better than one, and one is still usable if it's big enough. You want the fastest drives you can buy, which is currently measured in revolutions per minute (big flash drives will be different, but they're a ways away).

Western Digital Raptor hard drives are the best I know of short of SCSI drives, which require a special controller card and are way more expensive for less space. Raptors do 10,000 rpm and come in acceptable sizes, though you'll likely still need more than one.

They're good for holding temp/scratch files, since those files change the most and need the most speed. Hard drives are now often the slowest part of a computer, they have seen the least advancement in speed compared to other computer parts, but they've gotten a lot bigger. I use a 400 GB, 7200 rpm Seagate drive since I haven't built the optimum system yet, and I don't like carrying more than one external drive if I'm traveling. Seagate drives come with a five-year warranty, they're cheap, and I hear good things.

I have a digital external monitor I often connect to my Mac that comes in the form of ViewSonic's 22" VX2235wm, with a 1680x1050 resolution flat panel. Apple makes nicer, higher resolution monitors, but they also charge a lot more. I say they charge too much, because the Viewsonic is great! It's best to match the color profiles of the external monitor and the Mac, it doesn't match perfectly, but it's close. I have a Sony SD monitor that I can connect through a camera to preview work; it's second-hand and

I don't know the model number, but it has a great picture and it's about 27". I rarely use it other than when capturing, which isn't a very pro thing to do, but I need a FireWire converter box to get it back out of the computer, or to reconnect the camera to preview on the monitor, and I don't. If I'm making a DVD, I'll burn a DVD and preview it on my CRT TV.

SOFTWARE

I'm using OSX 10.4.9, which is also known as Tiger; by the time this book comes out I'll probably be on 10.5 which is Leopard. I'm too new to Macs to have gone through an OS upgrade; I doubt it will be significantly different, but you can read about Leopard's new benefits on apple.com.

I edit using Final Cut Pro because I know that it's better than Final Cut Express, which is better than iMovie. Better simply means more features. I don't know which ones since I don't use Final Cut Express. It's great software, very responsive, and easy to use. When I was on a PC I edited primarily in Adobe Premiere. There were other choices, namely Avid, but Premiere was easily accessible and more intuitive than Avid, though crash prone and more limited. Final Cut Pro, I feel, is more geared toward a younger generation that has grown up with computers, since I'm 25 that's me. You can pick it up and use it; it's not that complex until you choose to make it that way, mostly by changing formats.

Avid is the other main choice on a Mac, but with Avid I feel I need training and that it was made for people like Walter Murch who are coming over from a film and early digital background. Avid's GUI is not that easy on the eyes either. I've only tried Avid on the PC and I don't intend to try it on the Mac. Getting the footage into the editor is not as straightforward since you have to place it in bins that aren't intuitive. I never got very far past that; I just didn't take the time to learn Avid. Still I would like to learn it though, since I know it's quite capable.

I shoot high-definition, which is supported by all flavors of FCP, as long as updates are run and you're using version 5. iMovie also does HDV, that's because it's a versatile format and will soon be in many consumer-level camcorders. iMovie comes with the Mac and may be good for absolute beginners, I don't know since I've never used it. But unlike Windows Movie Maker decent results can be had with iMovie. It's seen getting extended use in the movie *American Pie Presents Band Camp* by Stiffler's little brother to produce a *Girls Gone Wild* type video. I'm sorry to use that example because it means admitting I've seen that movie. But the point remains, it can at least be used to do that and likely a lot more.

FCP Studio 2 has just come out. I don't have it yet, but it contains FCP 6 and a program called Color, which I hear is a formerly $25,000 color corrector that Apple bought and repackaged to make up for its shortcomings in color correction. In FCP 5 I color-corrected a wedding recently that made my renders take forever, hopefully the color program will shorten that. Further, the color correction didn't look as good as stuff that I've done with Premiere or After Effects on the PC. I was told by Mike Curtis at HD for Indies that the reason for that was because HDV wasn't as robust as other formats, but I feel that it's more to do with FCP 5's color capabilities based on my experience editing HDV with Premiere. Maybe Color will give me an answer. Check out the link for more on FCP Studio 2, there's demo videos on there, and it's pretty awesome.

http://www.apple.com/finalcutstudio/

FCP STUDIO 2 AND A LITTLE MORE ON HARDWARE

FCP Studio 2 isn't supposed to work with hardware that doesn't have a dedicated video card. A lot of that has to do with color correction in Color, graphics work in Motion, and all the hardware acceleration that comes with the dedicated video card. Apple is known to make good use of hardware acceleration. PCI-e is better than AGP which is better than regular PCI. All three of those are better than a card built in to the motherboard that shares memory with the RAM to do its job—a lot of this is just like PCs.

There's some debate as to whether or not you'll be able to use FCP6 with a MacBook (non pro) or Mac mini that doesn't have a separate video card. My view is that it'll probably work for basic editing, but when it comes to doing titles or more complex transitions than cuts and maybe some cross fades, it'll slow down and interrupt your work flow. If you think about it, when working with video, you really should have a dedicated video card with as much built-in memory as possible. It's just logical. Even if you're just doing cuts, at some point you may want to push and the option should be there. You should buy the best hardware you can afford, or you'll pay in time and maybe frustration depending on where you skimp. Get as much RAM as you can afford.

LAPTOPS

If getting a MacBook, get a MacBook Pro over a regular MacBook; 15" or 17", it doesn't matter. Never buy a used laptop, especially off of eBay. It's best to go through Apple, and you're never going to get a deal because Apple controls their products in ways I've never seen. I am an experienced eBay user, I bought my first laptop there, and Apple ended up replacing my hardware after it proved to be a lemon. I was lucky, because they could've easily told me no. In fact they did, but I was persistent, and got my newer, faster model after having purchased the Apple Care protection plan and having it crap out on me a month out of its original one-year warranty. It always helps to have Apple Care, which is Apple's extended three-year warranty. PCs have issues all the time with drivers and lots of other stuff. Macs generally don't and if something goes wrong finding help isn't as easy, so it helps to buy the plan. If you don't and you have an issue, Apple will ask you first if you have it, then if you'd like to buy it. It's both useful and they get commission on it, so it gets annoying hearing about it fast, but it's worth the $200 or so.

DESKTOPS AND A BIT ABOUT ROSETTA

In the industry, the main Apple you'll see today is the G5 tower that uses PowerPC processors and thus can't run Boot Camp/XP. That'll change soon, the reason being that Apple changed over to Intel processors. Adobe, makers of After Effects, Photoshop, Illustrator, and lots of other pro applications, had to run under a program called Rosetta to work on Intel Macs. This program slowed complex software like After Effects to 40 percent of its intended speed or less. Pros said to hold off and let Apple transition and Adobe catch up, and that's happening today so soon businesses will be transitioning. G5 towers can likely be had for relatively cheap as many come on the market during this transition. However, G5's aren't capable of running Boot Camp, which is really important to letting people transition.

There are likely other things that PowerPC Macs won't be able to do, but Apple is really good about supporting their older hardware since they control their hardware, unlike Windows which runs on any mishmash of parts you can find in the dollar bin at Discount Electronics. Apple knows the specs of every computer that OSX is running on and will say with software releases what levels of Mac are compatible and they've been tested to work. Microsoft likely doesn't have a single employee that can name all of even just the network card manufacturers that PCs running Windows XP can use, much less all the other parts. Apples use just a handful of parts and that's a key benefit for Apple reliability.

Desktops/Towers are generally better than laptops since you can add on to them more cheaply and easily, with a higher-power end product. Prospective buyers should focus on G5s if they're really low-budget and make sure they do their research as to what kind of graphics cards and other specific parts are best for these machines. Internet forums such as dvinfo.net's editing area can help in that decision-making process. They are going to be more limited on these boxes since they aren't compatible with Boot Camp and who knows what else from third-party vendors that choose to only support the

Intel Macs; that will probably be rare initially and uncommon in years to come because most Apple programs are written in Universal binary, which works on both.

The best choice would be to get a desktop with Intel processors, the more cores and processors the better, obviously the fastest that you can afford. They're the future. Pick the editing program that you want to use, likely Final Cut Pro, and see what it requires. Final Cut Studio is a group of programs, some have more requirements than others, here's the specs for FCP Studio 2:

http://www.apple.com/finalcutstudio/specs.html

Look at any third party programs you're into and see what they need.

There are a few plug-ins for FCP or Adobe Programs that aren't Intel-ready yet, but they will be soon or they'll go out of business. FCP's site says editing uncompressed HD requires 4 GBs of RAM, so only the highest of high-end Apple laptops can meet the minimum requirements for editing uncompressed HD. If this is something you'll be doing a lot of, get a Mac Pro Desktop.

One more thing that's very important to remember: *Do not buy a cutting edge new Apple product until it's been out for a year or so.* When they switched to Intel processors like my laptop, there were a lot of problems with the initial product, and I got stuck with one. Some were fine, some not. My replacement is a million times better. Apples should never be unreliable, but lemons do exist, and you'll know if you have one pretty quick. If you have three problems while under warranty, they're more likely to replace it, especially in the first year.

Elliot M. Smith, Austin, TX
July 2007

My Personal Windows Hardware

Starting with the core guts of my primary video box I will have to admit I am a bit less muscular than my friend Elliot's rig. One thing in defense of my box is that it has been on for 14 months 24/7 and has never crashed or locked up. I have yet to see the infamous "blue screen of death" common to earlier Windows systems. This system is the first rock-solid Windows box I've ever owned. Here's what I'm running under my hood and why.

MOTHERBOARD

The core of my system is an ASUS A8N-SLI Deluxe motherboard. I choose this board because it had the features I was looking for; a fast Front Side Bus, a nVidia nForce4 SLI chipset, PCIe video slots, USB 2.0 and FireWire input and output, 7.1 surround audio card. The board has a good design that allows for setting up FireWire and USB from the front of the box and/or the back panel. The board also has gigabyte Ethernet 1000Base-T built in and screams on my local gigabyte network. This board was at the high mid-range in terms of prices but ASUS makes a sturdy and reliable board so I didn't mind the extra few dollars.

PROCESSOR

The brain of my box is an Athlon 64 3600+ dual core 2.2 GHz processor with Hyper Transport. I have been using both Intel and Athlon chips for the last seven years or so. Both are reliable. AMD's processors are rated by their "series" numbers, which are designed to make them equivalent in performance to higher-speed Intel processors, even though AMD clock speeds are lower. For example, an Athlon 3600+ would theoretically be equivalent in performance to an Intel Pentium chip running at 3.6 GHz even though the AMD chip is running at about 2.2GHz.

RAM

I'm a bit underpowered in RAM—and will buy a couple more sticks soon—as I am now using only 2 GB 800MHz DDR SD RAM. If price was not a concern, I would be looking at screaming-fast registered RAM, which is recommended by lots of video pros. It is sure to be in my next box.

THE OPERATING SYSTEM

I'm currently running Windows XP SP2 with a couple of updates like the new Media Player codecs. It took some time to tweak all my Windows video applications to run at maximum efficiency. I visited user forums of others using the same hardware/software and learned some tricks to improve performance and stability. This is the primary reason I haven't made the switch to Vista; I have always been reluctant to buy a new OS on the release's first pass. More importantly, many companies haven't released final versions of Vista drivers for their hardware. Windows XP with Service Pack 2 has been running great on everything I own, from my Pro Tools rig in the studio to the video editing workstations. I realize that Vista will become inevitable; I expect it will be on my next new PC but I will keep my XP licenses for the foreseeable future.

VIDEO DISPLAY CARD

I'm viewing my work through the PCIe version of an nVidia GEForce 6600 with 256 MB of onboard RAM. The card supports the latest version of DirectX and the most recent shaders. I initially bought one of these cards for my game box and liked it enough to put one in my video box. I will be upgrading soon to a two-card system that will display HD as my first small step into the HD world.

CAPTURE CARD

I've been using a Canopus DV Storm 2 in a series of boxes for the last three years or so. Although it no longer supports the more recent versions of Premiere and other software, the box works great with Edius, the Canopus editing software. I use the box primarily for analog I/O from VHS, Hi8, Digital 8, and other older formats. You can find a good deal on this breakout box on eBay and in terms of hardware reliability, I have never had a grabage frame on this breakout box. Canopus has since been purchased by Thomson Grass Valley, and support for the older product line is rapidly fading.

HARD DRIVES

Most of the time I am working off the two drives inside the box, both Western Digital SATA Caviar series spinning at 7200 rpm and with 8 MB of onboard cache memory. The system drive is 80 GB and the video drive is 160 GB. As a core part of my toolkit I have a huge library of backgrounds, stock footage and photos, 3D models and other toys on an external USB 2.0 200 GB drive. I find myself reaching for this drive frequently, and it is almost always plugged in at the beginning of an edit. I have another 200 GB external USB 2.0/FireWire drive that I use with my notebook computer for editing on the road.

AUDIO COMPONENTS

I'm pretty wimpy on the editing box's audio configuration. I am using the ASUS motherboard's onboard 7.1 sound card (RealTek architecture) driving a set of Altec Lansing speakers with an 8" subwoofer. The speakers sold for under $50; one cool feature I like is that one of the desktop speakers has the control knobs on it and a headphone jack that mutes the speakers when plugged in.

Software

ADOBE PREMIERE PRO V2.0

This is my old tried-and-true editing buddy. Having used the program for the last four releases or so, I know my way around the software and am quite happy with the results. We will be looking at screens of Premiere throughout the book so I won't go into much detail here except to say the platform is a very good one for both new and experienced editors.

CANOPUS EDIUS 2.0

This is an older version of Edius that I have kept installed to use with my DV Storm 2 breakout box. Edius is a great application once you get used to the user interface, which is much different from other editors but quite intuitive once you get going. Another frequent use of Edius is for fine tuning streaming output via the Canopus Procoder LE output plugin. Even this light edition gives you a lot of power over your streaming output. Here's a look at the Edius workspace:

PHOTOSHOP CS

What can I say about the graphics program that the whole world ranks as number one? I doubt I can add much to the long list of endorsements except the fact that I use it almost every day. That being said, my favorite image editing program is . . .

ULEAD PHOTOIMPACT V11.0

I've been using this software since version 4.0 and for the price ($99), there is nothing better under the Windows platform. The newest version comes with more plugins and templates than you will ever need. For Windows users the interface is much more intuitive than that of Photoshop and the software sells for a fraction of the Adobe product.

PARTICLE ILLUSION 2.0 LE

I will be talking more about this cool program in the chapter on Computer Graphics. Using particle emitters similar to those found in feature films, this 2D software can add a lot of spice to a video. You can create explosions, starbursts, lens flares, smoke, water and hundreds of other particle-based effects very quickly. As with PhotoImpact, the price of admission ($99 SRP) makes this software a real bargain. Trial versions of the new version 3.05 are on the accompanying DVD in both Mac and Windows format.

BRYCE 6.0

I have been a Bryce fan for years and was somewhat dismayed when Corel bought the company and did nothing for a couple years. The software is now in the DAZ3D family of products and they have released two new upgrades in just the last year. Bryce is great for creating motion backgrounds and virtual locations and sets. Full versions of Bryce 5.5 for both Mac and Windows are included on the DVD.

VUE ESPRIT 6.0

This offering from e-onsoftware.com is the mid-range program of their 3D animation and environment creation software. The scenes you can create in Esprit are suitable for broadcast and even film use. The models created can be quite complex and the render times for even the shortest video clip can be huge. As an example I had a very complex (4,000,000,000+ polygons) that took almost 19 hours to render the first frame.

POSER 5 AND 6

I don't use Poser for its most common features—animating 3D characters—but I do use some of the props that come with the software. Frequently, I import 3D objects into a Poser set for lighting, which gives me great results with a pretty short rendering time.

COFFEECUP SOFTWARE

Here's another company that I am a true believer in. They make a variety of web widgets that can help you easily deploy photo albums with soundtracks, Flash-based video players, and just about every kind of desirable web widget known to man. Their HTML editor is top-of-the-line and the footprint is much smaller than other web page applications like Front Page or Dreamweaver. Because of this small hard drive footprint (15 MB installed), I use the application on my notebook computer for web page editing. A nice selection of Windows-based trial software is on the accompanying DVD.

Configuring the Video Drive

When you first purchase a hard drive for your video, under Windows there are a couple of things you want to do to prepare the drive to run as fast and efficiently as possible. On a Windows box, format the drive as one large partition and use the NTFS file system rather than FAT32, as I previously discussed. On the first boot with the new drive installed, go to the BIOS screen (usually accessed with the "Delete" key as soon as you see the BIOS splash screen) and set the drive for DMA/UDMA access and turn off any S.M.A.R.T. functions.

After the drive is installed, click on "My Computer," select the drive you just installed and select, "Properties." You will see a couple of tick boxes that should be unselected, especially the "Compress drive" option. These are background applications that take up RAM and processor resources. The "Compress drive" option is the last thing you want to do to a video drive. It compresses/decompresses the files on the fly and can slow you down to a crawl. If you are using an existing drive and experience sluggish response, you might want to check these settings.

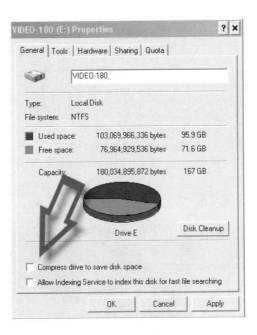

I also recommend defragmenting the drive on a regular basis and definitely before starting a project or just before final delivery, especially if you are writing to DVD. Defrag can be a long process so it's a good idea to start the defragmentation before retiring for the evening; a cleaner, faster drive will greet you for breakfast. If you want even better performance on your video project, format the video drive prior to starting the project. (Of course, formatting the drive will erase all information on it, so be sure you know what you are doing!)

Furniture

I know that furniture is not commonly thought of as gear, but if you are going to be spending countless hours hunched a computer monitor, you need to consider getting an ergonomic workspace together. Getting a chair with lower-back support, placing your monitor at a vision-friendly distance, and positioning your keyboard at a comfortable level will all leave you feeling much better at the end of the day and might make you able to endure longer days at your digital oars. Remember to step away from time to time, stand up, and stretch a bit. I'm not going to tell you that good posture makes a better video, but having a comfortable and ergonomic workspace can increase productivity.

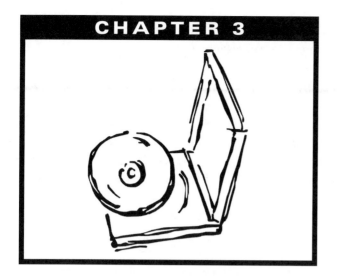

CHAPTER 3

Software Platforms

Regardless of whether you are a Mac or PC user, there are some common features in editing software on both platforms you should be looking for when considering a purchase. If you are on an extremely tight budget, the video editor bundled with either commercial platform—iMovie on Macs and Movie Maker on Windows—can create a simple video. You should find this on every new Mac or PC. These simple editors lack features compared to their more expensive counterparts, but a reasonably decent and simple video can be produced using these entry-level products. iMovie under OS X does have some keyframing features, where Movie Maker doesn't as of release 2.0. You can get something done with these tools but features-wise you get what you pay for. We'll be discussing keyframes a bit more shortly.

When making any editing software purchase, be sure to read the part about what the manufacturer regards as the minimum and recommended hardware necessary to run the application. As the words indicate, I recommend leaning towards the recommended hardware; the minimum will run the software but only minimally.

Although specifications are changing as I write this sentence, there are some major players that we should take a short look at. Remember that there is a mountain of information on these software platforms on the Internet, a great deal more than can be included here. That said, let's take quick look at the most popular platforms or at least the ones I have some experience with.

(Note that there are Linux programs like Kino (*www.kinodv.org*) that will do video capture and editing, but the feature set is lacking compared to the programs I will focus on. This is not a knock on Linux; Open source is a great software concept and I am anxiously awaiting great video editors for any open-source platform. However, the wait could be a long one. Video editing software is complex and requires a long development time.)

TIP

Just about all of these programs have a demo or trial version available on the Internet at the manufacturer's Internet site. Many of them are included on the accompanying DVD. Try before you buy.

Adobe

ADOBE PREMIERE

With robust support for both Mac and PC platforms, Premiere is the seminal desktop digital editing software and has had a long, illustrious career as top dog. (Adobe released the first version for Macs in 1991, long before most people considered the computer a workable video-editing tool.) I have been using Premiere since release 3.0, when I got my first trial copy "free" with a video breakout-box bundle. The upgrade price for each subsequent release is generally affordable. Other more recent software options are moving to dethrone Premiere, most notably Final Cut on the Mac platform.

One of the advantages to using Premiere is that it interfaces nicely with the other members of the Adobe family of products, most notably Photoshop and After Effects. The more recent releases of Premiere have made interoperability between the different Adobe applications as seamless as possible. Many of the key shortcuts, menu structure and features mimic the other Adobe products so that once you have a handle on one of them, you have a good head start on any of the others.

AFTER EFFECTS

Like Premiere, Adobe After Effects has become a standard in desktop video special effects. It is commonly used for compositing and animating stills and 2D objects in a 3D space. It is similar to Adobe Photoshop in its approach to layers. The application is also well suited for doing effects previsualization for film. With any effects application suitable for broadcast or film, you can experience some extremely long render times depending on the length and complexity of your animation. After Effects is no exception, but it does render considerably faster than most similar applications I've used.

ENCORE DVD

Encore DVD is a very easy-to-use DVD authoring program that gives professional results. I have been using it almost exclusively since the first version. The software makes setting up navigation, motion menus, and extra features quite easy and I was producing good looking DVDs in one afternoon of sitting down with the application, and without the manual after the first ten minutes.

PHOTOSHOP CS

Although not a video application, Photoshop is excellent for touching up stills or creating image files with an alpha layer for direct import into your editor. These images with transparency are easily imported, tweaked, and sent back and forth between the entire creative suite. Photoshop is the "world standard" for image creation and tweaking.

Apple

FINAL CUT PRO

This has become a first-tier application very quickly and is becoming the most popular editing system for Macs. There are many third-party plug-ins available, and the program enjoys a large and loyal user group. According to users who prefer Final Cut to other Mac editing applications, the big difference is in the workflow layout, which to them is more intuitive. Final Cut Pro is the heavy hitter on the Mac side.

MOTION 3

Motion 3 is a 3-D real time compositing environment as part of Apple's video suite. Multiple layers can be added to a 3-D environment and manipulated in 3-D space. This is Apple's answer to Adobe After Effects.

Thomson Grass Valley

Grass Valley has been a fixture in the video and film hardware industry for some time now and with the acquisition of Canopus has launched a new product lines for both prosumers and the high end video pro. This company is particularly well known for its breakout boxes that will allow you to capture a wide range of video sources and has every input and output known. The older Canopus breakout boxes can be found on eBay but use care: The plug-ins for Adobe Premiere have not been supported since Premiere Pro version 1.0. I have an older DV Storm2 card that I use primary for analog capture; the box will let me capture analog composite and s-video sources and I use this box a lot when archiving old footage for clients.

EDIUS

Edius was one of the first editing environments to be able to blend clips from different sources (SDV, HDV, SVHS, etc.) onto the time-line in real time. Although initially manufactured for use with Canopus breakout boxes, the recent versions of Edius work with any compliant FireWire channel.

Sony Media Software

VEGAS

The first time I ran into Vegas—which used to be called Vegas Video—was through a friend of mine who was in love with the software for audio editing! My pal was happier cutting and mixing audio inside this video application than in his audio software, and Vegas's full-featured audio toolkit is one of its main selling points. I used an older version of the program awhile back and the output is of high quality suitable for broadcast and digital authoring. Every Vegas user I know loves the software and I've seen a great deal of stunning output from Vegas systems.

SOUND FORGE

Although an audio application, the new version of Sound Forge has new features that might make a video editor or audio post engineer take notice. First you can now work with more than just two channels. Another handy feature is a video preview that will allow you to do a great deal of tweaking of your audio master. I sometimes fly my finished AVI or MOV file into Sound Forge for last minute touchups and normalization to the core video file.

Pinnacle Systems

PINNACLE DV-500

One of my first capture devices was a DV-500 system from Pinnacle. I used this system for about two years with Premiere and it was a fine architecture. In fact if you can find a used system, it might be a great capture device even today. Pinnacle makes a variety of I/O solutions at a very good price point.

PINNACLE STUDIO

Studio is a very popular consumer editing platform, primarily because it is the software included in lower end video bundles. I found the Pinnacle interface to be less than intuitive, but the program is stable, works fine for capturing analog sources and digital camera control, and comes with a good library of effects and transitions.

Avid

AVID XPRESS

Avid is the standard film and video editing software used in the professional film industry, but it is not generally considered a consumer or "prosumer" product. I have only spent a few moments at an Avid workstation, and I found the interface to be about as confusing as it gets. However, my friend who owned the system has output some of the best music video I've seen. For a long while the price of admission to an Avid workstation was prohibitive but they now have a more affordable pricing model. Judging by pricing I googled up on the web, however, an Avid system with all the bells and whistles can cost several times more than that of other editing platforms.

Ulead Systems (Corel)

PHOTOIMPACT

As I described above, the interface for this product is much more intuitive than that of Photoshop and the software sells for a fraction of the Adobe product. Although not as powerful as Photoshop in some areas, it is a superior value.

DVD WORKSHOP

This DVD authoring software comes in both a Pro and Express edition. Both are excellent, with the Pro product being a complete authoring platform that produces industrial strength DVDs with all the bells and whistles.

VIDEO STUDIO

This is ULEAD's primary video editing product and is commonly bundled with capture cards and breakout boxes. I've never used the product but it is quite popular at the consumer level.

COOL 3-D

When I wanted to do 3D animated titling the options a few years ago were few and expensive. I didn't want to have to become a 3D Studio or Maya ninja just to fly a bit of extruded text around the screen.

Enter Cool 3D. This application is great for creating nice animated text-based logo rolls. If you visit my video website, gregforestmedia.com, you will see that my site logo roll was done in Cool 3D. Since that time I have been using Vue Esprit for text animation, but the price point for Cool 3D makes it very attractive.

Steinberg Wavelab

Ok, ok. I know that Wavelab isn't for video editing. But since I mentioned earlier that Sound Forge was good for audio post sweetening, I had to mention that Wavelab will also give you a video preview and contains a lot of great sweetening tools for audio post. It also has a very reasonable installation footprint suitable for laptop computers.

Getting Started: Preproduction

You must start by making a number of important decisions for your video masterpiece, and some of these decisions may have an impact on the type of hardware and software setup you need to accomplish your goals. Let's take a look at the check list of components necessary to get the job done.

It All Starts with You

Any creative project starts with the artist's idea and vision. Music video is no different, but instead of focusing exclusively on what the music sounds like, we are looking at not only that but the artist's visual image. The music is the core of the project, but the images you project over the sound can be as compelling as the song itself.

In music video you can sometimes get lucky: The lyrics to the song can easily become the shooting script. But this isn't always the case. Here is the first verse of a song I wrote for this chapter. Ok, I'll be honest; I only wrote one verse of lyrics:

I woke up on another planet, one that had two moons
I hopped aboard my starship, with aliens singing my tunes
As I flashed through the star gate into a dimension quite unknown,
I saw Cerberus, Guardian of Hell, gnawing on a bone.

Can you see where my vision and my video content creation abilities might run into conflict? Here's another ditty:

She is the one I love, she is the hottest ever
I met her in a bar. She winked and pulled my lever
We danced the night away under an urban moon
I sat down at the table that night and wrote down this tune.

As you can see, the second set of lyrics might act as a script. I'm not saying that you can't create a two-mooned, alien-infested video, but it will take considerably more time, graphics, and computer resources than shooting your girlfriend at a local honky-tonk on a full moon. Fanciful computer graphics can be done in your garage but will take a lot more effort, as we will shortly learn.

It is not uncommon—in fact it is extremely common—that the images in a music video have no correlation whatsoever to the lyrics of the song. The video goes by with a flurry of shots of the band hamming it up and fast cut shots to B-roll material. Stock footage can be used. You see a lot of videos like this. Why? In two words, it's cheap and easy.

Live Or Lip-Sync?

A lip-sync or "concept" video has its one magic moment—the moment you drop the audio clip on the timeline. In terms of audio post, you're finished and can now focus your full attention on the visual aspects of the edit.

One of the advantages of recording a live video is that it usually takes much less time in the editing process, but the tradeoff is that you have to get the recording right in terms of both audio and video. If you have a three-camera shoot, at any given time during the performance one camera always has the best shot, so you will be inclined to use that camera for most of your money shots. Don't get too carried away with your best camera; remember, the audience wants to see changes on the screen. After all, this is video and motion onstage and in the editor is desirable.

Dissect the Song

Is the song going to be a script? Are you going to tell a story visually through the lyrics or is the performer going to be the focus of the video? If you use the lyrics as your script, how easy will it be to get the components together to tell the story? If the lyrics are telling a story in a linear fashion and the scenery is commonplace, you have a good place to start. If the song is more of a statement, "I love you," than an action, "you drove away," you have a bit more artistic room to move around in.

STORYBOARDING

Hollywood has a preparatory technique that helps the process of telling a story visually that you will find in almost every film project: the storyboard.

The storyboard is a group of pictures or images that tell the story visually. Storyboards can be as simple as stick figures or as complicated as graphic novels. Each picture in the storyboard can contain production notes on how each shot is to be accomplished. Information such as location, setting, camera and audio settings, camera operator instructions, the segment time and number gives you a "to do" list of the tasks that will comprise each scene of your video. It also gives you an overview of the whole piece, where you are, where you are going, and what the end result should look like. The storyboard is essential in saving you time and making sure you get the shots you need.

Before shooting begins, the storyboard is your guide, and modifications to the storyline or production tasks can be made before you roll the first frame of tape. Here is what two storyboard cards for an imaginary rock video set on a beach might look like:

musicoffice.com	PROJECT:	Beach Video
	Shot #:	001 Reel #: 001
	Description:	Setup for Beach Party -
		Guitar wails and scene starts
		Get Mike play slide guitar intro
	Trans/IN:	Straight Cut from splash
	Audio:	16-bit 44.1 lipsync... remember to
		capture ambience for 60 seconds
	Trans/OUT:	cross dissolve fade to black
	Time:	8 seconds
NOTES:		In edit zoom out from girl to full frame, sync straight cut in to the hard drum hit.
CAMERA NOTES/SETTINGS:		daylight shot, outdoors, SD
		001

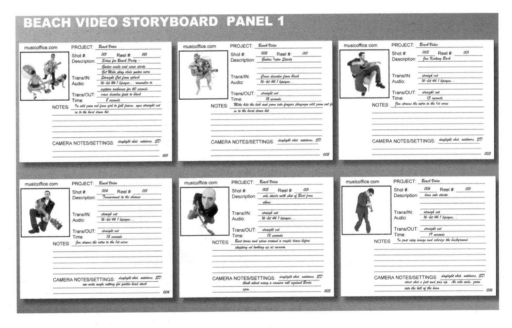

A bit further down the road one of your storyboard panels might look like this:

Storyboards can be as important as a script in a movie. If you are out on location and the storyboard calls for a five seconds of a traffic jam, there will be no need to waste time and tape getting a 30-second shot. Shoot only what you need. You can, however, do more than one take, and it is a good idea to have about two seconds of pre-roll and out-roll (starting the camera early and leaving on after action). This will leave you a bit of room to cover for transitions later, but it isn't necessary to shoot more than this. You will only have to trim the clips later during capture or editing. Keeping track of your clips is tedious and can slow you down a bit on location. But when you have conceivably hundreds of video clips, it is nice to know which is which and where each clip lays on the timeline in the editing process.

If you're averse to storyboarding and think it might be too much work, you should at least create a shot list for each location. Trust me, it will come in handy.

A music video doesn't have to be all music either. An artist can kick the video off with an entertaining personal anecdote as an intro into the piece; in fact a good career story can make a compelling video in itself even without music.

Notes on Copyright

In most cases the music video will be created using totally original content. This means that your team will be creating the video totally using content that you create. If using "royalty free" footage, stock footage or images, read the small print in the licensing agreement. The "royalty free" part of the license may only apply to use for non-commercial projects. This could be a speed bump in your DVD sales plan. If you don't have license to use an image or sound in your video, don't use it. And by all means, resist the temptation to drop in copyrighted audio or video from other CDs and DVDs.

Preproduction Meetings

Now that we have an idea about where the video is going, we should bring the other principals into the loop. Set up a meeting with every-one involved: band members, video camera people, graphic artists, and anyone else who is going to be involved in the production. If the people involved aren't all locals, start a blog or message board on the web, create an email list of the participants pointing to the web workspace and let everybody give input on the project.

Who will be wearing the producer's hat? Who is going to do what and when? What talent is going to be used in the video? Is it going to be a concert or lip-sync production? Even if you are running a one-man operation, it is a good idea to break the project down into separate production modules and address each separately.

Start with a timeline. Set a production start and end date. Can everyone fit inside that timeframe? If you are using photos, will the still photographer have the still images ready to go by the end of shooting? Focus only on the shooting aspect of the project for now; you can get into post-production issues later. The important part of this meeting is to get everyone on the same page and synchronized to the project timeline so shooting time and workflow are maximized.

Let everyone know that when they commit to a time and place, they need to honor the commitment. It can be sad when you have shelled out money to rent a video camera only to find that the friend who was going to bring the lights has decided to go on vacation instead. Let your people know that they are an important component to the production and that you and the rest of the team are counting on them to deliver on schedule. After all, if they weren't reliable and trustworthy, you wouldn't be talking to them, right?

Are you going to be incorporating still images into your video? Who has or will take the photos? Do some of them need to be scanned, or are they all in digital format already? Still photos can be a great component to a music video; you will see many with a staccato burst of dozens of stills in just a few seconds. A band with any following probably has fans who have taken photos.

FAN PARTICIPATION

Fan participation can be a big part of your production. Screaming fans look better than a bored audience and they can bring more than that to the table. You can bring your die-hard followers into the project by utilizing fan photos. I haven't called a fan yet that wasn't tickled pink to be a part of the artist's video project.

THE FAN SHOOTOUT

This is a great technique for quick content creation that will add a lot of spice to your finished product. Send out an email to all your fans and ask if any of them have digital still or video cameras. If you wind up with 10 fans that have MiniDV cameras, buy a box of tape and ask them to get to the gig a half-hour early with fully charged batteries. Have your fan shooters sign a video release giving full name and address so you can credit them, hand them a labeled and prestriped (see below) tape, and ask each individual to cover a specific part of the stage or band member for the whole show or until tape rolls out. Make note of what each fan is shooting. Tell them they can do anything they want except pause or stop the recording once you have instructed them to roll tape. At the end of the show, collect the tapes and thank the fans. You just added ten cameras to your shooting footage—and many hours to your editing time—but there may be some jewels in the footage. You can do the same for fan digital photo bugs; ask them if they have any killer photos larger than three megapixels that they would like to share.

Another thing to keep in mind is that the screen resolution for standard digital video is 720 by 480 pixels, so unless you are going to be zooming in and out of an image or panning across it, it need not be larger than that. We will be talking more about using stills and how they can improve your video in the chapter on editing.

ACTORS AND EXTRAS

Are you going to be using actors or extras? If so, the video release is very important. A good rule of thumb is to get permission and a written video release from everyone who will appear in frame. (Sample release forms are in Appendix C.) Make sure that the extras and actors also know when and where they are expected to be. If you are shooting live, be sure to get all your friends, family and fans to turn out; a live video with no audience looks pretty lame. (Unless, of course, your video is entitled "The Rock Tones: Rebels without Applause.")

Locations and Releases

For most videos, location scouting isn't really necessary unless you have something exotic in mind. If you are going to be shooting out in public keep in mind that some people, places, and businesses might not want to be in your video. If, for example, you wanted to shoot a few clips inside a nightclub where the band plays frequently, get written permission from the club. Venue releases are generally not necessary but if in doubt, get it in writing so it won't come back later to bite you. Project releases have been stopped dead in their tracks for something as trivial as not getting a release from a venue before the shooting. If you are up against a deadline and have to backtrack to get a release, the last thing you want to hear is the person that can authorize the release is on vacation.

Here is something to think about if you are shooting outdoors and are expecting to use sunlight as your primary light source. The best light for shooting is in the morning and evening, with the subject facing the sun. The sun is lower on the horizon, and if your subject is facing the sun you will get good light without the midday shadows that can ruin an image. If you are shooting in afternoon sunlight, you will probably want to bring along something to use as a fill light or reflector. You can also use any light colored object as a reflector. The subject could be next to a white-washed wall, or you could be reflecting light onto the subject with something as simple as a piece of white poster or foam board.

The quality of morning and evening light is also warmer and not as stark as midday light, giving your subject a golden, healthy glow.

Try to schedule your shoots in the time window for the best light in your region.

TIP

Another concern if you are going to be shooting a live concert outdoors is to try to avoid, if you can, the infamous "sundown show." A few years back we were contracted to videotape a large outdoor festival. The show would start about three hours before sundown and proceed well into the night. The act that would be performing during sundown was the most problematic because the light is constantly changing. I assume the same occurs for a sunrise show but haven't been called to produce one of those yet.

In full sunlight all our cameras are on the same page in light temperature and the same for after sundown when we are using stage lighting. The problem is adjusting the camera exposures on the fly while the show is running. We found that a communications system ("com") is almost a must to keep uniformity between camera shots. While one camera shot is up our director would communicate over the com set to the other camera operators directing them to tweak their exposure settings. The director would be doing this constantly during the sundown set to keep the light temperature as uniform as possible. It is a huge pain in the neck so if you have any pull regarding the artist's show time, I recommend either before or after sundown.

Shooting a live concert video can be a bit more problematic concerning releases. If you are the opening act for a major touring band, the venue or headliner might have a problem with audio and video recording. Be sure to check things out before the show by walking the venue. Clear everything with the venue and sound company well in advance of arriving to shoot!

When I was producing a music-video TV program awhile back, we made it a practice of having an audience sign-in sheet by the door. If an audience member wanted to be a part of the video, they had to sign the sheet granting us permission. Our audience release form (included on the DVD and in Appendix C) was just a paragraph at the top of the page granting permission and lines for name and signature and optional email—an audience member may later be a customer. Getting permission to use someone's image is generally not a problem, but an essential tool in any professional videographer's tool kit is a booklet of video releases.

Owning, Borrowing, and Renting Gear

Earlier, we looked at the features you should look for when buying a camera. I hope you ran right out and bought one with all the recommended features. If not, perhaps you can borrow a camera or two from friends. If you have any kind of budget and live near a large metropolitan area, gear rental may be an option. You can rent a camera for a few days for a fraction of the cost of owning it. It's just like renting a car; the rental company keeps the gear in their rental pool in good operating condition, and you can sometimes get invaluable advice from rental pros. Here is an example of what can be rented for what price; prices may be higher or lower in your region but here is a list from Middle America. Note that there are weekend and student discounts.

Camera	Daily Rate	Weekend Rate	Student Rate
Panasonic DVX100(A)	$75	$112	$50 /$75
Canon XL2	$125	$187	$95/$142
Sony HVR-Z10	$175	$262	$125/$187
Sony DSR-PD170	$95	$142	$75/$112
Panasonic HVX-200	$275	$420	NA
JVC GY-HD100	$225	$337	$195/$280

With any of these cameras, you could shoot a great music video over a weekend. Renting is something to consider if you don't own and can't borrow a 3-chip camera and want the highest quality possible.

Prestriping the Audio and Video Tapes

Prestriping the video tapes—basically, recording blank video on the length of the tape—before the shoot has a both an up and a downside. The downside is that it takes the playing time of the tape to stripe it and also adds to the overall wear and tear on the tape record head. The upside is when you are shooting with multiple prestriped cameras, if everyone has rewound to zero, when you say "three, two, one, start," all the cameras will be within a fraction of a second of each other in terms of timecode. This makes it much easier to sync in your editing setup. Also, you know ahead of time if any of your tapes are bad. Yet another advantage is that a pre-striped tape will not contain any timecode dropouts. Sometimes when a camera is stopped, perhaps to review a previous shot, restarting the recording again after the scene just reviewed may create a blank spot on the tape and timecode between the old scene and the new recording. If there is an interruption in the tape timecode, the camera will usually automatically set the counter back to zero and proceed. You could wind up with two places on the same tape with same timecode—not good. For these reasons, I recommend prestriping the tapes.

To prestripe a tape, put a new tape in the camera or deck and leaving the lens cap on or the video input of the deck unplugged, hit record and let the tape record black all the way through to the end without stopping. Then rewind the tape so it is ready to go. Now the tape has a continuous and uninterrupted timecode from start to finish.

Communicating with the Rest of the Team

If you are planning a live shot with multiple cameras, it is almost essential that the camera operators can communicate with the director or at least each other during the taping. Com sets with headphones and mics for four operators are found at most video rental shops and are well worth the money. We have also used small walkie talkies with earphones if the budget didn't support a real com system. The downside of the walkie talkie scenario is that the bleed from the venue sound can make it hard to hear—even with closed cup headphones. If you have no electronic options, a set of hand signals might suffice, but keep it simple. A line of sight to the director who will point at an operator and then maybe give the hand signal for zooming in is a common method. However, the hand signal method is less than optimal because it is very easy to confuse the signals and a line of sight between the operators may not be possible. And of course, while they're worried about hand signals, the camera personnel are looking at the director instead of the performer.

Here is an example of a communication between the director and operators during a live shoot. *Director: Camera three you have the shot. Camera two zoom in to the lead guitarist, hips to head. That looks good. Going to camera two. Camera two you have the shot. Camera one pull back slowly from percussionist to full stage. Standby.*

Going to camera one. Camera one you have the shot. Camera one, start your slow pull now. That's good. Camera two, zoom into drummer's face. Going to camera two. Camera two, you have the shot.

TIP

If you are using a com set to direct the show, keep the camera operators off the air. Unless there is a problem that a camera operator has to share with the director, the operators should remain silent and the communications one-way. The director is sending the instructions and any dialog between the camera operators about the upcoming lunch break might block out the director's transmission. Camera operators should be neither seen nor heard.

If no communication is possible, the director should designate each camera for only certain types of shots. If you can spare a camera, one should always be directly in front of the stage and panned out so the entire stage is visible. This is called your "master" shot and it never changes. The other operators can be directed to cover certain parts of the stage or performance; with proper direction in advance, duplication of shots and scenes is kept to a minimum. Your wide shot can save the day if the other cameras can't get a frame.

We've taken a look at what you should be thinking about prior to going out and shooting. We've laid out the best plan for locations, shots, talent, and shooting venues. Now let's have fun and roll some tape!

CHAPTER 5

The Live Shoot

On the Same Page

Decide in advance who gets what shots. On a three-camera shoot, you would typically have two tripod-mounted stationary cameras and a hand held or dolly operated "rover." Of your stationary cameras, one should be zoomed out enough to capture the whole stage and stay there the whole taping. As I said, this will act as your master shot.

If shooting indoors, have camera personnel wear black or neutral colors so that if they wind up in another camera frame, it will be as unobtrusive as possible. Underline to the camera operators that they should try to stay out of the other camera frames. Like a magician's act, it isn't magical if you can see how the trick is done.

Try to start the cameras simultaneously. Remind the camera operator of the prime directive: Do not stop recording until the show is over or a tape change is necessary!

Recording the Audio

If recording space allows, capture a bit of ambience of the audience entering. Thirty seconds to a minute should be adequate.

THE LIVE SWITCHER, OR FLYING WITHOUT A NET

We had a client who hosted a music festival that wanted to save a bit of money. We let him know that by just mixing the camera sources live and dumping the mix to one tape deck, we would cut massive amounts of post time but would be stuck with what we got. Like making a two-track audio recording, you are flying without a net. What you see is what you get as a final product. There will be no punch-ins to fix mistakes.

When switching live, it is almost mandatory that you create a separate multi-channel audio split from the FOH (Front Of House) or monitor console to an audio mixer/recorder dedicated to the video. The audio concerns of the main venue engineer and monitor mixer may be very different from what you need as a video producer. If you can get copies of the FOH mix too, do it. It can add ambience and audio coloration and place the viewer more realistically in the audio environment. In loud venues, you will want your video audio mixer as far away from the action as possible and wearing closed cup headphones. Sometimes even with good headphones, the venue noise may color what you are hearing. It is a very good idea to keep your eyes on the channel meters and solo each channel occasionally to make sure you are getting good signals. A strong signal on all the tracks is important if you have problems monitoring at the venue. This book is not explicitly concerned with the techniques of live sound recording, which have filled many authoritative volumes already. I will talk a little bit more about your audio signal path later in this chapter, but feel free to consult other sources, or talk to the FOH guy at the venue about what recording inputs he can give you.

For the director's preview in the trailer backstage, we built some little mini snakes that would run from the camera to the trailer that contained 100 feet of s-video cable and a balanced XLR cable for the com units.

If possible rehearse the show with the camera operators and the audio mixer. If you can spare the tape, let it roll. Try to tape the whole show with the same song sequence in rehearsal as it will be performed during prime time. If possible record the rehearsal to a deck for later B-roll or CYA footage.

Lighting Concerns

As mentioned in the preproduction chapter, the best light is light you have some control over. If you are shooting indoors, take a look at the subject with each camera. Where do the shadows fall? Is some kind of fill light going to be necessary?

A good example would be an Americana band shootout I taped awhile back. The event was at a large venue with a huge stage and lots of lights coming from above. The biggest problem we ran into was the cowboy bands where band members were wearing hats. It didn't matter if the performer was wearing a ten-gallon Stetson or a John Deere baseball cap, the shadows from the overhead light fell right across the face of the performers and looked horrible. We solved the problem in a somewhat gnarly slacker fashion by placing some construction site work lights down in front of the artists pointing upwards toward them. We put a steel-blue filter on the lights; our ad hoc Wal-Mart lighting kit saved the day and killed the hat shadows. This is why you see footlights in the better venues. Also review the preproduction advice concerning sundown sets.

Indoor lighting is a bit easier to work with because you have some control and consistency over the lighting environment. Once the stage is well lit, the job is done and further tweaking of camera exposure levels is unnecessary. I prefer indoor venues because they are predictable. Have you ever lost an outdoor gig due to a rain storm? Imagine a deluge from the sky not only washing out the show, but also pouring down on your gear.

TIP

Tape Rotation for a Long Shoot. *What happens when you have a three-camera shoot and the concert time exceeds the length of the tapes in the cameras? Most DV cameras will record from 40 minutes to an hour before requiring a new tape. To make sure there is no dropout in the performance footage it will be necessary to swap out the tapes in rotation during the performance. If you don't have a com set to the camera operators, you will have to use a time marker for each camera person. You might tell operator A to change out his tape at 55 minutes into the show, operator B to change out at 57 minutes, and* *operator C at 59 minutes if everyone is using a 60-minute tape. When swapping out tapes, don't rewind the tape you just shot; it burns up too much time.*

A great way to put "honesty" into a music video is to videotape the performance in a live environment. Instead of using a staged video of posturing and posing, recording live can give the audience an honest and straightforward means of displaying the band and its talents. I notice in my own collection of DVDs, 90 percent of the music titles are concert videos.

Top Ten Shooting Tips

1. Try to keep the camera steady. Use a tripod or set the camera on something stationary

2. Avoid using the zoom feature as much as possible. Never use the digital zoom.

3. When using multiple cameras, make your key shot a wide one.

4. Keep the sun over your shoulder except when shooting sunrises or sunsets.

5. White balance between shots; particularly when changing location or exposure settings.

6. If your camera has more audio inputs than just the built-in mic, use them.

7. Use the Rule of Thirds by dividing your screen into nine parts: Imagine lines like a tic-tac-toe layout. Place your subject where the lines intersect. Use full-face centered shots sparingly.

8. Make sure to have spare batteries, duct tape, and the essential toolkit.

9. Use the manual focus on your camera if available.

10. Enjoy yourself. This is supposed to be fun!

Getting Ready

THE BASIC TOOLKIT

Every shoot is different and some will require more gear than others. If you are shooting in sunlight, you may not have to bring lights, but indoors or at night you will probably need them. Beyond the obvious essential gear (cameras, recorders, tripod, camera accessories, etc.) here's what I am throwing in my car for the even simplest shoot before heading out to a live taping:

► Still Camera with fresh batteries and either a lot of film/memory free or some method of dumping the camera memory onto a notebook computer or USB memory stick.

► Duct or Gaffing Tape

► Slate clapper

► My Manfrotto 2930 Super Arm

► Extension cords and power strips

► Any necessary audio cable and a couple backups

► Small toolkit with pliers, wire cutters, hammer and the basic necessities

► Carabineers, C-clamps, and vise grips come in handy for clamping down lights and props

► Lens cleaners, extra video tape

► Trash bags or plastic sheeting to cover all equipment should it start to rain

Whole books have been written on methods of live recording, so I will just touch on some of the basics. What we are going to do here is set up for a live recording in a controlled environment. On this occasion, for a television show pilot series we recorded six musical groups in two nights at a small local summer theater during the off season. To entice the venue, we donated half the door receipts to the theater as rental for the room. There is a bit of an economy of scale in doing multiple acts in one shooting; the lighting and sound are pretty consistent, and the draw of three groups each night made filling the room much easier.

You might want to look at taping more than just your act as a way of cutting down expenses. Combining the promotion and production of the shoot can bring the price down considerably for each band when the costs are spread over all the participants.

SEWING UP THE LEGAL DETAILS

Before we ever got to the theater, we looked at what rights we would need to make things happen. The plan was to use the footage for a regional TV show showcasing new talent, so we needed to make sure that we had the rights to broadcast the material. So, our deal with the artists is very simple. The contract addresses two primary rights to the performance: broadcast and mechanical. The tapes and master edit will be owned by the company. The company has the right to use or not to use the material. We videotape the performer and are granted the right to broadcast the performance exclusively on TV and the Internet. The artist retains all mechanical rights in the performance and will grant to the company a non-exclusive right to manufacture enough DVDs or tapes to service the broadcasters. The company, in return, grants licenses for the artist or record label to use the video content on their website or other promotional outlet.

It's a pretty sweet deal. The artist winds up with a DVD and perhaps a live CD that they can do anything they want with. The broadcaster winds up with the right to broadcast the program.

This is also where the video releases for audience members come in. Some producers regard having the audience sign off on their participation in the shoot as unnecessary, but erring on the side of caution is always a good idea. It normally won't be an issue, but if the DVD would become a monster hit, and if it shows a very clear image of an audience member who didn't give permission to appear in the video, it could create legal problems. There are examples of video releases in Appendix C and on the DVD you can use as a starting place.

We told the audience before they entered the theater that we were recording and videotaping the show. Further, we said they would have to use our sign-in sheet to grant us permission, without any compensation, to use the footage of the show in any way we pleased and for whatever purpose. Being this general is a good idea. The audience grants their images to be used for both broadcast and mechanical licensing. If an audience member balks at signing in, tell him it is now a free show and he is welcome to enjoy it from the lobby.

Audio Signal Path

Keep it simple. Whether you are talking about audio or video, the shortest signal path is always the best signal path. Don't experiment at the venue; rehearse and have your act together before the taping. If possible, record a rehearsal and two shows so that you can edit together the best sonic material.

Use etiquette. Befriend the venue personnel; the FOH (Front of House) sound man has to be your best friend tonight. Always ask permission before inserting anything into the house system. Also checking the power grounding is a must when recording. Try to get your equipment on the same circuit as the FOH mixer.

SIMPLE SIGNAL PATH EXAMPLE

Let's start with a little six-channel powered mixer, in this example a Mackie. Many bands and venues use simple mixers like this, and most of them have the feature we are looking for: the channel insert.

A balanced (TRS) plug on a mixer can be used as a recording output. It is the best and easiest way to get audio data from the mixer into your recorder. The input signal is pre-channel/fader so that any EQ or effects added are not recorded; it's just the straight raw signal from the channel preamps. The trick is to plug the insert in *only halfway*. The tip and first ring on the TRS connector will then send the pre-amp output to the recorder. If you insert the 1/4'' plug in all the way, it will break the circuit and you will not get the signal.

Take a look at the front panel of this Mackie powered mixer:

If we zoom in a bit closer we can find our friend the channel insert:

On this particular mixer the insert is just above the line input. Insert your 1/4'' cable *halfway* into the insert plug and you are good to go. Repeat for every channel that contains a voice or instrument. You now have a balanced input for every channel on your recorder.

Another method if you have limited tracks on your digital recorder would be to take a stereo (or dual mono) feed from the FOH mix and set up two mics in front of the main speakers and back about fifteen to twenty feet if possible. You might want to insert a limiter on these channels if possible to keep from going over 0db while recording. In fact, I usually set my limiter to peak at about -3db so that I have headroom to add EQ or effects in post. Also make sure the camera mics are on. Even if you have only one stationary camera recording the entire stage, you can still get six audio channels to mix with: the stereo camera, the crowd mics, and the FOH feed. You can have all this without having to use channel inserts or splitters.

Ready to Rumble

Our setup for this live shoot was for three cameras. One camera is mounted on a rafter above and in front of the band shooting slightly downward. Another camera is off to stage left and is on a tripod with an operator. The final camera is our "rover," which is a handheld camera; the operator's mission to get in tight to grab our artist from down low in front and in back.

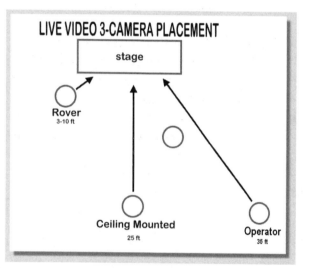

White Balance and Slate

If you are shooting with more than one camera, it's time to set them up. Have someone stand where the performer(s) will be with a piece of white poster board or paper. Then, have the cameramen point at this target and use the white balance feature of the camera to set a uniform color space between all the cameras. If you do this just before the slate, you can record the white balance test, leave the tape rolling, then slate and start the show. Hopefully, you will be able to do all of this in the space of a minute; valuable tape time is slipping away, so move fast. Having the white balance shot on the tape will let you A/B the different camera images when you get them in the editor, and it will give you a starting place to match and adjust color. You will see the differences in how different cameras define "white."

The Show

When getting ready to roll, have someone act as MC and get the crowd warmed up. Tell them you are taping the show for release and really appreciate their being in the house tonight. Tell them to please turn off any cell phones and pagers. Remind them that a large part of this concert video will be their participation and you are looking forward to a great time and show for all. If you know the TV broadcast date of the show, tell the audience so they can tune in to see if they got in any shots. If you don't know the broadcast date, tell them to check your website for the upcoming broadcast dates or view the show on the web. Then, have your MC use some high-energy shouts to get the crowd going.

If you are shooting in a large venue with a full house, get plenty of footage of the scene. Using a separate tape from one that will be used to tape the show, take wide shots of the large audience. If you have the opportunity to shoot from behind the artist, pull back to show the scale of the venue and take stills. Nothing helps an artist's visual impact with venues and agents more than the act in front of thousands. Sadly it is not always a perfect world; let's address the smaller venues.

Not too many people at the venue? The solution to getting a big look in a little club or with a small audience is to zoom that puppy in. A small room can look huge if the frame is being filled by the talent instead of the room. Shooting from in front and below the talent and from behind and below can make even the smallest venue look larger than it is. If fans are in attendance, tell them you want all of them down front and shoot them up close; you don't want the viewer to know that the whole audience is only the twenty people in frame. You can zoom into three of these audience shills and pan or pull back to the entire twenty before you cut to the talent. You have probably seen many close-up shots of artists down on their knees before the fans high-fiving some of them. Next time you see a shot like that, count the actual number of people in frame. That may be all the people in the building. Take lots of stills of the fans reaching for the band. At sound check, ask the band members to posture as though they are in front of a huge, ecstatic audience. Take lots of stills.

Here's a quick process list for the live shoot:

▶ Get release from artist to tape and use performance.

▶ Plan the venue, shooting team and overall production flow.

▶ Prestripe enough tapes to get you through the whole show, keeping in mind you might have to change out tapes mid-performance. Label the tapes according to camera/operator.

▶ Capture B-roll footage on a separate tape from the performance tapes of show setup, audience entering venue and any other "extra feature" material you can use for B-roll content.

▶ If a tape change is necessary, let each camera operator know when to swap tapes. Let each camera operator know what their primary focus will be during the show.

▶ About a minute before show time, start the cameras simultaneously, white balance them using the same target, slate each camera, then start the show.

▶ At the show's end, have the camera operators rewind their tape(s) and turn them into director/producer with any comments they might have about what they shot.

▶ Before leaving the venue, be sure you have the names of any people who worked or helped out on the project so they can be credited if possible.

Additionally, a Hollywood-style whiteboard clapper is a great tool. You can note reel, scene, and take number; if you don't have one, any loud sharp noise will do. A loud handclap will sometimes suffice. You can test whether you are getting a good slate by watching the meters on the audio equipment. If you're seeing a good spike when you slate, you're good to go and you'll be able to line it up later. I have found clap boards on eBay for between $10 and $50 depending on the quality. Digital clap boards are much more expensive and probably not something you will need this side of a feature film.

The lights go down, the van is loaded and we have shot a live video. All our content is labeled and we're ready to go on to the editing process. The live taping was pretty straightforward. Now let's take a look at shooting a lip-sync to see the differences in shooting and production.

The Poor Man's Dolly. Robert Rodriguez revealed a great deal of his low/no budget secrets in the extra features section of his El Mariachi DVD. Rodriguez used a wheelchair pushed by a friend as his dolly rig and got good results. My variation is to use a regular hand truck with the feet on the truck footing and again being pulled by a friend. If the assistant is pulling backwards, have someone there to guide him so he doesn't step off a cliff. Keep in mind that these techniques will only work on a reasonably flat surface. I have also seen sleds used during winter as camera platforms for downhill action.

CHAPTER 6

The Lip-Sync Shoot

Our live recording shoot was pretty straightforward. A basic lip-sync or concept shoot is similar; we will usually shoot an entire song from beginning to end with multiple passes. However, we will usually be doing it outside of the confines of a traditional music performance. If you are shooting any kind of abstract concept video, you will have to use extra care and forethought to plan what you are doing, or you will either get lost in a quagmire of clips or not have enough good footage. Where the live recording edit will have about 45 scenes and transitions over four minutes, the lip-sync will have many more different shots and transitions over about the same time period. This requires a great deal more content.

Our lip-sync artist is a local band called Someone Like You. The band revolves around singer/songwriter Josh Murley, and for the video we selected one of the shorter songs, "I Got Lost in It," from their upcoming CD. As mentioned earlier, the longer the program time, the longer the editing time for a lip-sync video. It's a pretty simple formula: a four-minute video will take twice as long to edit as a two-minute one.

The theme of the song is a common one: rock-n-roll love angst. The story is also familiar one: Josh has become lost somewhere along the way in the relationship that is starting to crowd the participants. It is my job to try and project that with what images I can muster in the time and budget allowed.

Keep in mind that musicians aren't actors, so don't try to get them to do too much. You might get lucky and have a Matt Dillon or Angelina Jolie in the band, but it doesn't do much good unless they are the lead singer and focus of the video. Music videos of band members cutting up and posturing are as old as the Monkees and still quite popular. Videos of this style are quick and easy; they can add humor and an informal and candid feel to the video. Even if your video is supposed to look like a jerky amateur home movie, get some good, steady and well-lit shots too just to show you can.

The lip-sync video can also be taped just like a live recording in a venue full of people except that the band is playing along to the studio track or a metronome click at tempo and not really performing the music. This could be problematic if the audience isn't in on the production. I might not be a happy camper in a venue where the opening act was lip-syncing their show and expecting me to applaud and rave about it. Although lip syncing has become much less of a scandal since the days of Milli Vanilli, most live performers are still expected to do *something* during the show.

You can also shoot a nice lip-sync with just one camera and location; for a solo singer/songwriter this is a great method. With one camera and tape you can take carefully framed and lit takes. If you make four or five passes of the whole song from four different well-lit positions, you will have a much easier edit similar to the live recording.

TIP

In the more rapid-fire edit of a lip-sync you will be moving from image to image much quicker. Start rolling the tape a few seconds before you fire up the jam box. Record only what you need but always start tape just before the beginning of the song. Again this will help you sync up the clips in the editing process. If you record just small parts of the song and start anywhere in the song but the beginning, you'd better know the tune inside and out as finding the exact insert spot on your editor's timeline will be harder and more time consuming.

The Tool Kit

Our lip-sync tool kit is essentially the same as the one we took out for the live recording with a few additions:

▶   Jam box with fresh and spare batteries. The jam box is a key part of the lip-sync, as it will be the audio cue for whoever is on camera and our editing cue for syncing the audio in the clips. While shooting the lip-sync, make sure the jam box or stereo is turned up loud enough for the camera's built-in microphones to pick it up clearly. The slate will act as our initial sync cue but on longer takes you may just want to use one phrase, even one word so hearing where you are in the song is important.

► Still camera with fresh batteries and either a lot of film/memory free or some method of dumping the camera memory onto a notebook computer or USB memory stick.

► Duct or gaffing tape.

► Slate clapper. You can also use any sharp loud noise; a hand clap will sometimes suffice.

► A couple pieces of colored poster board (light blue, orange, white, and red) to use as reflectors just outside the frame.

► If I have access to electrical power, extension cords and power strips.

► Small toolkit with pliers, wire cutters, hammer and the basic necessities. Carabineers, C-clamps and vise grips come in handy for clamping down lights and props. I have a handy tool called a Super Arm made by Bogen/Manfrotto that will twist and lock in any direction and will clamp on to just about anything: a lighting frame, pole, or ceiling joist. It is a tool I recommend highly.

► Lens cleaners

► Extra video tape

► Trash bags or plastic sheeting to cover all equipment should it start to rain

On Location: The Birth of Plan "B"

If you did your preproduction work, you have already mapped out where you are going to shoot. Everything was ready on the day of the lip-sync shoot; a variety of locations selected, the cameras loaded, and the band and crew showed up on time. In our case, we had a nice list of seven nearby locations and had prepared everything in advance, but all our great planning came to naught on the day of the shoot.

The problem was the weather. Torrential downpours and flash flood warnings didn't help the outlook for the rest of the day, or even the rest of the week. The band members live in different towns, not too far away but far enough to make rescheduling a problem.

I decided to utilize the time we had with the resources at hand so we shot for a couple hours against a green screen in my living room, planning to composite in the backgrounds later. This takes a lot more time at the editing end and is the least preferred way of shooting in terms of getting a quick delivery of the product, but without my location shots I had little alternative.

Keying and Mattes

Just about every movie you have seen in recent years that has any kind of special effects, the film crew was probably using blue- or green-screen compositing. The concept is essentially quite simple: You shoot your well-lit talent against a blue/green/chroma screen—we will call it green screen from here on. Then, later in the editing process, you use software to remove the colored background and create a transparent or alpha channel in the clip. Recently, entire feature films have been shot against a green screen because of some of its inherent advantages.

If you have a scene that calls for a sunset on a beach, or a planetary fly-by, it will be cheaper if you can bring the location to you instead of trying to buy time from NASA for your camera vehicle. Clips that have alpha channels can not only be laid on a motion background, but they can be also laid on top or below each other, which creates depth. Many feature films have composite layers over thirty deep.

Keep in mind when keying that you will have to do a bit of tweaking to get respectable results. I cheated a bit on the video and used Ultra 2 to get a quick key with an alpha channel. In this example I'm going to show how to do it inside Premiere.

TIP

When setting up to shoot a key and after you have the lighting as good as its going to get, have the talent walk out of the frame and shoot a few seconds of just the blue or green screen background. In some compositing software like Ultra 2, you can set the key of the background before the talent enters the scene. If your lighting is good, keying out the background is a one-click effort.

We start with a clip of our talent against a green screen. There are a couple ways to approach keying in this scenario. The first is to do the keying before you place the talent on the timeline background. In effect you will key the whole clip and resave it under a different layer with the alpha channel intact. Check your software to see if this is an option. If so, and drive space is not a concern, you may want to use this method. You will wind up making three clips from the same source material, but you will have your talent's segment ready to go with an alpha layer when you start your edit and changing the background or features of the key is easy. The other way I can approach it is to key inside the editor with all the backgrounds in place. I use a bit of both methods depending on the project.

GREEN SCREEN TO SAVE THE DAY

I have two green screens. One is a painted wall with the loudest "astro brite" green paint I could find at Wal-Mart. I also chose a flat paint as reflections aren't something I'm looking for in a composite background. It cost me one gallon to cover a 9' × 22' wall. My other screen is a 10' × 12' piece of bright green Lycra that can be stretched on a frame or pinned up to a wall. It is handy, and I bought it on eBay for under $50. Many models have grommets to make stringing it up almost anywhere easy, and it produces a nice even background.

In creating a setting for compositing, our primary concern is the color difference between the background and the subject. We want it to be as different as possible. A subject dressed in black against a true white background will be very easy to key. On the other hand, a person wearing a green shirt standing in front of a green screen will start looking like the invisible man when his chest disappears on the first keying.

TIP

A poor man's way to get a good composite background is to use a clear blue sky for the background color. As long as the subject is wearing clothes that are in stark contrast to the sky background, you can get a great key. The downside is you can only use this technique successfully with tight and medium shots that don't show the ground. In this scenario we break our rule of preferring to shoot in mornings and evenings. To use the sky as a compositing key color, you want the uniformly colored sky of midday.

The secret to compositing a good video from a green screen is essentially lighting. The more evenly lit the screen, and the more the subject stands out in contrast to it, the better. I start by lighting the subject straight on and then, while monitoring what it looks like through the lens, I adjust the backlights until there are as few shadows as possible. Also it is a good idea to keep your subject as far in front of the screen as possible, keeping the shadow the subject throws on the background as small and weak as possible. When the subject is close to the screen, light from the green screen is reflected onto the back of the subject, causing a green aura. This can be a problem to key out later so be careful.

For our shoot, we set up the boom box in the screen room, slapped a guitar on Josh, and made four passes of the entire song in front of the screen. I shot each pass from a slightly different angle and zoom. Once my shot was set up, I made minimal changes, only a slight zoom on occasion. Keeping the focal length of the shot uniform makes keying out the background a bit easier in editing.

Next we put the bass player in front of the screen and gave him two passes. The drummer lived locally so we decided to shoot his screens a bit later. The rain had stopped and although our primary lighting source (the sun) didn't show up, we still had a very short window to grab some location shots. I could see that only a small fraction of the shots we had scheduled were actually going to be shot so we winged it as we went along.

Everyone jumped in a car and headed downtown. I told Josh to drive and had a camera on him as he sang the tune to the CD player. It isn't the best material, but would work for inserts into our project and at this point I was grabbing all the content I could. Downtown, one of our locations was an alley that was only four feet across and we used a normal hand truck as the camera dolly. The bass player pulled me backwards down the alley as Josh walked towards me. I shot the band walking down the alley from the front then the back a couple times before the rain returned and our exterior location shooting ended for the day. Only a couple of the B-roll shots would require a sync. Those we taped from the beginning of the song on the jam box. The other shots were of B-roll material of the band cutting up a bit and these shots, not requiring sync, were just shot as they came up with no slating.

On the way back home, a friend called me and mentioned he was on the way to tear down the PA at a local venue. I asked if we could shoot a bit on the stage before he struck the stage so we ran over to the venue and got Josh onstage and in front of a mic. With the jam box wailing, Josh ran through the song with me shooting from low and in front of him, from above while standing on a barstool (have a friend hang on to you) and from below and behind. I tried to avoid any shot that would show the scale of the room and an empty room at that. These tight shots look great and I made three quick passes of the whole song.

The venue was small so all the shots were tight on Josh. The club had no theatrical lights but the funky outdoor floodlights didn't look too bad when I shot from below Josh and over his shoulder. It gave the illusion of a larger venue and added a bit of lens flare to give it zip. Next up was the bass player, who ran through the whole song a couple times with tight shots of the bass and a couple of rolls that I might want to insert later.

That wrapped up our first day of shooting. From start to finish, the shoot took about three hours and burned up about 50 minutes of tape on about 10 takes of the whole song and thirty B-roll clips. Not bad for a rain-out.

Additional Notes

GRAB A BIT OF AUDIO AMBIENCE

When on location you are ready to start the camera rolling on your lip-sync, take thirty seconds to a minute to have everyone be quiet and record the ambient audio of the location. If you are using one of the cameras for B-roll material, this would be the camera to do it on. If there are multiple cameras, drop a slate, record the ambience with all cameras and—*without stopping the cameras*—slate again before starting the actual shoot. This can give you visual markers in the editor and keep the cameras as close to sync as possible. The ambient noise can be used for effect; I sometimes bring in just a tad of street noise (sirens, traffic noise, etc.) under an urban scene before the music starts. If I was doing a cowboy campfire video, I might want the crickets and wolves howling in the background. Most of the time you will dump the ambient sound, but having it gives you one more clip on the timeline and one more option on the production menu. Of course, if you're sure you won't need it, don't waste the time.

TAKE PLENTY OF STILLS WHILE YOU'RE AT IT

While you are shooting the lip-sync, take plenty of photos. You will probably get quite a few you can use in the final edit and they can change the whole texture of the video in a few frames. Keep in mind that if you shoot at an image resolution higher than 720x480, you will probably want to crop or resize the photo later. In addition, any images smaller than this size will not fill the screen without stretching it out in the editor which can cause pixelization. So for most shots you can use one of the lower settings on the camera to something as close to 720x480 as you can get (1200 × 900 and 1600 × 1200 are common). If you are going to be using a still in your edit for motion, such as a zoom in or out, or panning across an image, then the larger the image resolution the better.

TIP

Here's a tip for Photoshop users that I found amazing. If you have a low resolution image that that needs to be of higher resolution and size, try this trick for almost lossless upsizing. In Photoshop (I'm not sure if this works on other photo editors) increase the size of the image by 10 percent (but no more) and resample the image. The resulting new file will be 10 percent larger and no appreciable artifacts have appeared. Repeat the procedure until you have the size you want. Depending on the individual image the results can be amazing.

TURN THE JAM BOX UP LOUD

Just as in the live recording, we will be using the audio tracks from the cameras to sync up our various video sources. While on location, be sure to turn up the jam box or other stereo you are using. You want all the camera microphones to pick up the audio track loud and clear. It also helps if you have a quiet location and keep the noise down on the set. As you will find out when we start to capture and edit the files, good audio markers are important.

Both the live recording and the lip-sync recording have been covered; we're ready to move on to post-production.

CHAPTER 7

Getting Ready to Edit: Capturing Video and Sweetening Audio

In order to edit effectively, we have to gather all the high-quality elements we are going to edit and import them into our editing software before we start. We may add new components as the project progresses, but all the basic digital assets should be in place before you start chopping up the files.

Speaking of chopping up files, when you capture a file to your editor and put the razor to it, you are not actually making any changes to the original file. The editor is not razoring your edits, just making note of the time locations on the file you are using. If at any time you don't like what you did to a clip, you can always return to square one with the original file. This is one of the most powerful features of non-destructive editing.

Setting up for editing is very similar regardless of whether you are producing a lip-sync or a live taping. In the lip-sync mode, you will probably use assets other than just the video footage; stills and art slides come to mind. All these assets should be imported into the project and placed in clearly labeled bins so you can find them easily.

TIP

Keep all the assets for the project in one hard drive directory. For example if your project is being stored on D:\MUSICVIDEO and some of the stills you are using are located at E:\PHOTOS\MUSIC\CONCERT2 copy all the stills you will be using in the E:\PHOTOS directory to the project folder. It's best to put them in a subfolder named, you guessed it, "Stills." This keeps everything nice and tidy, the computer is only working one hard drive, and when you go to backup the project during production or archive the project after the final edit, all the pieces are in one place.

Audio Capture

Consider the audio source when capturing to your computer. With your live shoot, your master audio mix will theoretically come into the project with your digital video. With a lip-sync or concept video, the primary audio track is probably going to be from a studio recording CD. If you're using a CD, you will be using the standard audio capturing rate, 44.1 kHz at a 16-bit sampling rate. All the audio files in the project should be on the same binary page without re-sampling or dithering. You don't always have the luxury of using the same bit and sampling rates; cameras often record audio at 48 kHz, for instance, but you should try to limit the amount of re-sampling that your program has to perform. Re-sampling degrades the audio quality and makes your rendering take longer. Most editing programs allow you to insert files of different sampling rates and bit depths on one timeline; if your editing program doesn't let you do this, you will have to convert all the audio to the same format before you import it.

Your software should let you choose the audio sampling rate when you create the project. In Adobe Premiere the new project dialog box looks like this:

In this example you would click on the "Custom Settings" tab to get to the screen where you can set the input audio sampling rate.

Now the audio files you capture from the camera will be at the same sampling rate as the primary source material. In the lip-sync mode it is common not to use any of the camera audio and after using the audio tracks for syncing, they are usually separated or unlinked from their respective video tracks and deleted.

EXTRACTING AUDIO FROM A CD

If you are using a track from an existing CD for the audio of your lip-sync video, just rip the song from a CD using your favorite tool. In this example, I am using Sound Forge 9 to extract the audio but you can use just about any audio player or ripper. The process is identical to ripping for MP3 except you will be saving a .WAV or .AIFF file instead of an MP3. You can use an MP3 as your base audio track but the fidelity will suffer when you re-compress the video for distribution—remember what I said earlier about compressing audio and video multiple times?

Note that Windows Media Player is probably not the application you want to use to rip audio from a CD. The program doesn't give you any options for saving files except in .WMA format, which is not compatible with all editors.

I start by telling Sound Forge what I want to do. Regardless of audio application, you should have little problem finding this common feature.

Then we have to tell our software which song it is we want to rip from the CD.

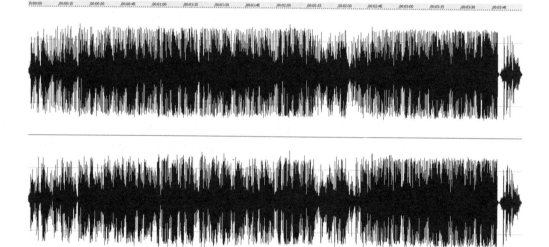

After extracting I have our familiar .WAV file.

If any additional audio sweetening is necessary for the video, this is the place and time to do it. Your audio is now saved to the video editing project directory after renaming it something a bit more personal.

AUDIO MIXING AND SWEETENING

When producing music videos, you can get all wrapped up in how everything looks. Remember, however, this is a *music* video and the audio is the foundation that everything visual is built upon. You should use the same care and attention on your audio files as you would on any CD project. In our experience, about half of the live video concerts we shoot wind up being not only video DVDs but audio CDs too. As an artist, this way you can kill two birds with one stone. After you have mixed your audio, you have not only a saleable CD product but all the audio for the video clip or DVD is a done deed.

For the purposes of this project we will be looking at a straight two-channel stereo mix. Surround sound is certainly an option if your hardware and software permit it, but deploying a surround mix for video is beyond the scope of this book. Check the web resources in Appendix B for more information on surround-sound mixing for video and film.

There are lots of books and resources available regarding mixing methods and techniques. If you are a musician or music producer, you probably already have a good handle on that but there are just a couple of concepts we should touch on in preparing your mixes for wider distribution than just a CD.

Remember, these files are multi-use assets. You may want to make a DVD, a web video for YouTube or Google, or MP3s for both streaming/downloads (low rate) and maybe for a promo pack (high rate). All of these mixes come from the same source material. When you have the final mix of a song ready to go and be bounced to a stereo file or routed to mastering hardware/software, make a few different mixes.

Here's a list of what I typically save for each song:

▶ The master audio file; generally a 16-bit, 44.1 KHz stereo file. Although 24-bit 48 KHz and 16-bit 32 KHz are also popular if the project is for video only. 16/32 is a common bit and sampling rate for consumer video cameras.

▶ A master audio mix with the lead vocal muted for live TV or event lip-syncing.

▶ A master MP3 at 256 kb/s streaming and various other MP3s at varying stream rates. Be sure when saving your MP3 files to insert the additional artist and song information into it. It can guide listeners to your website and brands the file as yours and the song title and artist name will show up on the screen of popular MP3 players like iPods. For uploading to a video streaming site like MySpace or YouTube, remember to encode your audio into a stereo MP3 at a bit rate of 192 kb/s and a sampling rate of 44.1 KHz.

▶ A full mix with the count left in or an audible slate to use as a cue when videotaping the lip-sync.

Copy the audio that you will be using in the video directly to the hard drive project directory where the video project files reside. It is now separate from the audio project and becomes part of your project inventory when you archive it at the end of the project.

rename file

This takes care of getting our primary audio bed ready and imported into the project. We're ready to start capturing our video clips.

TIP

Save your project frequently. As the project progresses I rename the project file so that I can return to milestones in the project. After I have the video clips all captured and on the timeline, I save the project as ready to edit with a name that includes the date. If you are going out on an experimental limb, save your project with an easy-to-remember name and do your thing. If the operation goes badly (the patient dies), you can revert to an earlier saved file in the project. Of course be sure to save your final edit as something like, "SongTitleFinal-01." The new editions of some popular editing programs automatically save past versions as part of your ongoing file, with a feature called "versioning." Check to see if your program includes this feature.

Video Capture

In this case I am using Adobe Premiere screenshots to illustrate, but the process is pretty much the same with all editing software. Upon opening our video capture window, the first thing we should do is to give our capture files a home and a name. Your editing software is set up to save the captured files to a specific location on the hard drive. Change those settings to reflect the location of your video project. (I have occasionally overlooked this procedure and have wound up searching for my files all over the hard drive.)

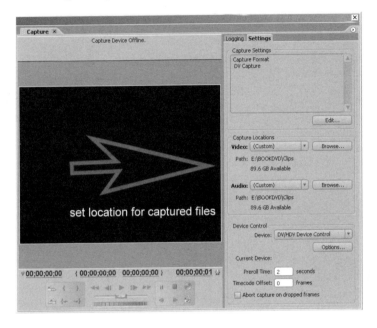

When capturing video, I start with the tracks that will require sync and get them on the timeline before I add any other B-roll cutouts, titles, or stills. Getting the foundation established sync-wise is my first mission.

We're ready to capture some video. After connecting the FireWire or USB cable into your computer, turn on your camera. The computer should notify you that it sees the camera after a few seconds; then, insert your first tape and *use the controls inside the software to operate your video camera or deck.*

Note that some consumer level cameras don't have a FireWire or USB connector. In this case you will not have any camera control from inside the software. In addition, you will have to bring your video into the project through a breakout box and will be capturing video at a degraded resolution using the analog-to-digital converter in the breakout box. You will have to start the capture sessions by hand on the camera itself. Click record in the software and play on the camera/deck.

DIRECT CAPTURE AND BATCH CAPTURE

Most video editing software will give you the option of batch capturing. This can be a very handy feature for an editor concerned about drive space. In the batch capture model, you scrub through the tape, fine tune locations with the scroll wheel and set multiple in and out points, giving each clip a name. As you proceed, a list of these in and out points is being compiled by the software and when you are finished, you start the batch capture with the editing software and camera/deck talking to each other while capturing clips. The camera/deck will fast forward, rewind and cue on its own; when you are finished you have all the clips in the editor with no bad takes. As a reminder, if you are going to use just a segment of a song, capture from the beginning of the song to the end of the segment if the segment is in the first half of the song. If the segment is closer to the end of the song you can capture from just before the segment starts to the end of the song and use the audio markers (hopefully applause) at the end for sync. Unless you know every beat in the song and where every word occurs, I don't recommend grabbing clips from the middle of the performance because it will be confusing when you try to sync it.

Regardless of whether you are working on a live shoot or a lip-sync video, you will be using the same methods for getting your project ready to edit. In the case of our live video, which is up first on our task list, we will capture the three camera tapes first and then any B-roll or other video. Into the camera/deck goes the first camera tape. I preview the first minute or so to find my slate then rewind to just before the slate and start capturing.

If editing a whole show, I capture the whole show. If editing just one song, I capture from about 5-10 seconds before the start of the song to 5-10 seconds after the end, or to just after the audience noise dies down. It will be harder to sync the clips that don't start after a slate, but during a live show slating every song is impractical. You should be able to find audio markers without a slate with a bit of practice.

Although every frame you don't use is taking up drive space and you shouldn't capture more than you need, give yourself a good amount of lead in and out (at least 1-2 seconds) for each clip you capture. This will leave you a bit of trim room at the beginning and end that can help with scene transitions later.

If you are capturing an entire live performance, you will want to start the capture before the slate and let the whole show run. You will repeat this procedure for each camera. If you are just grabbing one song from a performance, look for an audio cue before the start of the song. If you are lucky, the audience will give you hoots and hol- lers for cues, or perhaps the drummer or front man counts off the song. We will be looking at getting them in sync shortly.

When you are finished capturing, you will be prompted to name the file. In Premiere, you can also add some notes to the file, as pictured above. These notes can be very handy especially if there is more than one person working on the edit. Great-shot time loca- tions, and B-roll clip notes can be incorporated—something like writing a review of each clip so you know where the gold is.

After you have captured all the camera performance tapes, capture any B-roll or extra video you want. You can cut these clips much tighter than the full show/song camera tapes, but leave a bit of room at the head and tail of the clip to work with when creating transitions. After capturing your clips, your project inventory might look a bit like this:

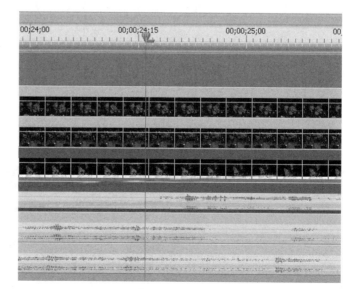

As you can see, we have each camera take in the bin and each one is clearly labeled. You can change the labels to something you prefer—such as "Camera Right, Rover, Dolly Cam"—if you so desire. Keep in mind that you are not altering the names of the original files, just the pointer to them. If you have other content you will be adding, now is the time to create some bins so the other content is easy to find. If necessary, create bins for B-roll, stills, and any other non-sync assets.

Selecting a clip should also give you information about time, bit rate, and other file information. Now we drop the video onto the timeline, each clip on its own separate track. If we enlarge the audio tracks a bit, we can see the .WAV files; this will be our signpost for cueing up the first audio track and then aligning the others to the same time location.

SYNCING THE CLIPS WITHOUT TIMECODE

Getting the sync right is crucially important in video. If one or more of your cameras are out of sync it can look like a badly dubbed 60s gladiator movie.

One of the video tracks will act as our master and starting point. Turn off or mute all the audio/video tracks but one. Zoom in to the audio track and let it play. As the .WAV file scrolls by and before the start of the performance or song, I look for an audio cue I can use as a slate. Remember back at the shoot how we underlined the importance of a good slate? Recall pre-striping the cameras and starting them simultaneously? Here's where those preproduction tasks come in handy.

On that first video/audio track, find the slate event and then mark the event with the software. This will be your reference point for the other tracks.

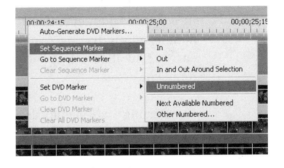

Now disable the audio/video track you just marked, and open another. Again scroll through the footage until you find the same event that you marked in the first file. When you find the event, drag it up or down the timeline to the place you marked the first file and line it up. Now you repeat the procedure with the other files. After you have gone through the files, you will have the clips aligned very closely as shown below.

Now zoom in further and tweak the audio files, lining them up frame-by-frame until they are in perfect sync. An easy way to test your camera sync is to view one video clip with the audio track from another clip. Any of the video clips should play fine with any of the audio tracks and vice versa.

Here's what my final capture and sync screen looks like just before I start editing.

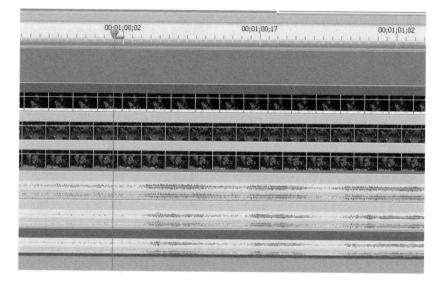

You can see that the audio files line up nicely. Very slight .WAV file offsets may be apparent when you have it synced, and this is due to the different camera distances from the subject; the closest camera gets the audio a few milliseconds before the farthest camera. Because we will be using a non-camera audio file as the primary audio source, worries about audio phasing problems are few as these audio tracks are rarely used; it is even rarer that you would use more than one. In fact if you want to free up a bit of screen space in your editing workspace, you can delete the camera audio tracks you don't need. Be sure to "unlink" the audio from the video so you don't delete your video too!

I trim the beginning of each file so that the clips all start at the same place on the timeline. The clips now line up like boxes of the same length with the beginnings and ends dragged to uniformity.

After aligning and syncing the clips, save your project with a name like "SongTitle-Sync," and you can now import the final audio file either from the CD for a lip-sync project or of the final mix from the live audio taping. Create a new audio track and drop the primary audio file into it. Now line that audio file up just like the ones you did syncing the camera video clips.

Once my "real" audio track is on the timeline and in sync, I do a couple of things to tidy up the work space and make it ready for the edit. First, I designate my starting point. At the beginning of the timeline I put two seconds of black, then I use the "ripple delete" feature of the editing software to line up all my tracks at the starting point. If you didn't leave any space at the beginning of the timeline, use your software to select all the clips and move them all in unison a bit further down the timeline. Then, delete the space between your initial black.

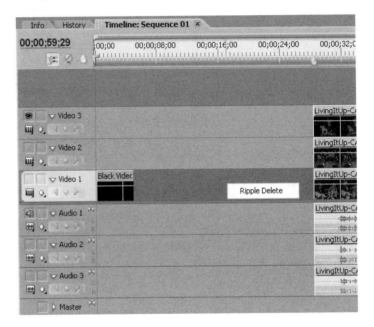

Here's what my workspace looks like before I start editing.

An option at this point is to unlink the audio and video tracks and delete any unnecessary audio tracks. With your mouse, select the video clip you want to delete the audio from, right click to bring up a drop down menu and in the software, select "unlink, separate, etc." from your options. Once unlinked, you can click again on just the audio track and delete it.

In our live recording scenario, I delete all the camera audio tracks except the last thirty seconds of the camera with the best crowd noise. I can bring this applause track up into the audio mix at the end of the song. The rest of the camera audio files are just taking up space and can be deleted. Remember when you delete the audio from the video clip, it is only happening inside the editor; no modifications are made to the original files, which still contain the audio tracks.

Adding the Other Media

If you haven't already created bins in your project for the still photos and any B-roll material you have, do so now and import them into the appropriate bin. You can change the name of any file in the editor to make a clip name more descriptive and again it will not affect the original file name; it's just an aid inside the editor for easy clip recognition. If you are using any sound effects or stingers, also create a bin for these files. "A place for everything and everything in its place," as my Dad used to tell me when talking about his tools. Your video tools should be equally easy to find and use.

THERE'S TREASURE IN THEM HILLS
While on the subject of other media you can add to your video, take a look at archive.org, particularly the Prelinger Archive. This library has archived hundreds of old films, TV shows, commercials and industrial videos that are in the public domain. There are many clips from the 50s and 60s and the quality, although not up to SDV levels, is adequate for filler. Some of these old video clips are awesome sources of images. If you use any of archive.org's material, be sure to give the credit where it is due.

Once you have all the assets for the project in the editor, the primary video tracks in sync and all the other material in place, save the project with a name like "ReadyToEdit." Inside your editor all the players are on the stage and awaiting your editing magic. We now have just a few more things to consider before we go to work with the razor.

CHAPTER 8

Editing

Before You Begin Editing

In the last chapter, we got all our resources into an editing project and have all the content arranged for easy access and use.

Your editing screen at the beginning of the edit process for a three-camera shoot might look something like this:

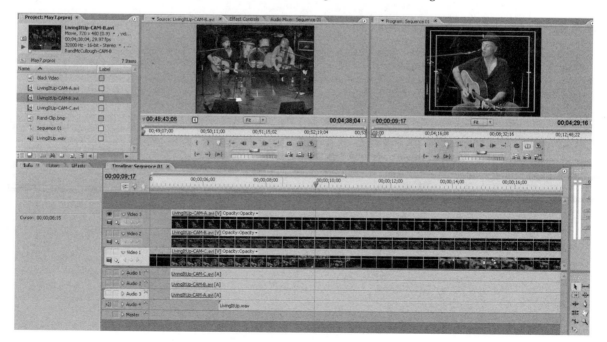

Produce & Promote Your Music Video

GLOBAL COLOR AND WHITE BALANCE CORRECTION

In this step, we will take a look at the footage and try to give uniformity to the white balance and color. It's important to match the footage from the cameras globally as well as you can before starting to cut. A uniform look lends consistency from one camera shot to the other. However, use color correction and lighting effects sparingly; a little bit goes a very long way.

If we made use of our camera's white balance feature when we started recording the video, we should be pretty close to viewing the same color temperature and exposure with all the cameras. Theoretically. CMOS chip sizes and brands, lens differences, etc., can make a perfect white balance difficult. If there is a big difference in the color depth and lighting temperature between the cameras, you can adjust these parameters now so that your clips are as uniform as possible. These changes aren't etched in stone but a cohesive color balance will make a better starting place. You may in fact wind up color correcting the video twice: once at the onset of editing to make the gamma and color temperature uniform between clips and again at the end of the edit to touch up any deficiencies that might be apparent in the overall final edit. Use care in color correcting your master edit; after a long render is completed or the DVDs have been burned there is no "Undo" button.

Select the clip you want to color correct, then select color correction from the video effects menu or list of your editing program.

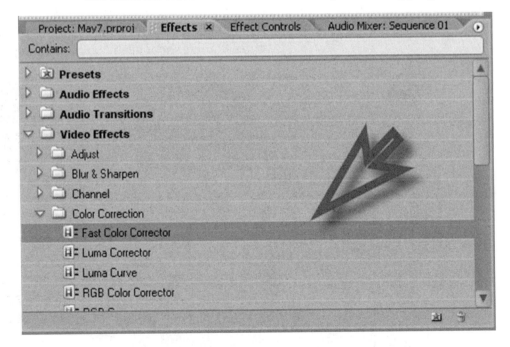

When you bring up the controls for color correction, you will probably see the standard color wheel. You may also have the option of splitting the screen so you can see the video both raw and with the color correction. The color wheel is easy to use; when you move the pip in a circular manner, the hue colors change. As you drag the pip towards the outside edges of the color wheel, the intensity or saturation of that color range is increased. Color correction is usually a very subtle process and it's easy to go overboard and oversaturate the image, so be careful. The color wheel can also be used for creating a color sepia tone if you want some of the clips to appear to be old film or still footage. Most programs also have presets; they might not do the trick completely, but could be good starting points.

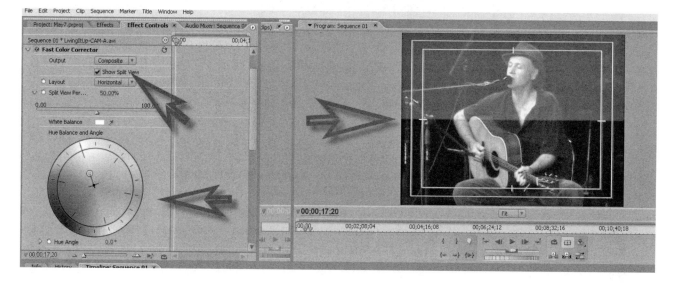

Experiment with small clips, and when you have dialed in the setting, save the project with a name like "Clips Corrected" or something similar. Depending on your editing software you can save the correction setting into your toolbox or, in the case of Premiere, you can select the clip that you just corrected, right-click on it and select "Copy." Then, select the clip for which you wish to reuse the color correction settings, right-click again and select "Paste Attributes." This feature will work with both transitions and effects in most video editing software.

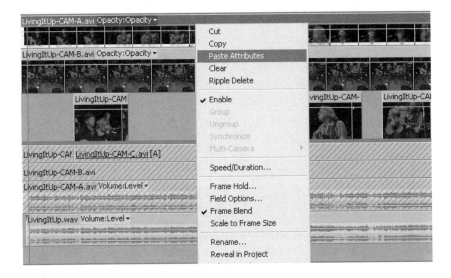

Note that depending on the number of video tracks or streams you are editing and the complexity of the effect or transition, you may require a render to see the fruits of your work. This will depend primarily on your system RAM and processor speed.

This has copied the color correction settings from one track to the next. Repeat as necessary for the rest of the video tracks. Keep in mind that you can change these attributes at anytime in the future. Many of the more "out there" music videos use the color wheel to create oversaturated and gnarly-looking clips. If you want to remove color correction from a clip or a just part of a clip, razor the beginning and end of the portion you want to de-correct, select the clip, right click and select "Clear" or "Reset" depending on your software. This will return the video image back to the state it was in before color correction.

Adjusting the gamma or brightness of the clip may also be necessary; again, a little goes a long way. If you add too much gamma, the video will start looking grainy and washed out. Too little and the image is dark as a dungeon. This is a procedure that only your eyes can judge.

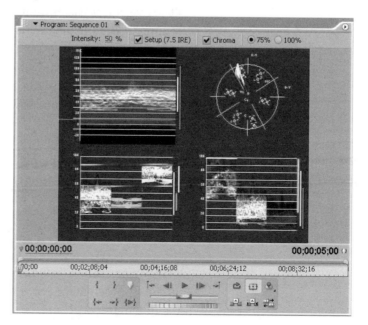

Oversaturating the gamma channel can also deliver some cool effects, especially when combining with a transition. If you stumble on an exceptionally cool setting, save it to your toolkit for later use.

If your software supports it, another way to check your color space is to use to use scopes. The scope will give you a visual representation of your color balance, gamma and other parameters. You can look at a scope view of different clips and see if your color tweaks on the clips look similar. The clips will never be completely identical, but if you are way off base, both the preview and your scopes will reflect the differences.

We now should have our video razor ready. The clips are in sync alignment, the audio tracks are locked, the images are as close to the same color balance and gamma as we are going to get. Let's get ready to rumble.

We are going to walk through both the live recording edit and the lip-sync process. We'll start with the live recording, as it is the easiest to edit.

TIP

Many DVDs contain "extra features" that will sometime include small behind-the-scenes clips and/or director's commentary. These can contain real gems and can be a great aid in learning how to create an effect or mood. The director lets you inside the production to see how she set up a scene or effect, or perhaps how she solved specific problems that arose during production.

The Live Taping Edit

In our example live-production edit, we are recording a popular regional singer and songwriter, Rand McCullough, from Austin, Texas. He is accompanied by Robert McEntee, who normally plays with Dan Fogelberg. We recorded the audio through a small Mackie PA system and only used four channels: two vocals and two guitars. We used the camera tape audio for the crowd noise and room ambience.

The live edit is easier than a lip-sync or concept video because at any time during the performance, one camera will have a better shot than the others. If your master-shot camera is stationary, you don't have to worry about it and you need only seek the "greatest hits" of the other cameras to find the good stuff. When the other cameras aren't cutting it, go to your reliable and uniform key shot.

This was a three-camera shoot. Two of the cameras were mounted and one was being carried by the "rover." One of the mounted cameras was doing the most simple but smooth shots, primarily wide shots of the whole stage, slow zooms, and pans. The rover got down and dirty setting up shots from just below, above, and behind the artist.

The rover camera generally has the most visually compelling shot. First, preview the rover by scrolling through the rover clip; then, delete the portions that are unusable. A good example of unusable footage is when the rover camera is moving to set up the next shot; you probably don't want the camera person's feet and the floor scrolling by in your video. Just use the razor to trim these segments out and you will wind up with a rover "greatest hits" laying on that video track.

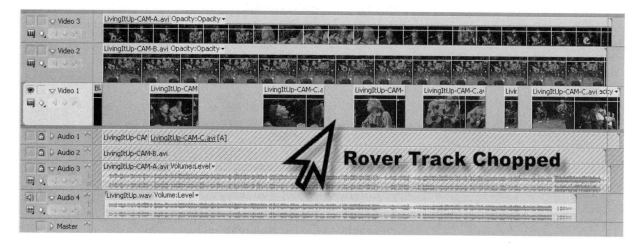

You can see that you will be able to go to a good shot on the rover camera six times during the song. Much of the last segment is a pan across the audience.

The next video line above the rover is the key shot. In this example, the key shot never moves or changes, so you know what that track is going to look like throughout the video. There is no need to preview the whole clip. Using this process of elimination, we go through the video slowly and find which of the three tracks give us the best image at any given time. When you get finished with deciding which camera works best at any given time, your timeline will look something like this:

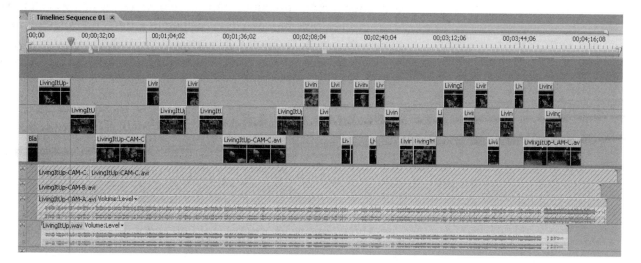

As illustrated, the roving camera is used almost every chance a good shot comes up on that track. There are only thirty edit points in this video, but we used the material to give us the best display possible. We could add more movement and activity, but giving the viewer time to actually see what's in a given scene can be as important as a machine-gun staccato burst of fast images that is common in the lip-sync. This is a major aesthetic difference between a lip-sync and a live video edit. We now have the greatest hits of all three video tracks and are ready to add transitions where necessary.

Edit Types

RIPPLE EDIT

If you want to make changes to a clip's duration without affecting any of the other clips on the timeline, this is the editing method of choice. If you shorten a clip, for example, it will pull the other clips a bit to the left on the timeline to close the gap created by the clip shortening. This is the most common method of editing and is appropriate for video sources that do not require sync. This is usually the default editing style on most NLE software.

ROLLING EDIT

This editing variation is similar to a ripple edit but the total program time can't be changed—good for use in a music video. When a clip is shortened, the adjacent clip's in point is changed to fill the gap created by the clip trimming. You can replace other clips on the timeline if just extending the clip following the cut is not adequate. This method requires manual tweaking.

SLIDE EDITING

What if you want to move multiple clips around your timeline without affecting the total time of the program? A slide edit will allow you to move multiple files or a whole segment around on the timeline. The software makes up for these changes by modifying adjacent files but leaving the total play time of the video intact. This method requires manual tweaking.

SINGLE-TRACK EDITING VS. A/B TRACK EDITING

These terms are referring to the user interface of the editor rather than an actual editing process. In single-track editing, you place two clips beside each other on one track; in A/B editing, you use two tracks to accomplish the same effect. It is about how the editing workspace looks, not behaves. Both are popular methods. In my case, for the first couple years I used A/B editing because it was more familiar to my older analog habits. I now edit exclusively using single-track editing because I have found it to be faster and it frees up at least two video tracks worth of space in my congested workspace.

Adding a Transition Between Video Clips

The most common way of getting from one image to another is the straight cut, sometimes called the hard cut. You move from one camera view to the other in the space of a frame and there is no movement or dissolve between the clips. The next most common transition and one we will use extensively in the live recording editing situation is the dissolve. This is where the image from one video track is mixed slowly into another video track; it's simple but sweet. It is the most common transition you will see in concert music videos.

You set the length of the transition between the clips usually by selecting how much of the two clips overlap each other. In addition, most video editing software will come with library of other, fancier transitions. In the live recording project, we will want to steer away from most of these. Our goal is to give the viewer something like the experience they would have if they were in the audience; cutesy transitions such as flying wipes, rotating cubes, and spheres might look good on your vacation video for Grandma but are not really appropriate for this application. In this case, less is more.

My method of setting up clip transitions now that I've found all the best shots is to pull all the video clips down onto one timeline. The results look something like this:

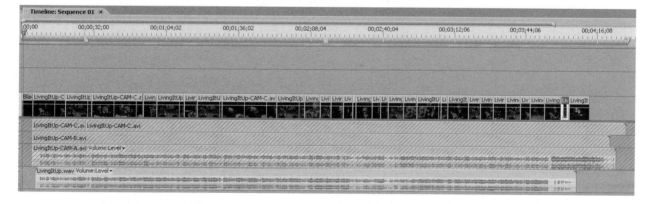

Play the entire clip through and see where the existing straight cuts will work and where you will want to add transitions. You can tweak the in and out points by just dragging the edge of the file to make it shorter or longer. A good point for an image change is where the song underlines something: the beginning of a verse or chorus, maybe a strong lick by the guitarist, or a massive downbeat by the drummer. The image changes should also be in sync with the audio track when possible.

After reviewing the song, I have found a few places where a cross-dissolve will work better than a straight cut. As we only have three video sources in this project, we need to do all we can to break up the video image with what few resources we have. A way to get a bit more mileage out of a transition is to make the transition long. Let's add a few transitions to our video.

At the beginning of the video we will probably fade up from black. Even though this will be the first transition seen by the viewer, it will be the last one we will work on; the beginning and end of the song will need a bit of special attention for titling so we will revisit them later in the edit.

This video is a straight-ahead performance, so the primary transitions will be the straight cuts that are already there and a few cross dissolves to break up the monotony. The additive dip to black dissolve is also applicable in concert video. One clip fades to complete blackness before the next clip fades up from black. The dip to black can be used to underline a dramatic change in the song or a "turning the page" event.

You just select the transition preset you want to use and drag and drop it onto the clips you want to effect. You may have to be zoomed in to get the precision you are looking for in the in and out points of the transition. Like the clips themselves, you can adjust the length of the transition by stretching either end of the transition to make it longer or shorter, or to show more of one than the other during the change.

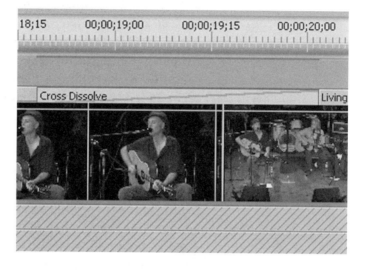

In your software, you should be able to preview your A/B clip transition from the actual video files. In Adobe Premiere you have a small check box for the option.

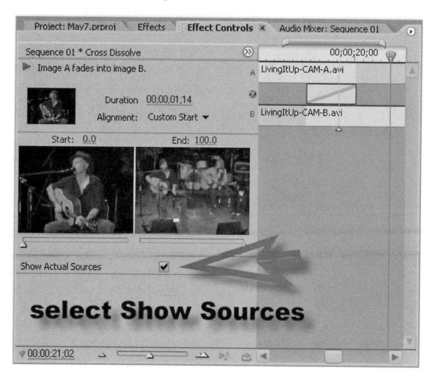

Adding Effects to Clips

Most video editing software programs, from the lowly Movie Maker and iFilm to the high-end products, contain a library of video effects. In my experience most of them are worthless. Liberal use of effects and cutesy transitions is the mark of an amateur in the video world; it's a sign that something's wrong with the content. Keep in mind that whatever the subject of your video, whether a musical act or a car documentary, it is the subject that is important, not your video editing tricks. Successful video editing should be almost invisible. The focus should always be on the artist and song. Any effect or transition that detracts from the artist's performance is counterproductive. Note that I will soon be eating these words when we go to edit the lip-sync.

KEYFRAMES AND EFFECTS

A powerful part of video editing available in most editing software is what is known as keyframing. A keyframe is a frame location in a video clip that is set as a marker for an action by the editing software; usually an event modifying an effect transition or audio plug-in. For example, you may want to add a colorization effect to a ten second clip, fading in and out of a color scheme over the clip. You set the first keyframe where you want the effect to begin and a keyframe where you want the effect (or transition) to end. The space between the start and end marker points are the "tween" spaces where the computer interprets the change and automatically calculates the changes in a linear fashion. You don't have to tweak every frame; the computer will do a lot of the work for you. For even finer control of the effect or transition, you can subdivide the transition down to the frame level for precision tweaking. Using keyframes gives you accuracy in transition and effect tweaking that just dragging and dropping onto a video clip won't give you.

You may already be familiar with keyframes. Keyframes are commonly used in audio editing timelines too. If you have ever used the volume or pan line in the WAV file view in your audio software rather than the faders when performing mix automation, you are using keyframes. The only difference is the audio marker is pointing at a specific sample or time location rather than a video frame. Video software can be also be generally categorized as "consumer" or "pro" by the availability, features and power of keyframes in the software. The cheaper or free software will have little or no support for this powerful tool.

Keyframes are a core component to any kind of computer–based animation. 3D objects in motion are all controlled by keyframes. When an orc raises his eyebrow in *Lord of the Rings*, the action is controlled by keyframes. Getting familiar with using keyframes is a valuable skill set in both video and audio production.

Utilizing Stills

Although we will be using stills more frequently in our lip-sync edit, they can also be used in live recording scenarios. A common trick is to use the last frame of the performance clip as a still background for credits to roll over. You can also utilize image files with an alpha channel for lower thirds and titling. An alpha channel turns the image background to clear or 100 perfect transparency. You can sometimes get a better title using Photoshop or other graphics software than you might get in the in-editor titling widget. Keep in mind to create and save your graphics file in 720x480 resolution and keep the alpha layer intact by saving as a .PSD, TIFF, or .PNG file. JPG and BMP files don't retain alpha layer information.

If you have an image larger than 720x480 pixels, you can adjust the image size in the editor and use pan and zoom effects as methods to put movement into a still image. You probably won't want to deal with images smaller than that. Most documentaries dealing with subject matter before the advent of film use this technique liberally. A good example of a documentary with virtually no video is Ken Burns's *The Civil War*. There weren't any IMAX cameras at the Battle of Gettysburg, but more than a few still photographers (called daguerreotype in those days) were on hand. The battle is immortalized on video because of these still photographers.

In our example with Rand, we are going to use the last frame of the performance edit as a lead in to the credits. We start by cueing up the last frame of the video and saving the frame as a still. In Premiere you choose "Export Frame" from under the Export options on the File menu. In other software I have seen this as a "snapshot" feature.

Name the file something memorable and save it. In the project still directory, of course.

Place the clip at the end of the timeline adjacent to the clip you exported the still from. Drag the still image length out a little bit and play the last five seconds of the clip. With the still butted up against the last frame of the clip, you should see the movie stop and the still displayed.

As I review the edit, I notice a problem at the beginning of the song. We snagged the primary audio from a CD track and noticed that the crowd noise at the introduction dropped off too quickly and sounds unnatural or canned. One of those camera audio tracks we unlinked from the video but didn't delete is going to come in handy during this quick fix.

I move to the end of our video and look at the audio waveform where the song has ended and the audience starts applauding. Make sure there is no audio from the performer ("thank you very much"). Using the razor tool, cut about ten seconds of applause from the audio track. Select the audience audio clip and copy it. Paste it into an existing empty audio track at the beginning of the song. If there is no audio track to paste to, create one.

I have a couple of choices on how to mix the crowd audio into the beginning of the song. Some editors, including Premiere, have an audio mixer function. If your editor doesn't have an audio mixer you can probably use the volume/gain keyframe feature from right on the timeline.

Another thing to keep in mind if you are creating a video with more than one song in it is that, just like video clips, you can add cross dissolves and effects to the audio tracks. Crossfading from one song to another is a popular way to segue from one song to the other, especially if the songs are in complimentary keys. A touch of long reverb can help round out a sharp song ending.

Titling and Credits

One of the most important aspects of finishing up your video clip is to brand it with a title or overlay. If you have a website, be sure to put the address in your video and make it prominent and easy to read even after the video servers have crunched it. The typical branding as seen on MTV is fine for something that will be broadcast or put in DVD format but will not be legible on most web video streaming sites. A good place to put your brand/logo is at the beginning and end of the video in high contrast and a simple, easy-to-read font. Your branding and titling is important and should be prominent and legible. You can use the titling feature of your software or create your own titles using an image editor like Photoshop™. First, let's take a look at using the title generator inside Premiere.

We are going to start with a simple lower third from the template library in Premiere. You can create your own lower thirds and other titles in any photo enhancing software that supports alpha layer file types like, .TIF, .PNG, and .PSD.

First we will set our timeline cursor to the place where we want to place the title. This will give us the screen view of the title being layered over the background. This preview feature is handy as it can keep you from displaying your title over something you want the viewer to see. In that case, either modify the title by placing it somewhere else on the screen or just move the title to a position a bit earlier or later in the video.

From the file menu or using the F9 key in Windows, start the titling applet. A common feature of almost all title generating software is a library of fonts that have already been tweaked for a display a bit more creative than just plain text on a background. Experiment with these settings and you will find some that you will use frequently. For now, we will use a Premiere template.

Notice the boxes around the image, the outer box is what is known as "action safe," meaning that if your primary motion is within the boundaries of the box, you should see all of it on any display. The inner box designates the "title safe" area. You need to place any titles or text-based effects within this inner box.

The lower third we want to use is selected from the template library. All you need to do is to type in the new text and you are done. If your text is longer than will fit in the template, lower the font size or perhaps even change the font so it will fit in the template. With the title applet open, from the Title menu select "New Title" then "Based on Template" as shown below.

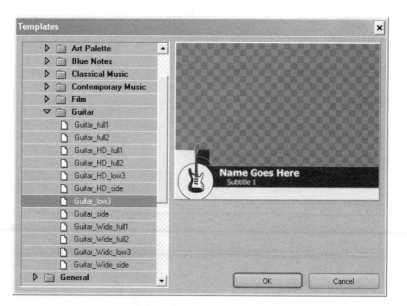

A menu of Premiere title templates appears and we will scroll down to the Entertainment tab and drill down to select the Guitar lower third template.

The rest is easy. Just place the cursor in the text boxes and change the text. We now have a nice lower third at the beginning of the song to brand it with our artist name. Another option would be to replace the guitar icon with your logo.

One last tweak and we're done with the title at the beginning of the video. Let's have our lower third fade in and out by placing a cross dissolve transition at the front and back of the title. In this example, I worked it both ways; at the beginning of the title I just dragged and dropped a cross dissolve from the Video Effects bin and at the end I used keyframes and the opacity line to fade out the title. The results are the same using both methods; it is a matter of personal taste as to which method you use. I have noticed that video producers who are also musicians tend to use the second method, using the time line keyframes because it is similar to tweaking an audio file.

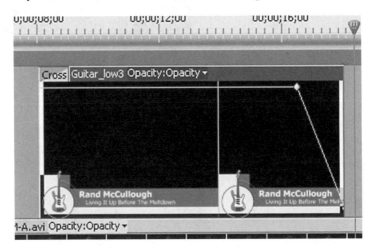

Our lead-in lower third title is in place, so now let's go to the end of the song and insert our industry-standard "MTV" overlay title.

During our edit, we ended the song with a freeze frame still of Randy waving at the audience. We will start our exit title at that point on the time line.

I have seen a few variations on this type of title but in general the title is four lines in this order:

"Song Title

"Recording Artist"

"Album Name or Sometimes the Label"

"Producer or Songwriter Name"

We are going to plug this information into the title applet. You have seen a number of MTV videos so you can tell about what size the screen font needs to be.

TIP

When generating text-based titles, especially these smaller titles at the end of the song, use a non-cursive font like Arial. Cursive fonts like Times do not display as legibly as the non-cursive types.

"Living It Up (Before The Meltdown)"
Performed by Rand McCullough
Wooden Fish Records
Written by Rand McCullough

In general, I'm a design-challenged person but as in using effects in editing, too many fancy titles racing around the screen is the sign of an amateur or someone with way too much time on their hands. Keep it simple. If you watch great titling on a feature film, the effect may be killer but the display is always subtle and understated; part of what makes a great title is that the eye is drawn to it. Also try to utilize the same look in terms of fonts, size, etc. throughout the video in order to keep the look uniform. In most cases, less is more.

ROLLING CREDITS

For most one-song music videos, the method above will be the only way to do titling. That is why you don't see long rolling credits at the end of songs on MTV.

Rolling credits would be applicable if you were creating a movie of an entire performance for distribution on the web or DVD. An entire performance will be closer to the length of a film and you can take the time to credit the entire production team. Let's take a look at creating a quick rolling title.

Again place the cursor at the location on the timeline where you want the rolling title to begin. This is usually the last frame of the video or the black at the conclusion of the song.

Type in your information in the same format you have seen in almost every movie you've ever watched. You may have to reduce the font size to get long names or titles on one line. I generally start my rolling credit off the bottom of the screen and at the end let the titles roll all the way off the top of the screen. You can modify the speed of the roll by right clicking on the title and from the "Speed/Duration" menu option reduce the speed to 50 percent for example and the titles will scroll by at half the speed. Save your project.

We now have our video clip complete from start to finish. We can start looking at the formats we want to output in. Or perhaps we might want to edit a lip-sync edit.

The Lip-Sync Edit

Where the live recording edit went quickly the lip-sync edit will go much slower. The live video only had about thirty cuts and transitions, add an introduction and exit title and you're done. In the case of the lip-sync we will be looking at many more edits and transitions. I edited the live video in just a couple hours. The lip-sync will take considerably more time.

We are going to create a new project folder on our video drive and place all our content in it. Then using the video editor, create a new project, again checking our audio bit depth and sampling rate to match that of the primary non-camera audio track.

Now we are going to create descriptive top-level bins into which we will import our content.

We are now ready to start importing the content.

A TWO-MODULE PROJECT

Because we didn't get the content we were looking for on our rainy exterior shooting day, our green-screen work is going to be the bed of this video. This created a lot of work in the post process because something has to be behind the green that we composite out. I used three applications to create the video animation backgrounds that would be the backgrounds for the green screen shots: Bryce 6.0 for quick clouds, Particle Illusion for emitter type effects, and Vue Esprit for panned landscapes. This portion of the project is a standalone edit in its own right.

Because it is going to take longer, I build my green-screen/CG base first. When completed this will be the key track that I will use as my fallback when I run out of our scant location shots. I have four camera passes of Josh in front of the screen from different angles and zoom levels. I also have two passes each of the drummer and bass player against the screen to work with.

After I have all the clips in and synced, the workspace is looking a bit crowded so I am going to unlink the audio from the video clips and delete the all the audio files except the main audio track. Doing this deleted four audio tracks and freed up a bit of space to make the visual side of editing a bit easier. If you think you may use some of the camera audio, composite an audio track of the material you're most likely to use and delete all the rest. In Someone Like You's video, we will be working off only the main audio so I deleted everything else.

After having unlinked all the audio files that we are not going to use, we free up some space by deleting them. In Premiere you can right click on the master box for any audio track and select "Delete Tracks" from the popup menu.

Another task box pops up. If you select "Delete Video Track(s)" and "Delete Audio Track(s)" with the "All Empty Tracks" option selected for both, you will strip unused tracks from the project and give yourself a bit more screen real estate.

When I'm finished I have one audio track instead of six and the workspace has become a bit tighter and video-centric.

Now we need to key the clips that are going to require alpha channels for our compositing. I use compositing-specific software, ULTRA 2, which can give me any easy alpha channel in sometimes questionable light but for now we will look at the keying features in Premiere. Keep in mind that the concepts are the same regardless of what software you are using.

Looking at the bass player's track we can see that our lighting is less than perfect. Multiple shadows are apparent. We may have to place more than one keying filter on the clip to get a decent alpha channel background. Let's see how a quick chroma key can help us drop out the green background.

We click on the Effects tab and from the Video Effects subgroup, select Keying and then Chroma Keying. Drag the Chroma Key selection and drop it on the clip you are working with.

Now select the Effects Control tab and click the arrow to bring up the options menu. The basic part of keying is setting the color range to be dropped out. Use the eyedropper and select a part of the screen that would be "midway" between the brightest green background and the darkest shadow in the green area.

Our green selection now shows up as our key color next to the eyedropper icon. Now we will spread the color range of the key a bit using the Color Tolerance slider. As we move it to the right, more of our green screen disappears. At a certain level we will start seeing our subject turn transparent; at that point, start backing off your settings a bit. You can further refine your key by setting the size of the edge, perhaps a bit of edge feathering to make our composite a bit less jagged. We have tweaked the chroma key, but we're still getting a few green screen artifacts in the background. If you are producing a New Age music video, leave it in to serve as an "aura."

To get a finer tuning on your key, you can use multiple filters, especially if you have less-than-perfect light. You can set each filter to cover a specific and smaller range of color for more precision in your key. In this case I have added a color key and used the same fine tuning tools as we just did with the chroma filter. I have stacked up to six different filters on one clip before to get a good key. Of course the number of filters you apply to a clip will add to the render times necessary to get a preview.

When we have tweaked as best we can we now have our bass player's clip laid on a motion background.

We will cover how to create your own motion backgrounds in the next chapter.

After repeating the process for each video track, we should now have all our clips on the timeline in sync and with an alpha channel. Much like our live recording edit, at any given time on the timeline there is one shot that is better than all others. To find the good shots, we will scrub through each video clip, while the others are turned off/muted, and razor out all the parts of the clip we know we are not going to use. Again, this creates a "greatest hits" for each video track. When we are finished our project will look much like our live editing start screen.

TIP

Quick and cool. You can use slow motion to lengthen or add drama to a clip and to cover up sync discrepancies. Also motion blur can be a cool effect for a video of ethereal subject matter.

FINISHING UP: TITLING AND CREDITS

Our titling will be a bit different in the lip-sync than the live video shoot. The end "MTV" type credits will be identical but we will go with something a bit more aggressive (if not creative) for the lead title on the lip-sync. The video opens with Josh walking down the alley and the next two clips bring in the other band members. I inserted one word of the band's name, Someone Like You, between each of these clips and made the font size large. I placed the titles on a black background and the effect works well with my introduction black and white clips.

At the end of the song I duplicated the live recording title credits, just replacing Josh's information for Randy's.

Our lip-sync edit is almost finished. Let's take a short look at some computer graphics tricks and ideas before we start outputting our masterpiece to DVD and the web.

CHAPTER 9

Computer Graphics

Because of our change in plans regarding the outdoor shooting, we had to use a great deal of our green-screen passes to flesh out our video. It takes a lot more work than just shooting live, but can also give your video an artsy, high-tech look.

Computer animated graphics can be a powerful addition to your video production toolkit. Since the days of Dire Straits' MTV smash hit "Money for Nothing" decades ago, computer-generated graphics and characters have become more common. I'm not a particularly talented animator, so I keep my backgrounds pretty simple. In the right hands, however, the technology can do amazing things.

The downside of adding computer-generated graphics of any complexity to your project is that the learning curve for 3D object creation and animation can be quite steep. Depending on length and complexity, the render times can also be really long.

CGI Software

Without going into a lot of detail, let me share with you the CGI software I use and what I use it for.

ADOBE AFTER EFFECTS

After Effects is the primary tool I use to bring two dimensional images, both stills and video, into a three-dimensional workspace. Its interface is timeline-based and very similar to Premiere, so navigating my way through its features is easy for any Adobe user. I use After Effects for keying out blue and green screens, flying in video images, and making logos. It uses layers like Photoshop does, so you can manipulate each component separately with a lot of control over each piece. I also use After Effects for creating logo rolls from alpha layered-images.

ULTRA 2

Although you can key out green or blue backgrounds in most video editing software, the results aren't always optimal. Ultra 2 from Serious Magic is a specific application for keying. In most cases, even using bad or uneven lighting the results of the key produced by Ultra 2 are astounding. Try pouring a glass of water from a pitcher in front of a green screen, and you will see what I am talking about. Most of the other keying features in prosumer editing applications don't get this kind of accuracy.

VUE ESPRIT

Vue Esprit is the mid-range environment and animation generator from a software company called e-on. I use the software to create environments when I don't have the resources to physically go to the location, which is often. I need a sunset on an island beach with slowly moving clouds, the waves rolling in, and a slowly setting sun. I don't have the money or moxie to fly to Jamaica for my 60-second clip, so I bring Jamaica to me via Vue Esprit. This application creates great environments, but can also create very long render times at higher resolutions.

PARTICLEILLUSION 2.0 SE

You can download a free 30-day version of this software with no watermarking or other limitations, and the software is only $99 for the SE edition. I use particleIllusion for creating motion backgrounds and adding effects to videos. Even in the SE version, you get a lot of control over the particle emitters and can get some very cool backgrounds very quickly. The advantage in using particleIllusion over other CG effects is that the workspace is in 2D and the renders are much shorter than with a render from within a 3D application. I find I can create dozens of eye-popping video backgrounds in particleIllusion in the time it takes to render one 3D scene of any complexity. I can layer multiple particle videos in After Effects for some great motion menu backgrounds.

Making Your Motion Background Clips

Any of the applications I just described can create motion backgrounds. Which tool you use is a matter of taste. Each piece of software approaches the content creation in a different manner; you can find lots of information on different applications and methods on the Internet. But how do get motion backgrounds into your project if you don't have any specific software?

USING STILL IMAGES

If you don't have access to software that can create animated backgrounds, not to worry, any photo or imaging software can help you create a still background that you can animate once it is in the editing software. Animating the still for rotation is straightforward and simple. First calculate how long your background needs to be. It should be at least a couple seconds longer than the video clip; leaving a second or two at the beginning and end will come in handy should you try any clip transition other than a straight cut.

I fired up my photo editor and created a new image, one about twice as large as my 720x480 project. On it I dropped one of the cute *Austin Powers*-style spirals from my texture library. The reason that I made the image large is that if I left it in 720x480 resolution, I would have a problem after the image has rotated 90 degrees; I would have had only 480 pixels to cover our 720 screen. At 1500x1500, not only will this problem go away but if I want to zoom in or out of our spiral, I have headroom to do so.

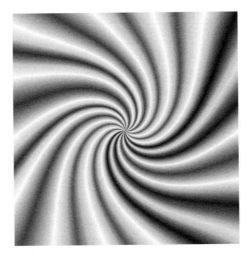

Animating this image is pretty straightforward from here. Our editor doesn't work in 3D space so we can only rotate the image on a 2D plane.

I usually start a new editing project each time I create a motion background. Doing this inside my main edit project will make keeping track of files a bit harder and when I make the short clip it will be in the native editing format and no rendering will be necessary to see it in real time. I animate the still and then render and import the finished movie clip into the project. On the other hand, if you are only creating one or two of these backgrounds you can do them inside the main edit project if you think the inventory is not getting out of hand. This is a very simple animation; we are just going to spin the spiral clockwise for a couple turns.

After selecting the clip, go to the Effects Control tab or the equivalent on your editor. In the rotation section set a keyframe on the first frame. Now scrub down the timeline to the last frame of the clip and set another keyframe. While remaining at the position, select the rotation dropdown menu and use the wheel to set your rotations. In the example below I have set the image to rotate almost three times in the eight seconds we need the clip. Run the project from the beginning of the timeline and our spiral should be spinning like Austin's time tunnel.

All you have to do now is to export the file as a movie clip. Remember to turn off the audio when rendering the clip; we don't need to make a separate audio track for sound that isn't there.

You now have a custom motion background created quickly and easily. You can place this below any video channel that contains an alpha layer and you have your *Austin Powers* time machine scene locked down.

USING PARTICLEILLUSION

Here's how I created most of backgrounds for the Someone Like You video. When you start particleIllusion, set your screen size large enough so that you can see all of the main view at your default file settings (720x480).

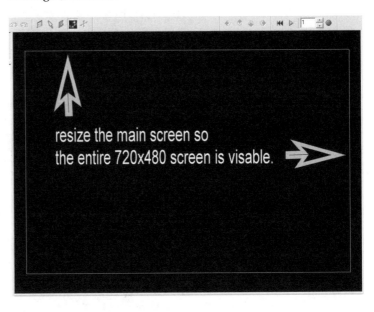

To the right you will see a list of the particles available in the loaded library. If you right click in that area, a popup menu appears and you can select "Load Library" from the list.

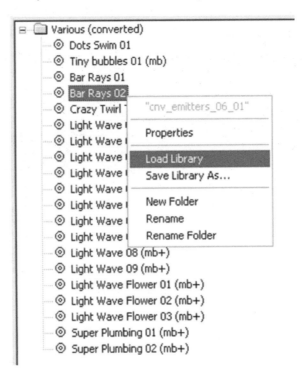

First, we will load the video background that we are placing the particles over. This is not necessary if you are just creating a background for a clip to lay over but it is a handy thing to know. You can import stills and video clips of various file types.

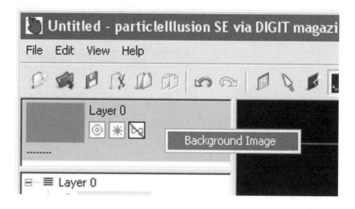

Load another library if the particle emitters in the default library aren't what you are looking for. When you select a particle emitter you will see a preview in the right screen.

You can move the particle effect or tweak it anywhere in the timeline. On the left screen are the particle parameters, you select the parameter you want modify and use the keyframe timeline below the main screen to set in and out points and changes in the particle emitter component. The left screen gives you a preview of the current particle selected in the library.

All that is left to do is to click on the red "record" button. Tell particleIllusion where we want to store the rendered file, what we want to name it, and what the first and last frame will be.

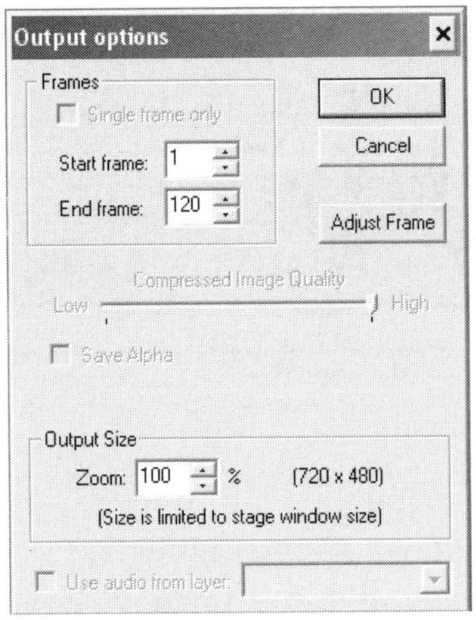

Note the output size is what we are looking for. Sometimes you can move the screens around inside particleIllusion and when you resize your preview screen, you are also resizing your output default so be careful. If you find the output size is smaller than 720x480, just move the boundary boxes of the main screen outward until you can see the whole full screen image. There will be a boundary box visible in the main screen.

The next box is asking how you want to encode this clip. The video codecs loaded on your computer appear in the drop down menu. For the best quality and compatibility, I always use the "Full Frames Uncompressed" setting as seen below.

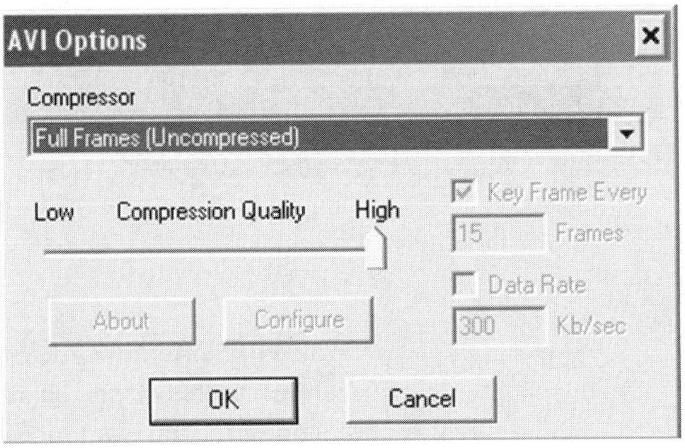

There are other particle emitter software packages out there, but I have seen nothing close to this price point. particleIllusion is also fun to use.

Now we have our edits finished, and before we take a look at our different output options for distributing our video, we have just a bit more special effects editing to do, for our DVD motion menus.

Creating a Motion Menu for DVD

Before we move on, we are going to make a motion menu for our upcoming DVD authoring session. I'm sure you have noticed that the slicker DVDs will have animations on their main menus. Some of these menus are in and of themselves works of art. A motion menu creates increased perceived value to the buyer. I don't expect to see motion menus on the Wal-Mart DVDs that have two movies on them for $4.99, but when I shell out $19.95 you better believe I want to be entertained!

Let's create a simple motion menu for Someone Like You using three components: photos, video, and particle backgrounds. Most good DVD authoring programs are able to import normal video and use it as the menu background. Normally, I would do the compositing in After Effects, but in this case we will do it in Premiere as the animation will be a simple one.

The easiest way to create a motion menu that doesn't jerk when it reaches the end and loops back to the beginning is to have an identical frame at both the beginning and end of the menu clip. The process is called looping and we will use a fade out and a fade in from black to keep things from jerking.

I open Premiere and create a new project named something like "MotionMenu-01." I will point it to a newly created directory named—yup, you guessed it—the "Motion Menus" directory. It's really important to keep things organized!

I am going to use a montage of music video clips, three B-roll clips, and a few stills to create a thirty second motion menu. From the file menu I create a block of black video and place it on the beginning of the timeline. Adjust the size of the clip to one second. We will build our menu from that starting point.

Just as we did in our other edits, we will be stacking the components up on video tracks above the time line. Since we will have to do a bit of work on the photos first, we will start there.

In your photo editing software, in my case PhotoImpact 11, open the image files you want to include in the menu. For this project I want one image of each band member. If I don't have stills, I use exported frames from the video to get the job done. The goal is to create images of the band members that have an alpha layer we can fade in and out.

I don't have any stills of the band, so I revisit my last edit and scroll down the timeline until I find a frame featuring the best image of the band member I'm looking for.

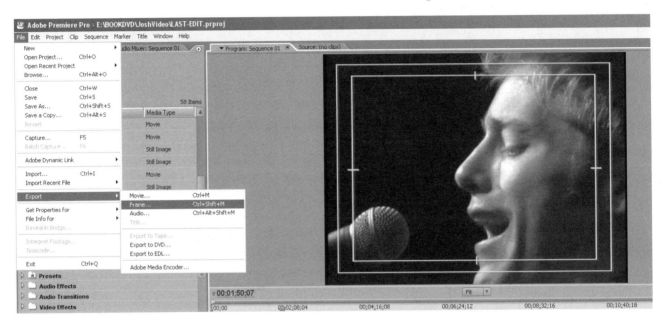

I repeat the procedure for the other two band members. I now have my raw material for the still photo part of the menu.

While I'm still in Premiere I look for three excerpt clips that are about 10 seconds long, the greatest hits part of the video. These will be layered under the stills. Tweak these shorter clips to taste, then render them to individual clips without an audio track. Save them to, you guessed it, the "MenuClips" directory. We'll be returning to them in a moment.

TIP

While setting this project up, I was moving back and forth between my lip-sync edit project and my new motion menu project. Little did I know until now is that when I select a clip in one project, I can right click on it, select, "Copy," open a completely different project, find a place on the timeline and just "Paste" it onto the time line. This is a very handy feature.

In your photo editor, pull up the three band member images and using the lasso tool, composite out the band member. Copy the image into memory. Create a new file with a transparent or alpha background and paste our band member into it. It should look something like this.

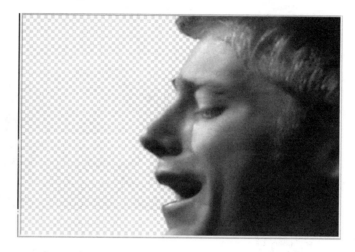

Now save these three files in a file format that supports alpha layers such as .PSD or .PNG and we have our alpha layer stills created and ready.

Back in the editor I should now have three video clips and three photo images. My one second of black awaits company on the timeline. I grab one of the video tracks and drop it next to the black. Now I put the color wheel effect on it and colorize it off the map. I also cut the clip speed in half so it appears as a slow motion shot. I repeat this with variations. I limit each clip to about ten seconds. Now between each clip, including the black starting point, I drop a cross dissolve from my transition toolkit. I add another second of black to the end and place a cross dissolve between it and the last clip also. My last touchup on the video side of things is to make these cross dissolves much longer than a normal one, so long in fact that the unaffected portion of the clip is only about 1/3 of the clip. It should look something like this:

This is the video bed we will use as the background for our alpha layer stills. Place the stills on a video track above the one we've been working on. Maneuver the clips around, try making them larger and smaller; don't be afraid to experiment. Make sure you stay well within the boundary line of our black video boxes at the beginning and end. Once you have placed your stills above the video and have them where you want them, again place a long cross dissolve at the beginning and end of each of these clips.

Preview your menu. Make sure you are in complete black for the first and last frame. Now is a good time to drop an audio file on the timeline. It can be an excerpt from the video file or something you create just for the menu. Again make sure it is an audio file that will loop nicely. In a similar fashion to our black first and last screen on the video side, you can have silence be the first and last frame of the menu. Use your editor's inline mixer or keyframe the volume fades from the timeline. Bring the audio up from silence to -3db or so and at the end of the file, then set the end of the fade back to silence. You can add audio at a later time if you don't want to now, but doing it here instead of when you are building the motion menus will save a bit of time; you need to create and tweak only one file instead of two. If it looks good, render the file to a new file name and save it to the MotionMenu directory. You now have a motion menu ready for your DVD project. And speaking of DVDs, it's time to make our own!

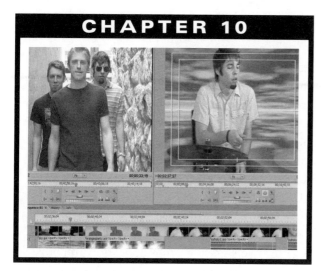

CHAPTER 10

Outputting and Delivering Your Video

After we have our editing finished, we need to get this great piece of work out to the world. The best video ever could be completely ruined by poor choices made while making the DVD or rendering for the Internet.

Making One Clip

I have found the following first step to be incredibly helpful: You should save your entire edit into one clip. Use your editor's export feature and create a new file of your total edit in whatever file format you have been editing in (MSDV, .AVI, .MOV, etc.). This is now your master video file. Although you can export from your timeline, it is often better and cleaner to make sure that you have a master video file on your hard drive in your uncompressed DV format. You can work from this file easily in your DVD program.

Don't delete the original project yet, because we will come back to our editing session again to output the movie for steaming. Let's start with making a DVD of our master file.

DVDs

DVD stands for Digital Video Disc or Digital Versatile Disc; it describes a set of related disc formats encompassing video, audio, and computer file storage on optical discs. There are lots of different flavors of DVDs: DVD-ROM, DVD+R, DVD-RW, and DVD-R. But don't worry; all these formats, after being finalized, will play on set-top players and computers. (Keep in mind that the computer also needs a DVD playing application, but these are generally standard nowadays.) A single-layer DVD contains approximately 4.7 GB of space, while the newer double-layer DVDs will store twice that amount. You can also buy double-sided DVDs that will store 4.7 GB on each side and can be flipped over for two separate programs. I don't recommend this type of media because one thumb print on the media and you can be out of luck.

You can squeeze more time out of a DVD by lowering the playback bitrate, but picture quality will suffer in direct correlation. DVD high-definition formats are now available; however, creating hi-def DVDs is outside of the price range of most musicians at the time of this writing. Once the BluRay/HD-DVD format battle is won, we should see the price of this larger storage medium drop considerably.

A DVD should be targeted to play without error or skipping on:

▶ Set-top standalone DVD Players

▶ Game consoles such as Sony Playstation 3 and Microsoft Xbox

▶ All computers with DVD-ROM drives

TIP

When I first started burning DVDs, I was dismayed to find that the DVDs I created wouldn't work on my top-of-the-line, progressive-scan DVD player. This player, which cost almost $300 when new, wouldn't play any recordable media. If it wasn't replicated in a factory, it wouldn't play. It is odd but the reality is that a $30 DVD player you can buy in any Wal-Mart is more likely to play recordable media of any format than an older top-of-the-line unit. If your DVDs are to be replicated (glass master) instead of duplicated, this incompatibility becomes a moot point.

There are a few more digital-video delivery formats out there such as VCD an SVCD, but with the low cost of DVD burners, players, and recording media, these formats are quickly dying. They were never popular in North America, anyway.

OUTPUTTING TO DVD

Let's walk through the creation of a relatively simple music DVD one step at a time. The DVD we will be authoring is the one that accompanies this book. For this example, I will be using Adobe Encore, but most other DVD authoring software will give you the same features, if not almost the same interface. In fact, the largest difference in the various authoring software I have used is the workspace look and the way the program handles the work flow. I have used a number of other authoring products but decided on Encore because, as I said, it interfaces easily with the other members of the Adobe software family and gets good results quickly. My second choice would be DVD Workshop from ULEAD, which is a very powerful authoring platform.

If you can't afford dedicated authoring software, a number of the programs that come with a DVD burner will create simple DVDs; some, like Nero, will allow you some simple and basic authoring features.

The first thing is to get all your content together that you will need to complete the DVD project. The inventory for this DVD example is:

▶   The main music clips (in this case the song videos)

▶   The motion menus background movie files

▶   The still menu backgrounds

▶   Music track for the motion menu (optional)

▶   The "Extra Features" files included (outtakes, making of, additional tutorials, etc.)

▶   Data files

▶   A logo roll for the first play and an FBI warning to strike fear into the hearts of DVD pirates.

Again, just like the editing portion of our project, we want to keep all of the DVD authoring files in our project directory. Just name a new folder "DVD" inside the project folder and you're good to go. If you wind up archiving the project, you will have not only the raw files should you decide to return for a new edit, but will also have the DVD authoring materials in the archive.

Let's get started. After firing up Encore, we are prompted for the type of DVD we want to make: NTSC or PAL. These refer to different video display standards and should not really concern you, because if you use a piece of gear acquired in North America, it's going to shoot NTSC video. Hence, you should select NTSC if you are in North America. If you are using the PAL system in your part of the world, select PAL.

In the world of DVD content protection, discs are also encoded for specific world "regions." This feature was added to the DVD format as a way of helping content companies limit piracy and control distribution of product. For instance, a Region 3 disc encoded in Asia will not play on Region 1 players sold in the United States. Most DVD authoring programs will create "region-free" discs that will play on all players, so it shouldn't be something you are particularly worried about.

Following is a chart of the different regions:

Region	Countries
0	No Region Coding
1	United States, Canada
2	Europe, including France, Greece, Turkey, Egypt, Arabia, Japan and South Africa
3	Korea, Thailand, Vietnam, Borneo and Indonesia
4	Australia and New Zealand, Mexico, the Caribbean, and South America
5	India, Africa, Russia and former USSR countries
6	Peoples Republic of China
7	Unused
8	Airlines/Cruise Ships
9	Sometimes used as region free

We will be using the NTSC Region 1 as our default for this exercise. You can also encode with Region 0 if you want your DVD to be region-free and playable just about anywhere in the world, if that option is available in your authoring software. This is a good option if your band wants to send DVDs to Europe or Asia.

Our opening screen project bin in Encore looks like this:

Similar in nature to Premiere, we see the content bin labeled "Project" on the left side of the screen. This is the bin we will populate with our content. Just double-click on the empty bin and add all the files you will need for the DVD project to the content bin. In comparison to our editing bin, you can see that there is a lot less content than we saw while editing our lip-sync video. Many DVDs are created with only one file: the video itself, which is configured to play once or loop over and over. We can get a bit fancier than that and will be placing multiple music videos, motion menus, and extra features on our DVD.

Our DVD workspace might look something like this:

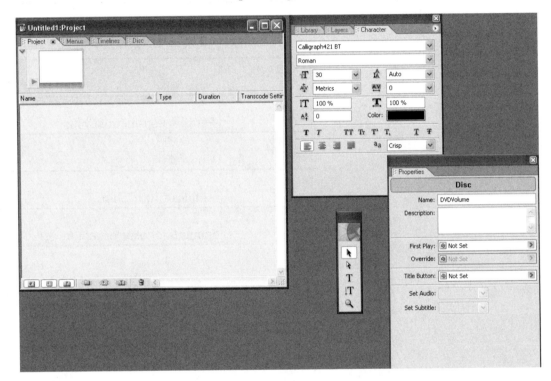

Our DVD is going to contain three separate music clips: the two we shot and edited, and an additional one-camera, one-shot clip recorded at a recent NAMM show. In addition, we will be adding some DVD menu files and motion backgrounds; on the data side we will have a mini website and data files easily accessed by any viewer with a web browser. That is one of the greatest features of a DVD; it is interactive. For example, if the viewer is watching the DVD on a computer and clicks on an Internet link, it will fire up the default web browser and surf to the location specified, which can be an Internet site or another file on the DVD. However, keep in mind that Internet or web features will not work on a standalone DVD player.

MENUS AND MENU STRUCTURE

Before we get started, we have to do a bit of DVD preproduction. It only takes a few moments to outline the menu structure and contents of a DVD. In this project, we will have a total of four menus on our DVD. You can look at the menu structure of a DVD in a similar fashion to a website. The difference is that you can set your DVD for "autopilot" navigation through the disc rather than having to click your way through a website. Your main menu is the equivalent of your home page. Here's what the structure outline looks like:

MAIN MENU

Rand McCullough Live Video

    Randy's Play Page Menu

        Play Video

        Return to Main Menu

Someone Like You Lip-Sync Video

    Someone Like You's Play Page Motion Menu

        Play Video

        Return to Main Menu

Randy Strom One-Camera Video

Extra Features

    Extra Feature Page Menu

    Data Files Menu

    Internet Resources Menu

From the Main menu, if you clicked on the Rand McCullough Live Video, it would navigate to the next menu, which contains an image of Randy, a button to play the video, and a button to return to the main menu. The Someone Like You selection option is very similar; it leads to a submenu. If you click on the Randy Strom option, it will immediately play the video with no menu and return to the main menu when completed or when the main menu button on the DVD player is pushed. The extra features option will lead you to another submenu, this time with instructions on accessing the DVD data files and Internet resources. The only motion menus will be the main menu and Josh's; the others will be still images cropped to 720x480 pixels.

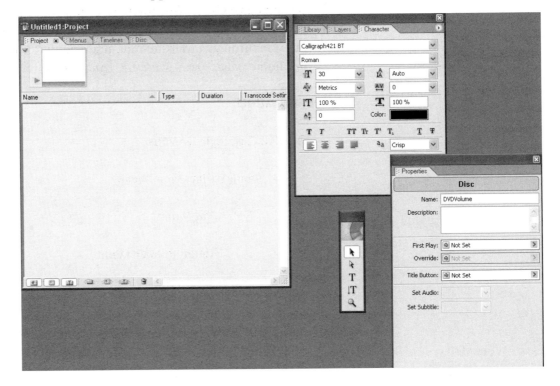

We start by filling the bin with our content. Our inventory list for this project will be:

Video

▶ Rand McCullough Video

▶ Someone Like You Video

▶ Randy Strom Video

▶ First Play (includes FBI warning and logo rolls)

▶ Main Motion Menu File

▶ Someone Like You Motion Menu File

▶ Tips and Tricks file

Stills

▶ Still for Randy McCullough Menu

▶ Still for Extra Features Menu

We will be adding data files to the DVD, but we don't need to be concerned specifically about the files yet. However, it is a good idea to keep the *size* of the data files in mind when authoring. You will add the data to the project last; make sure to leave enough room to fit the data files on the recording media.

FIRST PLAY

When you insert a DVD into a player the first thing you see are FBI warnings, logos, and other branding information. This is the frustrating first-play file that won't permit fast-forwarding or skipping. You too can create one of these nag files and you probably should. The FBI warning screen is on the DVD, and you can create your own logo rolls using alpha layer images and in your editor's titling feature. When done, compile and render them into one first play movie.

LAYING OUT THE PROJECT

The first thing to do is bring the content into the project by importing the files in our inventory. Our project inventory bin might look like this after all the assets are imported with timelines and menus created:

We are going to need four menus: the Main menu, Rand McCullough's menu, Someone Like You's menu and our Extra Features menu. These can be created from scratch or by using one of the templates provided. In the case of the template I selected, I don't like the menu background but I do like the font and a highlighting feature. So I am going to create a new menu using the blue grid template as a starting point. Clicking on the Library tab, I select the blue grid template, then I right-click and create a new menu.

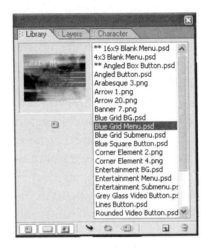

We now have our menu template in the preview window.

Under the Menus tab of the project bin we now see our new menu. I select it, right-click and rename it to MainMenu.

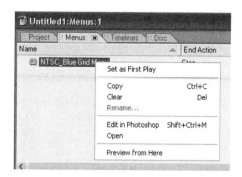

I repeat the entire procedure another three times, one for each menu that I will be using. When completed, the Menus tab of the project bin looks like this:

The next components we need to create are the timelines. Timelines need to be created for the video clips that will be accessed from a menu click; the motion menu files themselves do not need a timeline. Creating a timeline tied to a video clip gives you control over what happens when that clip is played. Once the file has completed playing, what happens next?

The first timeline we create will be the first-play. Create a timeline by selecting the first play video file, right-clicking on it and selecting "Create Timeline." Let's take a look at the timeline's properties.

By default, the name of the timeline is the same as the clip it references. Let's take a short look at the attributes of the timeline options. First the obvious; you can rename the file (again in the project only, not the original file). Since our first-play file is not interactive and we don't want anyone to skip our FBI warning and logos, we set up the first play End Action timeline attribute to go to the main menu when it has played. As you can see, the Override or Menu Remote option is "Not Set." This means that if the viewer hits the menu or next scene button on the remote control, nothing will happen. They are doomed to have to view the whole first play before taking the DVD driver's seat. If you are using other software, the concept remains the same; you want the first-play file to start your DVD and leave the viewer on the main menu. As you can see, Encore has a nice feature that gives you an estimate of the size of the file after encoding; this will help you stay within the boundaries of the DVD media's size limits.

Now we have created our first-play timeline and pointed it to the main menu. It's time to create our navigation tree from the main menu, so select the Menus tab from the project menu and double-click on it to pull up the main menu.

The menu template doesn't look too bad; if I were in a hurry I might just change the main title and a couple things and leave it substantially as-is. For our purposes, however, we need to customize it a bit for our DVD. Our main menu will have a motion background rather than a still image.

Go to the project bin and select MainMotionMenu.avi, which is the motion-menu video file we created in Chapter 9, right-click on it and select copy. Now we bring up our main menu and look at the properties tab. I place the cursor in the Video box and paste the motion menu file into the box. That has placed the motion video as our menu background.

From the project inventory bin, drag and drop an image to the menu. Now inside the menu select the image and from the Object menu select "Arrange" and then "Send to Back."

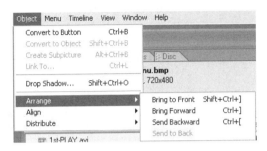

This will move your menu image to the back of the stack and the buttons will appear again.

Just a bit more tweaking and we will be done with the main menu. In terms of main menu properties, most of the default options are fine. One change we need to make is that after the motion menu has played, I want it to start back at the beginning and loop forever.

There are two ways to handle the audio on the main menu: If the audio is already inside your video file, you are done. If you want to use another audio file, remember that it needs to be the same length as your motion file; if the motion file ends before the audio, the audio will continue to play until it is finished and then restart the loop. The opposite occurs if your music clip is shorter than your menu animation. The best way to avoid these potential problems is to encode the menu audio when you are building the motion menu.

Now we have to address the buttons, which in this project are button text objects. I select the text link I want to work with; then, from the toolbar, I select the text tool. Clicking inside the text boundary of the text I want to change, I backspace or delete the old text and insert mine.

If you are unhappy with the location of the menu links, you can select them all and drag them to a different location on the screen. I lowered mine a bit to keep from covering up the artists' faces. We're almost through with the graphical component of the main menu. I now click inside the main menu text box and change the text to a two-line title, experimenting with different fonts and sizes until I find something that looks good and fits.

TIP

On the title, I wanted a shadowed look, so I selected the "How To Produce..." text box and, from the Edit menu or with a right-click, selected copy and then pasted it in place. Changing the color of one of the text box's fonts and scooting it over and up a bit will give you a nice shadowed look. Another cool way to approach this would be to have your menu's main title in the graphic or motion menu file that you are using as a background, which will give you more control over how the menu looks.

The menu setup is now complete and we can address the linking from the main menu to the other menus and clips.

Select the Rand McCullough button and from the Project inventory, drop the Rand McCullough timeline on the button. Now select the Properties tab and examine the button properties.

You can see that the link is now pointing to the Rand McCullough menu. When the link is clicked by the viewer it directs them to the new menu. The next video, Someone Like You, is treated in the same manner; just select the link and, from the inventory, drop the Someone Like You menu onto it. Our third video has no menu, so when we get to that link from the inventory bin, just drop the Randy Strom timeline onto it. When this selection is chosen by a viewer, it will launch the Randy Strom file immediately with no menu.

Let's take a look at Randy's Menu:

This menu is very simple. I dropped a frame from the video to use as the background and again moved it to the rear so the text links would appear. I point the "Living It Up" link to the video file by dragging Randy's video from the project inventory bin and dropping it on the text link. Also from the project inventory I drag and drop the main menu onto the "Return to Main Menu" text. That's it! Randy's menu is done. Select the "Living It Up" text and examine the properties.

As you can see the link is now set to play the first chapter. Because it's only one song, there is only one chapter. If the user hits the Menu button or next scene on their remote, they will be returned to the main menu, as that is the Override we selected for the text link.

You set the Override by clicking into the box and selecting from the drop down menu where you want the viewer to go. In most cases this will be the main menu, but if there are numerous tiers of menus, you may want to return the viewer to the previous menu rather than the main menu.

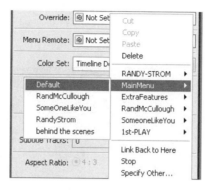

ADDRESSING LONGER FILES AND CREATING CHAPTER POINTS

The procedure I just outlined works fine for a project that has a few video and menu files. What if, on the other hand, we have a longer file, perhaps a feature film or a whole concert containing a number of songs? The way to link up your menu text or buttons is to create chapter points from the clip timeline. In all the authoring software I've ever used, this process is similar. Open the timeline of the clip, move the cursor to the point where you want to insert a chapter, right-click or select from a menu to "create/insert chapter point."

The first time you do this it will label the chapter as chapter 2. This is because the beginning of the clip has already claimed its rightful place as chapter 1.

Now you will select your menu text or button and drag and drop the chapter points onto the link. This is the way you would populate another common menu, the song or scene selection menu. Also, creating these chapter points in longer files lets the viewer skip to the next scene or song with the remote control.

Having used one method or the other, link all the newly modified text boxes or buttons to their appropriate timeline or chapter point. Repeat the procedure for each menu. The DVD now has four menus that look something like this:

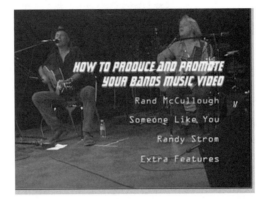

As you can see on our last "Extra Features" menu, there is little there except a notice that opening the DVD on a computer will lead to more features and a return to the main menu.

Before you build the DVD, one last step is to add the DVD-ROM content. You can create a stored website viewable through a web browser, or you can just insert more photos, MP3s and other goodies you may wish to share with the DVD viewer. Place all these digital assets inside your DVD project, then from the File menu choose "Select DVD-ROM folder." Browse to the folder containing all the digital assets and select it. If you don't have any digital extras, you can skip this step.

At the end of the process, test your DVD project thoroughly, using the program's preview feature to click on each link on all the menus and make sure that everything is working like it is supposed to.

The menus are created, the links are established. The dog hunts. It's time to burn baby burn.

TIP

Before burning your master DVD, it is a good idea to defragment your hard drives, or at least the one that has your DVD content. This will place all the DVD files (assuming of course they all reside in the same folder on your hard drive) next to each other; this, in turn, will make the burn go faster and more reliably by saving the read/write head a lot of work. I have never made a DVD coaster if I defrag before the burn.

BUILDING AND BURNING THE DVD MASTER

We have a number of options when creating our master DVD and we will address them each. From the File menu, select "Build DVD" and you will see the output options.

Let's take a quick look at the settings and what they mean.

► Make DVD Disc: This is the default and most common setting for burning a DVD. You can make one or set the number of copies you want to burn. On your first DVD, I recommend burning just one and testing it completely before burning numerous copies.

There may be some tweaking you want to do. You can still go all the way back to the editor and make changes as long as you save the resulting file with the same name and in the same place as the one you are replacing. That way all the information in your DVD build remains valid.

▶ Make DVD Folder: This option will create a DVD folder on your hard drive that is, in essence, identical to the folders you would create when you burn a real DVD. This lets you view the DVD from your hard drive if you have a DVD player installed on your computer with that feature. If you do, just fire it up and point it to the folder you just made. I don't use this feature often.

▶ Make DVD Image: This can be a cool setting, especially if you have a web site with a lot of storage space and a good bandwidth pipe. This option creates an ISO file on your hard drive that is identical to the one you would find on a physical DVD. You can upload this monster to your website. Users can then download the file to a computer and make copies of the DVD using Nero or other burning software. Not a great idea if you are selling DVDs, as obviously copy protection will not be available. But if the purpose of the DVD is promotions, you can just ask people, "Do you have broadband?" If so, tell them they can download your whole DVD from your site. It's a pretty impressive sales tool.

▶ Make DVD Master: This is the option to choose if you are sending the DVD project to a replication plant. You will need a DLT (Digital Linear Tape) drive or something compatible with the format to use this feature or the output destination will be grayed out on your selections. This format is not as popular as it once was, but is still the standard for high-end DVD authoring companies. Many replicators will now take either an image file or the DVD-R itself to work from, so check with your pressing plant before you buy a DLT drive!

I generally use the default settings when burning DVDs; they seem to do a fine job, but other options are available if you want to drill down further and really tweak your output. In Encore, there is a library of transcode settings that will let you select variable or fixed bandwidth, number of rendering passes and other options that can improve your DVD. From the File menu, select Transcode.

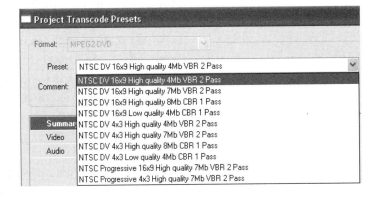

You can choose the screen aspect ratio, the overall quality, maximum bandwidth and the number of render passes. "More is better" applies when transcoding: The higher the maximum bandwidth the better, and using a two-pass render will produce the best results. Keep in mind that a two-pass render will, of course, take considerably longer than one pass.

It's a good idea to burn a few tests; a few blank DVDs won't break the bank, but they will let you see for yourself what the output differences are for the settings. Let's proceed with a standard DVD burn. Insert the blank media and after the computer has recognized it, from the File menu, again select "Build DVD disc"

The next screen depends on the option you selected previously. To burn a disc the menu would look like this:

The same screen for an image file would look like this:

The only difference is the output options. Click through to the next screen and you will have the option of bailing out or burning. Let's burn!

After the burn, your drive should open and reveal your DVD. Go kick back in front of your TV and see how it looks. Now let's take a look at outputting in a couple of other protocols.

Output for the Web

It's a good idea, while the files are still in place, to output for the web and other applications. When saving for web viewing, we need to consider some important threshold factors. First, what is our audience? If you are looking for new fans, you will probably want to share your videos on your website or something like YouTube. The tradeoff is always between file size and quality.

How long will a visitor to your website wait before the start of a streaming file? My goal is to have something for a visitor to see or hear no more than ten seconds from the time they click on it. I am making one major assumption regarding this benchmark: The visitor has a broadband connection. I hate to sound elitist, but experiencing the Internet over a dialup connection is a painful and time-consuming process, thankfully experienced by fewer and fewer people each day. The broadband pipe has been growing every year, and hopefully dialup will soon be relegated to the dustbin of network history.

I generally save a video file in two formats for the web: large and small. My small size is 340x280 and my large web format is 640x480. From inside Adobe Premiere, let's take a look at the export options available in the Media Encoder. Open the Media Encoder from the File menu, select Export, then Adobe Media Encoder.

The standard-issue streaming formats are available: Windows Media, QuickTime, Flash, Real Media and a variety of MPEG-1 and MPEG-2 templates.

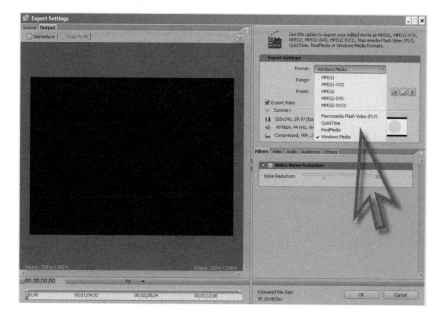

If you click on the settings box in any of the formats, you will find a wide variety of output options. My personal preference is to get as close to 256K as I can get for a streaming file. It gives a decent-looking video and doesn't take too long to start streaming under a broadband connection. If you are using a smaller screen size such as 360x240 or 240x180, you can increase the streaming rate a bit a get a very good-looking image.

QT 256 streaming NTSC

✓ QT 256 streaming NTSC
QT 256 streaming PAL
QT 28K streaming NTSC
QT 28K streaming PAL
QT 384 streaming NTSC
QT 384 streaming PAL
QT 512 streaming NTSC
QT 512 streaming PAL
QT 56K streaming NTSC
QT 56K streaming PAL
QT ISDN streaming NTSC
QT ISDN streaming PAL
QT alternate NTSC download
QT alternate NTSC streaming
QT alternate PAL download
QT alternate PAL streaming

FLV8 NTSC 400k

FLV audio 128k
FLV audio 32k
FLV7 HD 150k
FLV7 HD 400k
FLV7 HD 40k
FLV7 HD 700k
FLV7 NTSC 150k
FLV7 NTSC 400k
FLV7 NTSC 40k
FLV7 NTSC 700k
FLV7 PAL 150k
FLV7 PAL 400k
FLV7 PAL 40k
FLV7 PAL 700k
FLV8 HD 150k
FLV8 HD 400k
FLV8 HD 40k
FLV8 HD 700k
FLV8 NTSC 150k
✓ FLV8 NTSC 400k
FLV8 NTSC 40k
FLV8 NTSC 700k
FLV8 PAL 150k
FLV8 PAL 400k
FLV8 PAL 40k
FLV8 PAL 700k

Each of the output templates and default settings can be tweaked further. When the video tab is clicked, you can see the options available for the selected template. Also noteworthy are the Frame Width and Height boxes. This is where you can tweak your file size for the best possible upload to the video jukebox servers like YouTube and MySpace.

Filters | **Video** | Audio | Audiences | Others

Video Codec

Video Codec: Windows Media Video 9 ▾

Basic Video Settings

Allow interlaced processing

Encoding Passes: ○ One   ● Two

Bitrate Mode: Variable Unconstrained ▾

Frame Width [pixels]: 320

Frame Height [pixels]: 240

Frame Rate [fps]: 29.97 ▾

Pixel Aspect Ratio: Square Pixels (1.0) ▾

Advanced Settings

Decoder Complexity: Auto ▾

Keyframe Interval [seconds]: 5

Buffer Size [seconds]: ● Default ○ Custom 1

Average Video Bitrate [Kbps]: 208.00

All the formats have their strengths and weaknesses. Here are the results of a little shootout I did on the lip-sync video. I benchmarked the parameters that are most important to me:

Format	Render Time	File Size	A/V Quality	Play Time
Windows Media	23 min – 2 pass	7.4MG	5	5 seconds
QuickTime	22 min – 1 pass	6.8MG	4	5 seconds
Real Media	14 min – 1 pass	6.2MG	5	7 seconds
Flash Video	20 min – 1 pass	5.7MG	4	12 seconds

And the winner is . . . Windows Media. The Real video had slightly more color depth but took longer to stream, the QuickTime file looked good but the audio fidelity was inferior to the others, and the Flash video didn't look quite as good and the launch time was the longest of all the formats. Overall audio and video quality was a tie between Real and Windows Media, but the launch time and Real Network's limit on free video streams per server knocked them down to third place in my ratings.

As you can see, the time to render our four-minute video is two to five times the running length of the clip except in the case of the Flash video. Another important note regarding the Flash render, at least using the encoder in Premiere: A temporary QuickTime file is made on the fly while the render is under way. For our little four-minute clip, this temporary file rendered to over 7 GB! The file disappears after the render but make sure you have enough drive space for this bloated temp file when rendering to Flash.

The upside to using Flash is that the video can't be saved to a hard drive by the viewer. The downsides are the resources required to create the file, as mentioned above, and the fact that a visitor to your site may not have the Flash Player installed. For Flash video creation under Windows, I first output a high quality AVI or MOV in the screen size I'm looking for, and then use the CoffeeCup Flash Video Player to convert the file and create a video player for the file that is then uploaded to the site. This widget also creates the HTML code you will need to insert into the page, a literal Flash for Windows one-stop shop. A trial version of this software is on the DVD.

IMPROVING QUALITY

Using the default settings for creating files to upload to the services will work fine, but if you want to stand head-and-shoulders above the crowd, look at the parameters that the video services allow when uploading a file. The file size limit is 100 MB, and any of the files listed in the shoot-out would still leave 90 MB of possible video resolution unused.

A way to experiment with different settings is to render the file in different formats and sizes, then upload the files under slightly different names and run an A/B test at the video site itself. Keep the video that displays the best, then delete all the rest. This can act as your template setting for your next project.

Archiving Your Project

You have worked and re-worked your masterpiece and delivered it in every format you can foresee using. Now comes the choice as to whether you want the work you have done to be etched in stone forever, or whether you want to have the option of revisiting the raw files to make modifications to the project later.

If you are sure you are happy with the end product for now and all time, after burning your DVD master and a backup, delete all the working files and free up space on your hard drive.

On the other hand, if you think you may want to tweak things at some time in the future, you will need to backup/archive your project.

ARCHIVE BACK TO TAPE: AN INEXPENSIVE SOLUTION

A great way to make backup copies of your edits and to keep everything in the first generation digital domain is to print your edit back to the same type of tapes you initially captured from. Remember, a DVD uses MPEG-2 compression, and you won't be able to go back to the original uncompressed file. In the case of the Someone Like You video, the tape I shot the band on was a 60-minute tape. After all the location and green-screen shots, I had only used around 48 minutes of tape. I just plugged my camera back into the computer using the FireWire cable, cued the tape up to the end of my previous shooting, and printed the video back into the camera. If you are archiving a longer performance, use a new tape.

KEEP THE HARD DRIVE

With the price of hard drives continuing to fall, putting the whole project—including the raw video captures, images, final edit print, and DVD images—onto an external drive can be an affordable option. This is the method I use for all in-house projects and I recommend it to all my clients. If for any reason you want to return to the project, you have everything sitting right where you left it. This is a huge benefit. If you really want to rock, defragment the drive before you put it in a box on the shelf.

CHAPTER 11

Using the Web

The best and most obvious place for new artists to showcase their talents is on the Internet. At your website, you will have complete control over what the visitor sees and hears.

A common mistake that people make is that they throw together a site, email a couple friends, and wait for the surge in traffic. Sadly, it rarely comes. A successful web promotional campaign takes lots of work. The "build it and they will come" business plan is not a business plan. If you want to have a high rating on Google and other search engines, you will have to work your site almost daily.

If you don't have a site yet, you might think about getting one. There are thousands of web hosts out there with the capacity to stream audio and video. Finding a good one is not too hard. Many DSL and cable ISP accounts come with a small website, usually giving you about 5 MB of space. Resist the temptation to put up your band website there. Although this is adequate for a few pages and maybe one MP3, it won't cut it for streaming video. Another downside of using your provider's "free" website is the actual address. What will be more impressive to a visitor, surfing to mykickbuttband. com or music.users.kickband04567.myfreewebsite.com?

Getting a Domain Name

One of the problems in getting your own website is that the domain name may already be taken. More generally, of course, the more unique your band name is, the easier it will be for you to promote it on the Internet. Here's how to check to see if a name is available:

▶ Surf to netsol.com. (I only use this site, Network Solutions, for site name searches. I don't host or register my sites through them, it's too pricey.)

▶ Look for the WHOIS link and select it.

▶ Type in the name you would like to have for your website (e.g. kickbuttband.com) and start the search.

▶ If the name *is* taken, try another site name. A common workaround to the site name not being available is to add the word "music" to the website address: kickbuttbandmusic.com, or perhaps kickbuttmusic.com. You can use other variations like kickbuttbandrocks.com.

▶ If the name *isn't* taken, I recommend going to 10-domains. com—or a similarly priced budget domain registrar—and register the domain name for around $7 annually and pay to hold the name for a year or two. It is not that expensive and secures your site name.

▶ If you are *really* serious about your website and the branding of your band name, register all variations of the name you can find in order to stake out a larger claim to your internet real estate.

My company owns musicoffice.com, musicoffice.net, music-office.com and .net, themusicoffice.com and net. As you can see, it would be quite a task for someone to snag a name similar to mine. Owning this web turf adds value to your band and business. Dropping $100 on your domain name through 10-domains or a similar service is a good investment for your career in the long run, if you can afford it.

Hosting Your Domain

A friend of mine is a local internet-service provider who I helped when he first started his business. In exchange, I got free hosting for years. Since then, my site has grown and so has my online résumé.

My friend is not geared up to have his bandwidth monopolized by my 3 GB of online video and hundreds of MP3s, so I moved the site to powweb.com to keep the friendship.

For music and video streaming, a website can require more than what is generally available through an internet provider. I live in a small town, and when I went to the local telephone and cable companies looking for a deal, I was sadly disappointed. Other than the included 5 MB "mini-website," the cable provider didn't offer any other web hosting services. The phone company would expand their basic package or host my domain name with enough space for a couple MP3s and maybe one video for $19.95 a month. This is typical of the deals you will find through the common hosting players. Try to avoid any website host that is "template" based; your site will look just like everyone else's on the host's server. You will have to search further to find what you are looking for. Here is a list of the basic necessities of a robust music website:

- ▶ Storage Space: More is better. I am hosting at powweb.com; for a very reasonable annual fee I get 300 GB of space, unlimited email accounts, multiple SQL databases, and lots of other cool "click and deploy" features. This is enough server space for hundreds of MP3s and around 50 feature films at DVD quality. My web creativity is not hampered by storage space.

- ▶ Email: You should expect at least 25 email accounts with a package. Another thing to check on is what file types are prohibited by your hosting company's mail servers. File extensions like .EXE or .BAT may be prohibited by the provider to defend against viruses and spyware. This is generally not a concern; you can transfer files with these extensions via FTP. Speaking of FTP . . .

- ▶ FTP Access: Any host should allow you to access your site through FTP. Another common method of updating sites is Microsoft Front Page because of its simplicity. A website needs to be configured at the server end to use Front Page so if that is the software you prefer, make sure your host provides the Front Page server extensions on your site.

- ▶ CGI Script and Database Capability: Many websites today are database-driven. ASP (Active Server Pages) under the Microsoft platform is a technology commonly found on websites, and for other platforms various flavors of the PHP database platform are available.

- ▶ Bandwidth: This can be a spoiler if you are cursed with success. Most providers have a meter on the bandwidth your website uses. You will get a monthly allocation and will be charged for exceeding it. Read the small print in your hosting agreement and see what the monthly bandwidth allocation is and how much you will be charged should you go over. In the case of powweb.com, your monthly bandwidth or file transfer allocation is 3,000 GB a month. If you exceed that, my friend, you are now famous.

► Reliability: I usually stay with the big players with large server farms and a huge bandwidth pipe. A very important service that every web hosting company should offer is daily backups of your site and an easy method to restore the site from a previous backup should one of your experiments go south and/or the site crashes. A good way to check a web host's customer satisfaction is to just Google the host and see what comes up with users who have posted to online forums.

Promoting Your Site

Google my name and you will probably see me in about half of the first page of the search results. If it weren't for that darn mathematics professor at the University of North Carolina who stole my name and keeps writing books and papers, I would probably be top of the list! I wish he would be less prolific. Maybe the book you are now reading will dethrone him for a few months.

People ask me how much I had to pay to get that high on the Google list. The easy answer is, "not a dime." It's impossible to pay for placement on Google's regular search results, anyway. The hard answer is I work my site almost daily.

META TAGS

One important component that I have found to bringing traffic and search engines to my site is the META tags on each page. The META tags give the search engines information about the page and site. Here is the wrong and right way to do a META tag:

Wrong Way

<meta http-equiv="Content-Language" content="en-us">

<meta name="GENERATOR" content="Microsoft FrontPage 5.0">

<meta name="ProgId" content="FrontPage.Editor.Document">

<meta http-equiv="Content-Type" content="text/html; charset=windows-1252">

This is the default set of META tags you will get in Front Page if you don't add anything to the tags. As you can see it is a nice ad for Microsoft Front Page but doesn't say a thing about you or your music. Here is another example:

Right Way

<meta http-equiv="Content-Language" content="en-us">

<meta name="GENERATOR" content="Greg Forest Elves">

<meta NAME="Title" CONTENT="Greg Forest's Website">

<meta NAME="Author" CONTENT="The Music Office">

<meta NAME="Subject" CONTENT="Greg Forest, Musician, Writer, Producer Home Page. Free MP3s and Video">

<meta NAME="Description" CONTENT="Greg Forest's Eclectic and Alternative Music and Video Streams">

<meta NAME="Keywords"CONTENT="Greg Forest, Greg Forest Band, alternative music, punk folk music, cow metal music, free video, free mp3, live concerts, Austin music, free music video">

<meta NAME="Abstract" CONTENT="Greg Forest, Musician">

<meta NAME="Copyright" CONTENT="© 2008 Greg Forest/The Music Office">

<meta NAME="Publisher" CONTENT="The Music Office">

<meta NAME="Revisit-After" CONTENT="7 Days">

<meta NAME="Distribution" CONTENT="Global">

<meta NAME="Robots" CONTENT="All">

The most important lines of the tags are the Subject, Description, Revisit, and Robots. These are the tags that the search engine bots drop into their database. Do not put too much information in the tags, and keep it honest. Just because you played a gig once in Mobile, Alabama doesn't mean you should put it in your META keywords. The search engines look at context, and your score will go down at the engines if you are promoting content that isn't there. The last few lines give information specifically to the bots with recommendations about when to revisit and what content will be changing.

Here is a screenshot of my site's web statistics for the first 14 days of May 2007:

Robots/Spiders visitors (Top 10) – Full list – Last visit			
17 different robots*	Hits	Bandwidth	Last visit
MSNBot	472	11.98 MB	14 May 2007 - 23:54
Yahoo Slurp	204	15.63 MB	14 May 2007 - 23:43
Googlebot	143	63.73 MB	14 May 2007 - 21:51
Alexa (IA Archiver)	54	680.11 KB	10 May 2007 - 18:23
Unknown robot (identified by 'robot')	12	326.15 KB	14 May 2007 - 23:31
AskJeeves	9	456.01 KB	13 May 2007 - 08:17
BecomeBot	8	175.71 KB	14 May 2007 - 15:03
Speedy Spider	7	283.83 KB	14 May 2007 - 21:39
findlinks	5	223.50 KB	11 May 2007 - 12:49
Asterias	5	1.18 MB	13 May 2007 - 20:38
Others	18	818.38 KB	
BecomeBot	8	175.71 KB	14 May 2007 - 15:03
Speedy Spider	7	283.83 KB	14 May 2007 - 21:39
findlinks	5	223.50 KB	11 May 2007 - 12:49
Asterias	5	1.18 MB	13 May 2007 - 20:38
Others	18	818.38 KB	

As you can see, I have an average of 78 search-engine bots visit my site every day. It looks like MSNBot is the hardest working, but Google is still coming by more than ten times a day. Why? Not only are the META tags accurate and descriptive, I change the content on my home page almost every day. This is important.

Although the exact method of hashing web data and giving it a score is proprietary to each search engine, there are some common denominators in how they all look at a page or site. A search engine spider/bot may look at your site and find the following:

First Visit

▶ What is the title of the site/page?

▶ What are the central key words and description of the site?

▶ Do the keywords and site information generally match the text on the page?

▶ Enter all this into the database

Second Visit

▶ Has anything changed since the last visit?

▶ Back at the search site database, has anyone searched for this site and/or clicked through to it?

▶ If so, how many?

The web spider or bot comes by and takes a snapshot of the page. It returns in the future and notices that nothing has changed. At an even later date it will return and if it finds the page hasn't changed, the page ranking is lowered as the content is static and unchanging unless being offset by numerous user queries for the site. With good META tags and compelling and changing content, you should be able to get to the first page before too long. If, on the other hand, your META tags are inaccurate—in the early days of the internet people would drive traffic to their auto parts website by putting "sex sex sex" in the description META tag—this will hurt your score and could ruin a relationship. The major search engine bots and spiders, especially Google, are savvy to most of the tricks and overdoing it can hurt your score more than help it. Repeatedly searching for your site from the same IP address is futile.

Even if your META tags are good and your content constantly changing, you have to prime the pump a bit. Have every person you know with ten seconds on their hands to go to Google and run a search for your website and click through to it. Repeat this procedure on the other search engines. As the search engines guide more traffic to your site, your ranking improves. If you fall down on updating content, you will see a corresponding drop in rankings unless the click-throughs from visitors at the search engine are numerous.

Creating Flash Photo and Video Animations

One of the most common ways to display your web photos and videos is by creating Flash animations. The presentation looks slicker than just sticking your media on a page, and you protect your content because visitors can't just right-click and download the image or video. Many photo and video editing programs have this feature available as a web export option. If your software doesn't support a Flash export, do a Google search for Flash animation tools. In Windows I have found a couple tools for very little money (under $40) that will create both photo slideshows and video animations. Converting DV to Flash will probably take a bit of rendering time for the downsample but the results can be easier to access and protect. The accompanying DVD contains trial software of Flash creation tools.

E-Commerce

Merchant bank accounts, CGI gateway programming, and monthly banking and service fees scare many people away from selling on their websites. There is a certain level of sale that needs to occur to make all that worthwhile. To get started, you can set up a PayPal account in a few minutes and be selling your product. You will be able to accept major credit cards and e-checks. PayPal charges more than a commercial bank discount rate, but the difference is negligible when dealing with small volumes. The convenience of having PayPal do the invoicing, reporting, and even print the shipping labels can be a great time saver.

Using Free Web Services

If you are on a tight budget and your own website is not an option, or you want to test the waters before you make an investment, you can use one of the free web services to promote your group. There are new video-content sites popping up every day of differing qualities and purposes. For this book I will be covering three websites that can really help you get your video viewed: MySpace, YouTube, and Google Video. Keep in mind that these video servers use their own compression algorithms and your video is likely to lose a little to a lot of quality when the server is finished with it. That is why the information in the previous chapter is so important; sending the web server the best video image possible will help you retain the quality of the original file. There is a list of other video servers in Appendix B.

MYSPACE

MySpace is the leader in online music pages. It is a cost-effective (free!) method of getting your band and music up on the web and can be used in conjunction with your website rather than in competition with it. Remember, any exposure is good exposure. Using MySpace, a number of bands have been lifted out of obscurity and actually sold a lot of CDs and merchandise. In this section, we will set up a MySpace page for music.

There is more than one type of account at MySpace and you will want to sign up for the Artist rather than the Personal account. This type of account gives you more exposure as a musician and artist, and allows you to host your own music and videos. Click on the Music link at the MySpace homepage.

Home | Browse | Search | Invite | Film | Mail | Blog | Favorites | Forum | Groups | Events | Videos | Music | Comedy | Classifieds

You will see on the next page the Artist Signup Link. Click it.

Music Classifieds | Artist Signup

The next page is the copyright warning letting you know that posting music you don't own is forbidden. Heed the warning and click through.

Musicians - SIGN UP FREE HERE!

> **Warning** - MySpace Music accounts are for MUSICIANS, not fans. Uploading music you did not create is a violation of MySpace's Terms of Use and may be against the law. If you are not the musician who created the song or that musician's agent, do not upload it. Even if you lawfully own a copy of the music (for example, you bought the CD or downloaded it from an internet service), this does not give you permission to upload the music to MySpace. If you violate this rule, your account may be deleted.
>
> If you would like to show support for a musical group or artist, create a fan club in our GROUP section here.

Fill out the sign-up form that comes up on the next screen.

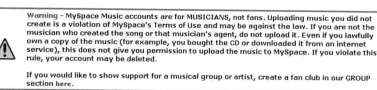

Sign Up!	
(orange fields required)	
Please enter a valid e-mail address. You will need to confirm your e-mail address to activate your account.	
Email Address:	gregforestband@musicoffice.com
Confirm Email Address:	gregforestband@musicoffice.com
Band Name:	Greg Forest Band
Password:	********
Confirm Password:	********
Genre:	Alternative
Country:	United States
Zip Code:	78028
Preferred Site & Language:	U.S.A.
	☑ By checking the box you agree to the MySpace Terms of Service and Privacy Policy.
	Sign Up

MySpace now asks for a little more detail that will help guide visitors to the type of music you play. This will fine-tune your musical genre even more for better search results.

Please complete your registration!

Sign Up!	
Your MySpace URL:	myspace.com/ gregforestband (e.g. http://www.myspace.com/yourbandname)
Genre 1:	Alternative ▼
Genre 2:	Folk Rock ▼
Genre 3:	Psychobilly ▼
Website: :	gregforestmedia.com
Current Record Label: :	OverDue Records
Label Type: :	Indie ▼
	Continue

That takes care of the online registration process. You will be prompted to verify the account and email address by checking your email box and clicking back to MySpace to confirm your account and identity. Now we have to populate our MySpace web with digital content. We will start with photos and then upload MP3 and video files.

Uploading Photos to MySpace

This is pretty much self-explanatory:

Upload Some Photos!

Share your photos to let friends and other members see who you are

Photos may be a max of 600K in these formats: GIF or JPG [**help**]
Photos may not contain nudity, violent or offensive material, or copyrighted images. [**photo policy**]

If you don't see the Upload Photo form below, click

Upload Photo	
	Browse...
	Upload

Skip for now

Let Your Friends See You!

Uploading MP3s to MySpace

Uploading an MP3 at MySpace is a breeze. Click on the Music tab and select upload. Browse to your MP3, select it, and click upload. You can upload up to four songs of up to 10 MB each. The first song you upload will be the default play when the visitor arrives at your web but you can change this setting later to change the site feel a bit. Remember to encode your audio into a stereo MP3 at a bit rate of 192 kb/s and a sampling rate of 44.1 KHz. Don't forget to embed your file information, such as song title and artist name, to brand your song and allow the information to be viewed on MP3 players.

[Return to Main Edit Page]

Select MP3 file to Upload

You may upload a maximum of 4 songs.
You must own the copyright for the Music you upload. [music po

If you don't see the Upload MP3 form below, click here

```
Upload MP3
        Filename: 7-10-2006TooMuch.mp3
        274432 of 5483278 bytes (4%)
```

Uploading Video to MySpace

There are limitations in both file size and format in what MySpace will allow you to upload. Acceptable file formats are: .avi, .asf, .dv, .wmv, .mov, .qt, .3g2, .3gp, .3gp2, .3gpp, .gsm, .mpg, .mpeg, mp4, .m4v, .mp4v, .cmp, .divx, .xvid, .264, .rm, .rmvb, .flv, .mkv, and .ogm.

The file formats are plentiful and it is very likely that your output will be compatible; heck, I've been a video producer deploying on the web for years and I have never heard of some of these formats! The size limit is 100 MB, which is adequate for a good-looking one-song video. Remember that the page visitor is not going to be viewing your video in high resolution so I would recommend that you compress your video file to the maximum size the site allows or as close to it as you can get. Big file means big information. If data is going to be stripped from the file by MySpace to accommodate their compression codec, it is a good idea to give the server as much information as possible. Consult the Output chapter for more information on maximizing your video for the web.

To get started, from your MySpace home page click on the "Videos" link. You will see the following tabbed page appear and from there select the "Upload" tab.

Home | Browse | Search | Invite | Film | Mail | Blog | Favorites | Forum | Groups | Events | Videos | Music | Comedy | Classifieds

Videos | Featured | Videos | My Videos | Upload | | Search Videos |

This will bring you to the screen where you enter the description of your video. Users at MySpace will create search strings out of certain words, so you should use words in your description that are likely to show up in search results for your genre. You get 3,000 words for the description field; you probably want to create a detailed description—perhaps with band bio and other promo information—offline using a word processor so you can spell check and tweak your grammar. You can then paste your grammar- and spell-corrected entry into the MySpace field. Three-thousand words is a lot of words, so you can tell a long story. Tags are very similar to the keywords of a META tag. When entering your tags, separate them with a space. Put in four to ten tags. If I were in an Americana singer/songwriter band, my video clip description might resemble this:

Title: Down On Rebel Road

Description: "Down On Rebel Road" is the title song of Nine Second Ride's new CD on Wang Dang Doodle Records. The song is penned by front man Hunk Williams, who wrote all the original songs on the CD. Nine Second Ride saddled up in 2002 when bassist Mark Mywerds and guitarist Don Inthedumps decided to form a casual band to play . . .

Tags: Nine Second Ride Country Punk Wang Dang Records Mywerds . . .

Category: Music. Entertainment.

Click the box that says you understand the terms of the agreement and pledge your firstborn to MySpace. Now let's upload the video.

Upload Video: Step 2

File Size Limit per upload: 100MB.
Acceptable formats: .avi,.asf,.dv,.wmv,.mov,.qt,.3g2,.3gp,.3gp2,.3gpp,.gsm,.mpg,.mpeg, .mp4,.m4v,.mp4v,.cmp,.divx,.xvid,.264,.rm,.rmvb,.flv,.mkv,.ogm.

Note: If you upload porn or unauthorized copyrighted material, your MySpace.com account deleted. Terms and Conditions.

Upload Film
Browse...
Upload

You're good to go on MySpace. Now contact everyone you can to add to your friends list. MySpace is perfect for music networking. It was designed for music sharing, so get out there and share!

YOUTUBE

YouTube is the most popular video site and also has a special category for musicians. Surf to YouTube.com and click on the signup link.

Create Your YouTube Account

It's free and easy. Just fill out the account info below. (All fields required)

Account Type: Standard
    Standard
    Director
    Musician
    Comedian
    Guru

Email Address:

YouTube Username: check
    only contain letters A-Z or numbers 0-9

Password:

Confirm Password:

Country: United States

Postal Code:
    Required for US, UK & Canada Only

Gender: ◯ Male ◯ Female

Date of Birth: — — —

Verification:
    Enter the text in the image   2 NgU V
    Can't read?

☑ Sign me up for the "Broadcast Yourself" email
- I agree to the terms of use and privacy policy.

Sign Up

After you have filled in the blanks you will prompted to check your email for confirmation of the account. After checking your email and returning to the site, you will be ready to upload your first video. Click on the "Upload New Video" button to get to the next screen.

This screen is where you tell the viewer about the clip. Type the title of the song and any notes you want to share with viewers into the appropriate boxes. At the bottom of the screen you will see the "Upload a Video" button. Click it.

Video Upload (Step 1 of 2)

Title:	I Got Lost In It (For A Minute)
Description:	Someone Like You's new music video from their upcoming CD. Recorded at Studio Gazelle and videotaped at The Music Office, Someone Like You displays why they are growing in popularity.
Tags:	eone like you alternative music texas music
	Enter one or more tags, separated by spaces. Tags are keywords used to describe your video.
Video Category:	Music

Broadcast Options:	Public by default	choose options
Date and Map Options:	No date or location has been set	choose options
Sharing Options:	Allow Comments, Video Responses, Ratings, Embedding by default	choose options

Upload a video... Or Use Quick Capture

YouTube is similar to MySpace in the size and types of files accepted by the service. It is unlikely that you will have any problems uploading a file in any common format.

Video Upload (Step 2 of 2)

Select a video to upload.

WinMedia256.wmv   Browse

Upload Video

Do not upload any TV shows, music videos, music concerts, or commercials without permission unless they consist entirely of content you created yourself.

By clicking "Upload Video," you are representing that this video does not violate YouTube's Terms of Use and that you own all copyrights in this video or have express permission from all copyright owners to upload it.

After browsing to your file, click on the "Upload Video" button. It will take a few minutes to upload your video depending on the file size and your Internet bandwidth. When the upload is complete you will get the message below.

Video Upload - Upload Complete

Thank you! Your upload is complete.
This video will be available in My Videos after it has finished processing.

Embed this video on your website.
Copy and paste the code below to embed this video.

```
<object width="425" height="350"> <param name="movie"
value="http://www.youtube.com/v/nVX4PP6hajQ"> </param> <embed
src="http://www.youtube.com/v/nVX4PP6hajQ"
type="application/x-shockwave-flash" width="425" height="350"> </embed>
</object>
```

Upload another Video   Go to My Videos

Click on "Go to My Videos" and you will see that your video is now in your YouTube inventory. You can modify your description of the video, delete it, or add more clips from this page.

My Account / Videos

My Videos - Favorites - Playlists - Inbox - Subscriptions

My Videos

My Favorites

Create Playlist

Upload a Video

Copy Videos To: ⸺ ▼

☐ Remove Video

I Got Lost In It (For A Minute)
03:49
Someone Like You's new music video from their upcoming CD. Recorded at Studio Gazelle and videotaped at The Music Office, Someone (more)
Tags: someone like you alternative texas music
Views: 1   Added: June 20, 2007, 10:29 AM
Comments: 0   Broadcast: Public Video | **Live!**
Playlists: 0   Raw File: WinMedia256.wmv
                                                      URL: http://www.youtube.com/watch?\

Edit Video Info

Make Channel Icon

Copy Videos To: ⸺ ▼

The first step in promoting your recently posted video is to stuff the ballot box, so to speak. Get every band member, fan, friend, relative, and anyone else to go view the video and give it a great rating and review. It takes views to get a buzz going; high ratings and good reviews initially help. Of course, the actual content of the clip has a lot to do with it too.

A good way to get folks to visit your video is to ride on the backs of those who have gone before. Run a quick search of something similar like "awesome guitar solo" and see what comes up. Examine the list and see who is getting the most views. Click on that video. When the clip comes up see if there is an option to "Post a Video Response." If the option is there, post your video as a response. Repeat this procedure with small alterations to the search string, something like "awesome alternative rock" or similar. An hour of doing this should bring you an increase in your video's views.

If you have tried all these promotional tricks and the results are still unsatisfactory, step back from the project a few steps and give it an honest appraisal. What is different between the clips that are getting thousands of views and yours?

GOOGLE VIDEO

Like all the other free sites, Google requires you create a Google account. I'm not going to repeat the account creation procedure; it takes maybe a minute if you type slowly. Verify your new account from your email box and you're good to go. Once we get to the welcome page, there is a button to upload video.

Google Video BETA   **Upload and share your videos**

All fields are required.

Video file: `D:\WinMedia256.wmv`   Browse...

We accept AVI, MPEG, Quicktime, Real, and Windows Media. Learn more.
If your video file is over 100 MB, please use the desktop uploader.
No copyrighted or obscene material.

Title: `I Got Lost In It`

Description:
`The new music video from Someone Like You.  This tune is a teaser from the band's upcoming CD to be released later this year on OverDue Records`

Include details such as location and story summary

Genre: `Music & Musical` ▼

Language: `English` ▼

Access:
  ⦿ Public - your video will be included in search results.
  ○ Unlisted^New! - your video will **not** be included in search results. Learn more

  ☐ I agree to the Upload Terms and Conditions.

  Upload video

Fill in the blanks and you're good to go. Google is actually the quickest site to get signed up and your video launched on; the whole process took about five minutes with a broadband connection.

Video uploads may take a while depending on
your internet connection speed.

Please do not close this window, as your upload may be cancelled.

Cancel upload

I haven't found in Google the easy networking and sharing tools that are on MySpace and YouTube, but Google is the 2,000 pound web gorilla. In fact, Google now owns YouTube, but as long as the company keeps Google Video alive, you will want to have a presence there.

IN CLOSING

I hope by now you have a handle on the basics of music video production and some idea of the power that a great video and strong
promotional effort can bring to bear in promoting a music career.
As you can see, music video production can be a lot of hard work,
but I am here to tell you that it is worth the effort. Remember
to keep pushing and don't let up. Use the Internet; use bulletin
boards, blogs, and community sites to tell people about your work.
The web is a tapestry of information and you never know which
thread could weave the robe of your success.

Keep your eye on the prize. Success in the music business
requires sustained effort and focus, and it rarely happens overnight.
Not only does the public need to know about your band, they need
to be reminded frequently. So remind them.

Don't forget to check out the DVD that came with this book. There
are many resources, web links, and special offers included on it. I
will also be posting more content for readers at musicoffice.com, so
drop by and register for goodies like free background animations and
software widgets. Please join the online community of music video
enthusiasts we are building there.

Music is a gift. Start giving.

Greg Forest
Kerrville, Texas
Fall 2007

Glossary of Terms

The video industry, like any other, has its own jargon. I am going to skip most of these terms, but there are a few that you will need to understand in order to make the best video possible and communicate with the like-minded. There are a number of other resources in the other appendices for further study of video and film terminology.

ASPECT RATIO

Aspect ratio describes the relative horizontal and vertical sizes of a video image with the most popular being 4:3 (standard definition TV) and 16:9 which is the wide screen or "letterbox" size now emerging in HD standards. 16:9 will soon be the standard for digital and broadcast video. If a graphic has an aspect ratio of 2:1, it means that the width is twice as large as the height. If you are tweaking stills or video in a project it is important to keep the aspect ratio the same so that images don't look "squeezed." If you are going to be using full screen photo images without any effects, cropping them to the aspect ratio and pixel size of the screen (720x480) will give you the best display.

ALPHA LAYER OR CHANNEL

The alpha layer in a video is that part of the video shot that is clear or completely transparent. It is used for combining multiple scenes into one layered and merged image. See Compositing for more information.

B-ROLL

The B-roll footage or stills are injected into the video to break it up stylistically. Backstage shots, the band goofing off and photos are the most commonly used types. B-roll footage can save the day if you wind up in a portion of the video where there just isn't a compelling image. You may be able to correct the problem by inserting a still or machine gun series of unrelated shots. You should have lots of B-roll material on hand when you begin editing.

CCD

The term CCD stands for Charge-Coupled Device. The CCD is the backbone of the video camera. The CCD converts the light coming through the camera lens into electron stream of varying charges and then into the huge number of pixels that comprise a video image. The image from a 3-chip (3 CCD) camera with each chip 2/3 inch will be far superior to a single-chip (1 CCD) camera with a 1/4 inch chip.

CMOS

CMOS stands for Complementary Metal Oxide Semiconductor and is the other method of converting light rays into electrons and a video image. This is an uncommon digital format more popular with scientists viewing MRI or CAT scan images than musicians.

CODEC

A codec is a compression algorithm and is short for compressor/decompressor. Video requires a great deal of bandwidth and to better utilize the available pipe, compression is used to get more information moved around faster. Be wary of codecs, many are proprietary and when you render your final movie you may find that others cannot view it because their computers don't have the codec to do so. Another consideration is that codecs compress the data, and different codecs have different priorities regarding picture quality. If you have the resources to capture and edit video in uncompressed format, do so and worry about codecs at the backend when you have to compress the video to make a DVD or streaming web video.

COLOR TEMPERATURE

Not all light is created equal; anyone who has shot a home movie has seen the difference between outdoor and indoor lighting. The film and photographic industry has catalogued the characteristics of different kinds of light. The unit of measure is "color temperature" in degrees Kelvin. Simply put, the higher the temperature, the more red the image will appear. As in all things digital, more is better. Here's a basic chart of light temperatures.

Lighting Type	Temperature (in degrees K)
Candlelight (low lux)	2000
Sunset	3000
Typical 100 watt light bulb	3200
High Wattage Fluorescent Light	5000
Sunlight	5500

COMPOSITING, GREEN/BLUE SCREEN

Compositing is all the rage these days. The technique has become so advanced that many feature films are using locations much less because it is easier to create virtual locations and sets. The actors are filmed against a well-lit blue or green screen. In the editing process using compositing software the blue or green background is removed leaving a clear or "alpha" layer. When this is composited or layered over the background of the fires of Mount Doom, you have Frodo in a world of trouble.

CYA (Cover Your Ass)

CYA is another corporate concept that has moved into mainstream art. If you are responsible for a project or component, make sure you justify what you're doing with self serving reasoning. In video it can also mean shooting a lot of video you won't use and keeping your original content on file forever.

DATA RATE

Data Rate is the speed at which your computer, cable, hard drive, or peripheral can move data through the pipe. It is a very important term in digital video and can be misrepresented easily. The most important consideration when looking at the data rate of a device is the rate of Sustained Input/Output. As an example, most hard drives are designed to dip onto the platter once in a while to update the data a given application is writing. In digital video—particularly in capturing and editing—the hard drive is accessed continually and the pedal is to the metal for long periods. In editing, you might be reading two or more video streams for an effect or transition which will at least double the data rate necessary before introducing error.

DEFRAGMENTING HARD DRIVES

Defragmenting your hard drive often, particularly your video drive, is a good idea. Essentially defragging consolidates files that have become fragmented—broken up into smaller components and stored in different locations on the drive—and puts them into one larger and more cohesive file at one location on the platter. Because the drive head is pulling data from one location when addressing a file rather than jumping all over the drive platter, your system will run faster and defragging cuts down on the hard drive's work load.

DEPTH OF FIELD

Depth of Field (DOF) is the distance in front of and beyond the subject that appears to be in focus. It is the range that defines "in focus." Changing the depth of field in a shot can dramatically alter a video or still image and help in creating a mood or emotion. A narrow DOF will give you a subject in focus but everything just in front and behind will be blurred, the blurring increasing with the distance out of the DOF. On the other hand, a shot with a wide DOF may have the foreground subject and the background in perfect focus, a feature of wide angle lenses.

DISC PRINTING

Also known as on-disc printing, there are basically only three flavors. Screen printing is done by replicators and is usually 300 dpi resolution. Ink jet printing is a popular format at the consumer level and can produce a very nice-looking disc. Thermal printing, in both color and black and white is very desirable because of the speed of printing and the industrial strength of the printer. My color inkjet takes about 3 minutes to print out a 300 dpi disc whereas my Rimage printer spits out a fully printed disc in about 20 seconds. If you are making lots of copies, the thermal printer is the way to go. The downside of thermal printers is the cost, which is many times more than an ink jet printer. However, the lifespan of a thermal printer is much longer and the per-unit print cost is the least expensive for do-it-yourself printing. I can get a few hundred color prints out of my ink jet before it screams for more cartridges; the thermal printer will do about 1500 before needing a new ribbon.

DUTCH ROLL

Although called by many names, this is a simple 90 degree roll where you start the shot 90 degrees off axis and turn the camera until the image is upright. You can also reverse the procedure for an oddball effect. The trick to the roll is to keep the target centered throughout the whole roll. Although it is the simplest of camera tricks, it will take practice to do it smoothly.

DVD

DVD is the standard for digital video delivery. Here is a brief look at the family of DVD formats:

▶ DVD-ROM: The format found in "store bought" or replicated discs. These discs cannot be recorded over.

▶ DVD-RAM: This is a recordable format that is falling out of favor. DVD-RAM was more popular in the early days of DVD technology because it was the first format that could be recorded on multiple times just like a recordable CD or floppy disc. Many DVD-RAM recorders required media that was in a protective case that makes it totally incompatible with all set-top boxes and the lion's share of computers. Steer clear of this format.

▶ DVD-R: A write-once format that is very popular because the media is inexpensive and getting cheaper each day. In fact, the price of quality DVD media is almost on par with the price of a quality blank CD.

▶ DVD-RW: This is the common rewritable format. The disc can be used over and over. I don't recommend using the DVD-RW for delivery as they are too easy to erase. Also the write speed on a rewritable disk is considerably slower than a write-once format.

▶ DVD+R: This format is similar to the DVD-R format, also being a write-once product. In early versions the +R format was a bit faster writing than the –R format. Most DVD burners and players are now compatible with this format and I use DVD+R media frequently.

▶ DVD+RW: This format is the rewriteable cousin to DVD+R. A popular format, DVD+RW media can be found in most electronics stores.

FIREWIRE

Originally developed in the nineties as a new high speed data pipe, FireWire is now a standard. This is the most common input/output protocol for transferring digital video back and forth between camera and computer. There are two flavors of 1394: the original 1394, sometimes called FireWire-400; and the newer 1394b or FireWire-800. iLink is Sony's take on the protocol; it's different only in name.

FOH (Front of House)

This term refers to the main sound console and operator that is feeding the audio to the venue crowd. This is a great source of audio if you can befriend the FOH engineer.

INTERLACED/PROGRESSIVE SCANNING

Interlaced scanning shows half of an image (on the odd rows of pixels) every sixtieth of a second, and then it shows the other half (on the even rows) the next sixtieth. Therefore, it takes one thirtieth of a second to show a complete frame, giving a frame rate of 30 frames per second (or, if you are picky, 29.97 for NTSC video.) Progressive scanning shows the entire image every sixtieth of a second, so the frame rate is twice as high, or 60 frames per second. A progressive image will give you a superior display.

IMAGE STABLIZATION

There are various methods to stabilize an image from in-camera software to hardware like a Steadicam, which actually holds the camera itself steadier when shooting. The hardware solutions can be quite expensive and the formula of dollars spent to quality of product is again in play. On the other hand, for those of you with smaller digital cameras I have found a widget at http://littlegreatideas.com/steadycam/ that is kinder on the shooter's budget and works pretty well.

I/O

I/O is an acronym for Input and Output used in describing just about everything digital or electronic.

KEYFRAME AND TWEENING

Keyframing in computer animation is a frame drawn directly by the editor or animator which is at an important point in the action, such as the beginning or end of a movement. The frames in between keyframes can be generated by the computer through a process called "tweening." By setting multiple keys in a scene or action, precision is attained; the more keyframes, the more accurate the movement or effect.

LOW LUX

A much-used video term to describe the camera's ability to capture light in low-light situations. Many cameras can go to a very low lux but the images are less than optimal. Except where the concept calls for it (e.g. faking a night vision shot), steer clear of shooting in low light. Video loves light.

MANUAL FOCUS

Your consumer camera probably came out of the box ready to point and shoot. Where possible use a video camera that will allow you to focus manually. On some consumer cameras this is not an option, but it can make a world of difference in a video production. Pulling focus for dramatic effect is one of the oldest tricks in the film/video book.

MEGABYTES/GIGABYTES/TERABYTES

Does this sound like a lot to "byte into?" These terms describe an amount of digital storage available in memory, hard drive space and throughput. A decade ago, a megabyte was an impressive chunk of data; today it isn't enough for one second of uncompressed video. If you are producing a video of any length, say beyond 45 minutes, you will probably be in the terabyte realm before you know it. If you want to start thinking about terabytes, just add another three zeros to the gigabyte column.

MEGAPIXELS

A megapixel is one million pixels, or a square image of 1,000 × 1,000 pixels. To get quality print output, you will need at least three megapixels. Most new digital still cameras are at this specification or higher. As in most things digital, more is better and the higher the megapixel images size, the more you can work with it and the larger the quality printout can be. A digital camera that is rated at 3.1 megapixels should have at least a 2048x1536 display size or 3,145,728 pixels. This is the low end of current digital photography, with high-end imaging hardware clocking in at over 30 megapixels.

MiniDV, DVCAM, DVPRO, DIGITAL 8

These are just some of the different digital camera tape formats out there with MiniDV being the most popular.

NLE

Non Linear Editing. In the old days, to edit multi-camera video you needed a synchronized video deck for each tape you wanted to edit. You had to physically fast forward, rewind and move forward and back frame by frame in some cases to make an edit. Needless to say, this was gear-intensive and time-consuming, not to mention a complete pain in the neck. With digital video, once the shots are in the computer and lined up in sync, you can just go to work moving from any part of the video to any other part without waiting for external devices to sync and start rolling.

PROCESSOR SPEED

This is the speed that your computer is rated for raw processing power. Needless to say, faster is better. And "pretty darned quick" is the default for video editing. For reliable video editing and reasonable render times, you will need a processor running at 2.0 Ghz at the low end.

PIXEL

A pixel is one of the many tiny dots that make up a video image. Display screens, now including televisions, are measured in not only the screen size but the pixel size. Likewise for video formats that are described by the number of pixels that can be displayed horizontally. The number of pixels on your cell phone will be much smaller than the number on your HD display. The more pixels, the higher the resolution of the video image.

QCIF/CIF/SD/DV/HD

These are the most common video display formats and the ones we will be touching on in this book. The range (in pixels) of display formats range from 160x120 in QCIF (suitable for an email video to Grandma), to the 352x240 of CIF (if Grandma has broadband), on through standard DV at 720x480 to the mountaintop at HD 1920x1080. There are other incremental standards such as 1280x720, but we will be sticking with the major players. You may see the letters "i" or "p" used in display formats; this is the specification for "interlaced" or "progressive" scanning.

RAM/ROM

RAM and ROM are different kinds of memory storage. ROM stands for Read Only Memory which is usually memory embedded in a chip to help it function. In the real world you can't access ROM memory in your applications. RAM on the other hand is Random Access Memory, and it is what can add real muscle to your computer. The more RAM you have installed on your computer, the better. You can never have enough RAM installed on your computer.

REAL TIME

The term "real time" can be something of a misnomer. The term is supposed to mean viewing your clips and edits in the time it takes to play it. To view a 60-second video clip or edit in real time would take one minute. Many vendors claim that you can do multiple streams of video and effects in "real time" but this claim is also dependent on the muscle of the editing computer. Many newer editors use a trick called "look ahead caching" which means that while you are looking at a scene at one minute your computer may be rendering an edit two minutes further down the timeline in the background. When you get to that later segment, is has already been pre-rendered into a cache file and it displays in real time. If you stack a number of video tracks onto your timeline, sooner or later, and most commonly sooner, you will leave the realm of "real time" and enter the dark realm of "rendering."

RENDERING

Rendering is sometimes called the "R Word." Rendering is creating a preview of a transition or effect or finalizing a video edit from many files into a finished movie or clip. There is a direct correlation between the complexity of the effect or transition and the time it takes to render. All 3D development, effects and compositing software will require rendering at some point. Rendering times are also tied to the computer doing the rendering; faster computers produce faster renders. Even with a fast computer, renders can be agonizingly slow. I have seen 10-second segments take a week to render at high resolution. If you delve into Computer Animation at all, rendering will rear its ugly head very soon in your learning curve.

Large scale projects (and even some smaller ones) will use a network of computers to break up the rendering job and spread the render over many computers via a network. Render "farms" are just large arrays of fast computers on a fast network working in concert to spit out scene renders as quickly as possible. I have a small render farm at my office utilizing older PCs (Pentium 3 and 4) that were collecting dust to help carry some of the rendering weight at my studio.

Another important concept to keep in mind when rendering: The computer doing the rendering will not be able to do much else during the render so it is not a good idea to check your email or run any other applications on the rendering box. It can easily impair the render process and sometimes even the file. The last thing you want to see is a render error message three or four days into a complex render.

RGB/COMPOSITE VIDEO

A standard video output (usually the yellow RCA) for attaching to a television or VCR. This is commonly used to preview the output of your production on a standard TV set. The composite output's Big Brother is s-video. A component video out streams three colors separately: Red, Blue and Green (RGB).

SHOT TERMINOLOGY

ECU: Extreme Close-up (the guitarist's fingers in frame)

CU: Close-up (the guitarist's whole guitar in frame)

MS: Medium (the whole guitarist in frame)

LS: Long Shot (the whole stage in frame)

XLS: Extreme long shot (the whole stadium in frame)

SLATING

Slating is creating a noise, visual cue, or both to set a specific time marker on a camera tape or film roll. One of the big advantages to the new generation of video products is that the necessity for time code has waned. With a strong slate at the beginning of the shot, synchronizing multiple cameras and audio sources becomes pretty easy. You will see how important slating is when we get to the editing section.

SMPTE

SMPTE stands for Society of Motion Picture and Television Engineers. The society is known as a governing board for video and film standards. SMPTE is most often found used in the context of timecode, with SMPTE timecode the standard for film and video synchronization.

STORYBOARD

A cartoon or graphic novel that is created prior to shooting and used in conjunction with the script that will show how every shot will look. Storyboard panels can also contain production notes for the camera personnel and crew.

STOCK FOOTAGE

Stock footage is footage that has been shot by someone else that you are using (with permission of course). The major TV networks as well as many film and production companies sell footage from their archives. There are many stock footage companies and web sites. Check Appendix B for some of their web addresses.

SVHS

SVHS was an interim device to television format that took the video image higher than standard VHS and boosted it to about halfway to the DV standard now in place.

TIMECODE

When you record onto digital video tape you are also recording time code. For most applications in this book you will not need to think much about time code except when prepping tapes for a live video shoot. Keep in mind that when you are about to stop recording a video shot, give it a couple of extra seconds past the content you want so that you can insert the next shot over the preceding one instead of having blank space on the tape. If there are breaks in the digital video track, it will reset the counter on the tape to zero. Where timecode (particularly SMPTE) comes into the picture is when you will be using your content for use in film. Every frame of a film is time stamped and composers can shape the music to match the scene easier with time code than bars and measures.

USB

Intel wasn't about to sit still and let lowly Apple set the standards, so USB was born. It is much the same as FireWire and also comes in two flavors, USB 1.0 and USB 2.0. The newer USB 2.0 is faster and I'm sure the data rate battle will continue with further upgrades to both platforms.

VIDEO FORMATS

▶ AVI: The AVI file format is the default standard for Windows-based video. Keep in mind that all AVI files are not equal and use different codecs (see above). The AVI file is generally preferred by pro editors as the format can be captured in uncompressed format.

▶ ASF: Active Streaming Format. A format that is about a decade old and already becoming a dinosaur. It was developed primarily for Internet streaming but has now been displaced by other formats with higher resolution and frame rates.

▶ DivX: This newcomer to video formats is becoming very popular because the underlying codec produces good compression while retaining a large amount of video information, resulting in a better image.

▶ MPEG: This format was introduced by the Motion Picture Experts Group and thus the name. There are different flavors of MPEG formats. The MPEG-1 is an older audio/video codec that was commonly used on training video CDs and DVDs and has a lower resolution of big brother MPEG-2 which is the default for DVD video. MPEG-2 is also the compression engine of most camcorders that store the information to disc.

▶ Apple QuickTime: One of the most popular streaming formats currently on the web. Developed by Apple the QuickTime format is well known for its quality output on both Mac and PC platforms. The MOV file format that QuickTime produces is readable by just about all video editors regardless of platforms. Many digital content creators use the QuickTime MOV format as the way their content is delivered – again because of the low loss of quality and still delivering that quality in a relatively small file size.

▶ RealVideo: The darling of Real Networks and is another of the popular streaming formats. Although popular, I rarely used the RealVideo format due to licensing restrictions on the number of feeds a site can stream simultaneously before having to buy seat licenses for viewers. I suspect this pricing model will change soon if it hasn't already. RealVideo delivers high quality streams and does a nice job of compressing files to a manageable size.

▶ WMV: This is Microsoft's primary streaming format and is the answer to QuickTime. The format is very popular because in preparing for delivery there are a number of options for maximizing quality against file size and the encoding widgets are free from Microsoft. This is the most popular streaming form on the web today.

VIDEO STREAMING

If you have ever played a DVD on your television or watched a movie on satellite TV, you have been watching a video stream. By the time a video frame gets to your TV, it has been compressed and streamed down the pipe. Your DVD player is streaming an MPEG-2 file to your TV when you are watching *Kill Bill II*. Every web video you have ever seen was streamed to your computer.

WHITE BALANCE

Again, most consumer cameras handle white balance much like focus, that is, automatically. Look for cameras that will allow you to set the white balance manually. You may have to spend a few more moments with your nose in the manual to figure out how to do it, but it can be a great help when working with one or more cameras. The color white is created by the sum of the other colors in the rainbow. If you have more than one camera you can point them all to the same white subject (usually a piece of paper), zoom in to fill the screen and set the white balance manually. That way the different cameras see the same thing as "white." It can speed color correction in editing if the different video sources are all starting on the same page regarding the color palette; white balancing accomplishes this.

Internet Resources

The quickest and easiest way to access this list is to use the website that is stored on the DVD-ROM portion of the accompanying DVD. Just put the DVD in your computer's DVD player/burner and go to the "Web" folder. Open the file "index.html" and you will be at the home page. You can also access the DVD extra content files in this manner.

Free Video Sites

The following are web addresses for uploading and sharing video. They all basically follow the YouTube model, although some have slightly different features and streaming video bitrates. As there are more coming online every day, you should do a Google search of "free video servers" to get the latest list of sites. Here are some of the more popular:

- ▶ www.youtube.com

- ▶ www.myspace.com

- ▶ www.video.google.com

- ▶ www.video.yahoo.com

- www.dropshots.com
- www.uncutvideo.aol.com
- www.zippyvideos.com
- www.lulu.tv
- www.photobucket.com
- www.guba.com
- www.tinypic.com
- www.ourstage.com
- www.vmix.com
- www.dropshots.com
- www.ourmedia.org
- www.veoh.com
- www.supload.com/free-video-hosting
- www.astravideos.com

Stock Footage Providers

- www.archive.org
- www.freestockfootage.com
- www.itnsource.com
- www.artbeats.com
- www.digitaljuice.com
- www.footage.net
- www.revostock.com
- www.blueskyfootage.com

- ▶ www.filmdisc.com

- ▶ www.videosource.com

- ▶ www.rocketclips.com

Tutorial/Instruction

- ▶ www.halleonard.com

- ▶ www.appleproaudio.com

- ▶ www.adobe.com/ap/products/tips/premiere.html

- ▶ www.timtv.com/mv-101.html

- ▶ www.pingmag.jp/2007/05/18/ big-in-japan-making-j-pop-music-videos

- ▶ www.howstuffworks.com/video-editing.htm

- ▶ www.desktopvideo.about.com

- ▶ www.digitaljuice.com

- ▶ www.musicoffice.com

Duplicators/Replicators/Blank Media

- ▶ www.kunaki.com

- ▶ www.cdrom2go.com

- ▶ www.discmakers.com

- ▶ www.oasiscd.com

- ▶ www.musiciansfriend.com

- ▶ www.mfdigital.com

- ▶ www.diskfaktory.com

- ▶ www.communitymusician.com

Copyrights, Clearance, and Publishing

▶ www.copyright.gov

▶ www.harryfox.com

▶ www.bmi.com

▶ www.ascap.com

▶ www.sesac.com

Forms

Here is a short library of the basic forms and releases you may find useful throughout your video shoot. Most of the forms are variations of a talent release. Getting releases, especially from primary talent who will get a lot of screen time, can be important. I have seen projects shut down because written clearance wasn't received by the producer. It can be very difficult to clear these matters up after the DVDs have been pressed or the program material aired.

Keep in mind that just about any large broadcaster is going to have you sign a release indemnifying them from any liability. Should a station get sued, when the trickle down legalities are finished you will probably be the wet one.

Also included are the Library of Congress copyright forms that would be suitable for a video producer or broadcast series. You can also find these forms on the accompanying DVD in PDF format.

PRODUCTION COMPANY/PROGRAM
VIDEO TAPING ARTIST CHECKLIST

Greetings!

Welcome to "Program Name!" We are proud to have you aboard the pilot production of this exciting new video and radio program. To get the best results for your taping, we have assembled this checklist of options and pre-production issues so that your video and audio taping is the best possible.

PERFORMERS

Please list the names of the performers in your group and the instruments they play, as you would like them to appear on the video and radio credits.

In space below, please list the performers, from stage right to left and the instruments they play. See the example:

Example:

Joe Smith, bass; Jill Jones, vocals; Bill Sanchez, drums; Amy Jones, guitar; Sam Smith, piano.

PERFORMER	INSTRUMENT
_____	_____
_____	_____
_____	_____
_____	_____
_____	_____
_____	_____
_____	_____

REPERTOIRE

2.   Please list the songs in the order that you will be performing them and, if you know the information, the songwriter and publisher. If you need more space, add an extra piece of paper.

Song Title   Writer(s)   Publisher (ASCAP, BMI)

_____   _____   _____

_____   _____   _____

_____   _____   _____

_____   _____   _____

_____   _____   _____

_____   _____   _____

_____   _____   _____

_____   _____   _____

_____   _____   _____

_____   _____   _____

4.   If you would like, we can insert your logo, still photography or other images into your video segment. If you would like to include other images, please mail them to The Program Office, Program Address, Somewhere, CA 98765 to use as soon as possible for scanning and setup on one of the video decks. Please send high quality images in PDF, PSD, TIF, BMP, PNG or TIFF format – Internet GIF images are generally not suitable. We will not include any logos or other artwork unless we get them ten (10) working days before your performance. If you have graphics containing an alpha layer, this is preferred.

5.   We will interview you briefly before or after the show. To make things easier, we will allow you to choose the questions you would like our host to ask. On a separate piece of paper, please list enough questions to fill a five-minute interview.

6.   We may shoot a brief chroma (green or blue screen) shot of the band before the taping. This is just a short shoot of the group in front of a green/blue background so we can fly the image into another background. PLEASE DO NOT WEAR BRIGHT BLUE OR GREEN during this part of the taping.

7.   If you have any other questions, please give us a call at:

Office Mon-Fri 10-4	123-456-7890
Office fax	123-456-7890
Producer cell	123-456-7890
Venue Phone	123-456-7890

Please return this at your earliest convenience, as we need to develop the cue sheets for the video director well in advance of the show.

We appreciate this opportunity to video tape and record you and are looking forward to seeing you at the venue. Welcome Aboard!

Sincerely,

Mr. Producer

PRODUCTION COMPANY/PROGRAM
VIDEO AND RADIO BROADCAST/RECORDING AGREEMENT

THIS AGREEMENT is entered into this _____ day of _____ February 2___, by and between Program Production Company (hereinafter referred to as the "Program") and _____, (hereinafter jointly and severally referred to as the "Artist).

FOR AND IN CONSIDERATION of mutual covenants set forth, the parties do hereby agree as follows:

Artist hereby grants the Program permission to record Artist's performance for the purpose of video/radio/Internet broadcasting at the following date and location and under the following terms:

1.   NAME OF ARTIST: NUMBER OF ARTISTS:

2.   PLACE OF ENGAGEMENT:

3.   DATE OF ENGAGEMENT:

4.   HOURS OF ENGAGEMENT:

5.   LOAD IN TIME

6.   The Program hereby warrants and represents that the use of the Master recordings of the Artist's performance shall be used for the sole purpose of broadcast on the video/radio program with the working title "Producer's Program Name." The working title of the program may change. Copies of recordings embodying the Artist's performance shall not be licensed, leased or sold to any other person, firm or corporation for any purpose other than for broadcast of the Program.

7.   Artist grants to the Program, in perpetuity, exclusively and universally, broadcast rights in and to that portion of the Artist's performance that is embodied in the Program. These rights are granted for all broadcast media including but not limited to broadcast television, cable, radio and the Internet. These rights are assignable to third parties by the Program under the terms herein.

8.   After mixing and editing the performance, and within 180 days of the performance date in Section 3 above, Program shall deliver to Artist at the address specified below, the final mix and edit of the audio and video broadcast master recordings (hereinafter the Master Recordings). Audio masters shall be delivered in CD format and video masters shall be delivered in digital MiniDV format.

Artist may purchase the separate camera tapes and the multi-track audio recording masters at the Program's cost for the blank tape.

9.   With the exception of the broadcast rights granted in Paragraph 7 herein, all mechanical rights to the Master Recordings, both audio and video are granted to the Artist. These rights are assignable by Artist and Artist may use the recordings for whatever purpose desired including but not limited to, the manufacture and sale of CDs, videos, DVDs, and multimedia products.

10.   Should Artist use portions of the Program in products offered for sale to the public (e.g. our final audio mix), the Program production credits shall remain within the video and the following shall be displayed on any product packaging.

Excerpted from The Program Name
Produced by Mr. Producer for Wang Dang Records

11.   Artist grants to program the right to utilize Artist's name, likeness, logo, signature facsimile or other image for Program promotional purposes.

12.   Upon completion of Artist's performance, Program will deliver to Artist a rough mix of the audio recording in CD format and the live video mix in VHS format.

13.   Artist has the option to buy additional copies of the rough taping for the following price:

- Cassette dub: $10.00
- DAT dub: $20.00
- CD dubs $20.00
- VHS dub: $15.00
- DV/MiniDV dub $25.00

14.   On each copy of the Program distributed to radio, television, the Internet or other broadcast medium, the following will be printed and included in the Program credits:
- Artist's name and the names of any additional performers in Artist's band.
- Artist appears courtesy of "_____" Records.
- The song titles, songwriter(s) and publishing affiliate (i.e. BMI, ASCAP) if any.

15.   This agreement shall be binding upon and inure to the benefit of the respective parties, their successors and assigns, and shall be governed by and interpreted in accordance with the laws of the State of _____.

16.   This agreement contains all the understandings, oral and written, of the parties and super-sedes all previous agreements.

17.   If any portion of this agreement is found to be invalid or unenforceable, it shall not affect the balance of this Agreement.

The Parties hereto have read, understand and agree on the terms and conditions set forth in this Agreement and by setting their hands to it do so agree.

_____

For Artist

Address that Master Recordings should be sent to and contact phone number:

_____

_____

_____

_____

Mr. Producer, for Program
The Company Name
PO Box 1234
Podunk, SD 67890
(123) 456-7890

PRODUCTION COMPANY/PROGRAM
AUDIO/VIDEO CONSENT TO RECORD

The undersigned hereby grants The Producer/Production Company and its assigns the right to record my image and voice for the purpose of the broadcast recording of a live concert. The Production Company and its assigns are hereby granted the right to use my image and voice for the commercial exploitation of the concert being taped with no further compensation by The Production Company, except as provided below.

The taping will take place at:

The Venue
123 Main St.
Anywhere, NM 98765
(123) 456-7890

Saturday April 1, 2009

The free or discounted admission to the concert you receive shall be the only compensation due the undersigned for granting this release.

Your name and phone number are mandatory to enter the concert – providing your email address will subscribe you to our mailing list and is optional.

PRINT YOUR NAME	SIGNATURE	EMAIL – To get on the list

PLEASE - NO IN OR OUT AFTER THE SHOW HAS STARTED. PLEASE TURN OFF CELL PHONES AND BE QUIET DURING TAPING - YOUR COOPERATION IS GREATLY APPRECIATED.

PRODUCTION COMPANY/PROGRAM
Location/Venue Release Form

Dated: As of _____, 20__

Venue Name
Address
City, State, ZIP

Re: Location Address: _____

Dear Sir or Madam:

This is to confirm the consent and agreement of _____ ("Licensor"), in consideration of _____ [Insert any compensation terms or delete line] [and] the possibility of publicity that The Company ("The Company"), its agents, licensees, assigns, successors, parents, subsidiaries and affiliates, and each of their respective employees, officers, directors, shareholders, agents and representatives are hereby granted the right and license to enter and remain upon the premises located at _____ __ ("Location"), and to make use of such premises and related Property, from _____ [Insert date] to _____ [Insert date] (plus any reasonable number of re-shoot days subject to availability of the Location) in connection with print, graphic, audio and/or visual or other content, projects, campaigns or programs, and derivative works thereof [known as "_____"] (the "Project").

Further, Licensor irrevocably grants to The Company the following permissions, rights and licenses in and to all property, both real and personal, located at such Location (collectively, the "Property").

In consideration of adequate consideration, the receipt of which is acknowledged, Licensor agrees as follows:

1. **Special Terms and Conditions**. *Any reference to terms not described below should be entered here. Insurance, hours of operation and access are commonly found in this clause.*

2. **Scope.**

   (a) The right and license to photograph, record, depict, represent and otherwise make use of the Property. Without limitation, the Property includes any and all names, addresses and trademarks connected with the Property and any signs, artwork, sculptures, pictures, fixtures and other personal property located thereon, and any logos and verbiage contained thereon in connection with, or as part of, the Project, the right to refer to the Property by any real or fictitious name, the right to attribute any real or fictitious events as having occurred on the Property and the right to reconstruct or recreate the Property or any part thereof for use as a set for shooting, photographing, recording and/or filming of the Project.

   (b) The right and license to reproduce, publish, distribute, exhibit, sublicense, advertise and otherwise exploit any and all productions and materials, in whole or in part, in connection with the permissions, rights and licenses hereunder, including, without limitation, the Project and the advertising and publicity therefor, and in commercial tie-ins and any merchandising or other commercial exploitation of the Project and the allied, ancillary and subsidiary rights thereto, by any and all methods and manners and in any and all languages, formats and media (including, without limitation, film, television, videocassettes, DVDs, interactive devices and Internet and on-line systems etc.), whether now known or hereafter devised, throughout the world, in perpetuity, without limitation or restriction of any kind and without further payment of any kind.

(c) As between the Licensor and The Company, The Company shall be the sole, exclusive and perpetual owner of all right, title and interest in the Project and any photographs and recordings made hereunder in connection with the Property including, without limitation, the copyright and all renewals and extensions of copyright therein.

3. **Representations/Warranties/Indemnity**. The Licensor represents and warrants that the Licensor has the full right and authority to enter into this "Location Release" and to grant to The Company all of the rights set forth herein and that the consent or permission of no other person or entity is necessary to grant the permissions, rights and Location Release.DOC licenses contained in this Location Release. The Licensor agrees to indemnify and hold harmless The Company and its parent, and its and their agents, licensees, assigns, successors, subsidiaries and affiliates, and the officers, directors, managers, equity holders, agents and employees of each of them, from and against, any and all losses, costs, liabilities, judgments, damages, claims and expenses (including reasonable outside attorneys' fees and costs) of any nature arising from any breach or any alleged breach by the Licensor of any representation, warranty or agreement made by the Licensor in this Location Release.

4. **Miscellaneous.** Neither The Company nor its agents, licensees, assigns, successors, parents, subsidiaries and affiliates shall be obligated to photograph scenes or make recordings at or otherwise use the Property, or make any actual use of or reference to any photographs or recordings made at the Property, or otherwise depict or refer to the Property in the Project, or produce, publish, distribute or exploit the Project. The Licensor hereby irrevocably waives and relinquishes any right to seek or obtain, for any reason whatsoever, an injunction, a rescission or termination of this Location Release or any rights hereunder, or any other form of equitable relief against The Company, or otherwise interfere with or impair the development, production, publication, distribution, exhibition, advertising, publicizing or other exploitation of the Project, the Licensor's sole remedy with respect thereto being an action at law for damages (if any). The Licensor shall have no equitable or legal cause of action against The Company or any third party on the basis that The Company's use of any photographs or recordings made at the Property is, or is claimed to be, defamatory, derogatory, denigrative, untrue, censorable or violative of anyone's rights of privacy or publicity or other personal and/or property rights except insofar as The Company is in material breach of any restrictions specifically set forth in this Location Release (if any). The Licensor acknowledges and agrees that any breach by the Licensor of this Location Release will cause The Company irreparable harm, and therefore, that The Company shall be entitled to injunctive or equitable relief (without obligation to post bond or surety or establish harm) in addition to all other remedies available at law or in equity, in any court of competent jurisdiction. The Company may freely license, sublicense and assign, in whole or in part, the Location Release or any of the rights hereunder.

This is the entire agreement between the parties relating to the matters herein and subsequent to execution cannot be modified without written consent of the parties hereto and shall be exclusively governed by and construed in accordance with the internal laws applicable to The Company, 123 Elm St., Somewhere, CA 99012

Sincerely,

_____

For The Company
AGREED AND ACCEPTED TO:
[Insert Name of Licensor]

If you are in agreement, please sign below and return.

_____

LICENSOR

PRODUCTION COMPANY/PROGRAM
SIMPLE MODEL RELEASE FORM

I, _____(Model)_____, for due consideration, hereby grant my permission to

_____ to use my photograph, photographic likeness, and/or

reproduction thereof, in whatever capacity as they see fit, including, but not limited to exhibitions,

illustrations, and advertisements.

DATE: _____

MODEL: _____

PARENT: _____
(if required)

PRODUCTION COMPANY/PROGRAM
Photography or Graphic Image Release Form

I, __*Photographer/Artist*__ hereby grant to __*The Producer*___ the right to use non-exclusively the photographs or images listed below for the sole purpose of broadcast and promotion of __*The Program*__.

I hereby state that I am fully empowered to grant this license and have all rights in and to the images described herein. I warrant and represent that I am the lone copyright holder and that the photograph or image listed below is not encumbered or otherwise pledged to any other entity that would be in contradiction of this grant of license.

Use of the images below is for the sole purpose of the promotion, and broadcast of ___*The Show/Artist*__. This license is not for the mechanical reproduction of my images except for the purposes of promotion or broadcast.

Usage of the image for t-shirts, posters or any and all other goods or commercial exploitation is not granted herein.

Photograph or Image Details

Title of image:_____

Today's date _____

Country _____

Photographer/Artist's Name: _____

Street Address _____

City _____ State/Province _____

Zip/Postal code _____ Email address _____

Phone _____

DVD BREAKDOWN

My company shot a local annual music festival—primarily for streaming on the Internet. The festival producer had the foresight to budget tape into the production so we could go back and edit shows. A few months later inquiries were made about producing a television show using the footage and selling DVDs of consenting artists through the web and traditional distribution outlets.

The scenario below produces a product with a suggested retail of at least $19.95; with wholesale around $ 15.00 and distributors cost around $ 14.00. The first run per unit cost will be approximately $11.00. On subsequent runs the cost should drop to around $8.25 as the production/editing/DVD authoring costs were recouped on the first run. The Artist and/or any of the other non-mechanical royalty partner(s) may purchase the product at the best distributor's price. This would give the Artist and the other per-unit royalty partners an incentive to retail the product. This deal could also be structured to cut The Music Office's post-production fees at least in half for a $1.00 per unit royalty paid at royalty distribution.

	Description	Unit Cost	Units	Amount
1	Production/Shoot (one 45-minute show)*	$ 500.00	1	$ 500.00
2	Coordination (Titling/ Releases/Accounting) **	$ 20.00	4	$ 80.00
3	Audio Post (Mix/Transfer to 24-bit 48Khz) **	$ 30.00	8	$ 240.00
4	Video Post (Video Capture/Sync) **	$ 30.00	4	$ 120.00
5	Video Editing/Mastering (broadcast ready) **	$ 65.00	16	$ 1,040.00
6	DVD Authoring/Mastering **	$ 65.00	8	$ 520.00
7	VHS/DV/DVD/CD copies/ mastering media **	$ 100.00	1	$ 100.00

	Description	Unit Cost	Units	Amount
8	DVD Replication **	$ 2.50	1,000	$ 2,500.00
9	Publishing Mechanical ** (a reduction negotiated?)	$ .08	1,000	$ 800.00
10	Artist Royalty ***	$ 1.50	1000	$ 1,500.00
11	Festival Royalty ***	$ 1.50	1000	$ 1,500.00
12	Festival Record Label Royalty ***	$ 1.50	1000	$ 1,500.00
13	Administration Fees ***	?		
TOTAL COST PER DVD PRODUCT RUN (1,000)		$10.40	1000	$ 10,400.00
Location Production Costs (PAID) *				$ 500.00
Post /Master/Replication (PENDING) **				$ 4,680.00
BACKEND COST (Royalty) **				$ 5,220.00
Ongoing Administration		?		
Second and Ongoing Runs		$7.80	1000	$ 7,800.00

*   The paid up-front costs include preproduction, location shoot, equipment rental, and original tape.

**   The pending up-front costs include video post/editing, DVD authoring/replication and publishing royalties.

***   Backend Costs include per-unit royalty payments to the Artist, The Festival and The Festival Record Label

COPYRIGHT FORMS

Even if you have done your work and branded or digitally watermarked your work, it is a good idea to consider officially copyrighting your work. A small bit of prevention can go a long way in keeping thieves at bay. Your claim to a song or video's ownership has to be stronger than the thief's. Although you can affix the copyright symbol on your work immediately and claim it as yours, a Library of Congress registration is the most iron-clad legal claim for an artistic work. Here are a few of the more commonly used forms for music, TV serialization, and video.

Commonly in commercial CD or DVD projects there are two components to the product: the underlying, intangible songs (Form PA), and the specific performance of the songs captured on the CD or DVD (Form SR). Each of these two components has separate copyright protections.

FORM PA
This covers a wide variety of Performance Arts works including songs, theatrical and film works—just about any art that is performed. This is the most commonly used form for songwriters and music publishers.

FORM SR
This covers the audio recording only. To further protect the release you can file a form SR for both the audio CD and the video DVD. It is redundant, but if you wind up in court suing someone it's nice to get to beat them over the head twice. This is the most commonly used form by record labels.

FORM VA
This is the form you would use for graphics, photos, design layouts, and other works of visual art. Not only are the songs and performances protected, but the cover art should be, too.

FORM SE
If you are broadcasting with regularity—say on a local cable access show—this is the form for you.

FORM RE
This is a copyright renewal form. It can extend the life of the copyright. Another method of extending a copyright would be the lengthy "director's cut." It is usually filed at a later date than the commercial/theatrical release and encompasses content not included in the original release. However, copyright lasts so long

that your great-grandchildren might need to use this form for a song you write today.

FORM CON

If you are filling out Form PA and have more collaborators in the piece than the form allows for, you file this form with the PA to expand the number of claimants. You can use multiple copies of Form CON if one isn't enough. This is commonly used when a large band or ensemble all contribute to a musical work.

COPYRIGHT TIPS

Library of Congress registrations are getting a bit pricey—$45 at the time of this writing—so many artists are sending in their work initially as a compilation encompassing a number of songs/clips rather than a single work. The contents of the compilation are afforded the same protection. Then, you can register an amended copyright later, culling out any part of the compilation for its own separate copyright. You will notice this option in Form PA.

You can get all the copyright forms you need on the DVD, or surf to copyrights.gov and run a search.

Not only has the price of registering a copyright gone up recently, but the time it takes to get your stamped registration back has become incredibly long. Ten years ago you could expect the form back in 90 days; waiting times of over a year are common these days. Pay with a check, and at least you will know the date that they stamped you inbound.

Form PA

Detach and read these instructions before completing this form.
Make sure all applicable spaces have been filled in before you return this form.

When to Use This Form: Use Form PA for registration of published or unpublished works of the performing arts. This class includes works prepared for the purpose of being "performed" directly before an audience or indirectly "by means of any device or process." Works of the performing arts include: (1) musical works, including any accompanying words; (2) dramatic works, including any accompanying music; (3) pantomimes and choreographic works; and (4) motion pictures and other audiovisual works.

Deposit to Accompany Application: An application for copyright registration must be accompanied by a deposit consisting of copies or phonorecords representing the entire work for which registration is made. The following are the general deposit requirements as set forth in the statute:

Unpublished Work: Deposit one complete copy (or phonorecord).

Published Work: Deposit two complete copies (or one phonorecord) of the best edition.

Work First Published Outside the United States: Deposit one complete copy (or phonorecord) of the first foreign edition.

Contribution to a Collective Work: Deposit one complete copy (or phonorecord) of the best edition of the collective work.

Motion Pictures: Deposit *both* of the following: (1) a separate written description of the contents of the motion picture; and (2) for a published work, one complete copy of the best edition of the motion picture; or, for an unpublished work, one complete copy of the motion picture or identifying material. Identifying material may be either an audiorecording of the entire soundtrack or one frame enlargement or similar visual print from each 10-minute segment.

The Copyright Notice: Before March 1, 1989, the use of copyright notice was mandatory on all published works, and any work first published before that date should have carried a notice. For works first published on and after March 1, 1989, use of the copyright notice is optional. For more information about copyright notice, see Circular 3, *Copyright Notice.*

For Further Information: To speak to a Copyright Office staff member, call (202) 707-3000 (TTY: (202) 707-6737). Recorded information is available 24 hours a day. Order forms and other publications from the address in space 9 or call the Forms and Publications Hotline at (202) 707-9100. Access and download circulars, forms, and other information from the Copyright Office website at *www.copyright.gov.*

PRIVACY ACT ADVISORY STATEMENT Required by the Privacy Act of 1974 (P.L. 93-579)
The authority for requesting this information is title 17 *USC* secs. 409 and 410. Furnishing the requested information is voluntary. But if the information is not furnished, it may be necessary to delay or refuse registration and you may not be entitled to certain relief, remedies, and benefits provided in chapters 4 and 5 of title 17 *USC.*
The principal uses of the requested information are the establishment and maintenance of a public record and the examination of the application for compliance with the registration requirements of the copyright code.
Other routine uses include public inspection and copying, preparation of public indexes, preparation of public catalogs of copyright registrations, and preparation of search reports upon request.
NOTE: No other advisory statement will be given in connection with this application. Please keep this statement and refer to it if we communicate with you regarding this application.

Please type or print using black ink. The form is used to produce the certificate.

 ## SPACE 1: Title

Title of This Work: Every work submitted for copyright registration must be given a title to identify that particular work. If the copies or phonorecords of the work bear a title (or an identifying phrase that could serve as a title), transcribe that wording *completely* and *exactly* on the application. Indexing of the registration and future identification of the work will depend on the information you give here. If the work you are registering is an entire "collective work" (such as a collection of plays or songs), give the overall title of the collection. If you are registering one or more individual contributions to a collective work, give the title of each contribution, followed by the title of the collection. For an unpublished collection, you may give the titles of the individual works after the collection title.

Previous or Alternative Titles: Complete this space if there are any additional titles for the work under which someone searching for the registration might be likely to look, or under which a document pertaining to the work might be recorded.

Nature of This Work: Briefly describe the general nature or character of the work being registered for copyright. Examples: "Music"; "Song Lyrics"; "Words and Music"; "Drama"; "Musical Play"; "Choreography"; "Pantomime"; "Motion Picture"; "Audiovisual Work."

SPACE 2: Author(s)

General Instructions: After reading these instructions, decide who are the "authors" of this work for copyright purposes. Then, unless the work is a "collective work," give the requested information about every "author" who contributed any appreciable amount of copyrightable matter to this version of the work. If you need further space, request additional Continuation Sheets. In the case of a collective work such as a songbook or a collection of plays, give information about the author of the collective work as a whole.

Name of Author: The fullest form of the author's name should be given. Unless the work was "made for hire," the individual who actually created the work is its "author." In the case of a work made for hire, the statute provides that "the employer or other person for whom the work was prepared is considered the author."

What Is a "Work Made for Hire"? A "work made for hire" is defined as: (1) "a work prepared by an employee within the scope of his or her employment"; or (2) "a work specially ordered or commissioned for use as a contribution to a collective work, as a part of a motion picture or other audiovisual work, as a translation, as a supplementary work, as a compilation, as an instructional text, as a test, as answer material for a test, or as an atlas, if the parties expressly agree in a written instrument signed by them that the work shall be considered a work made for hire." If you have checked "Yes" to indicate that the work was "made for hire," you must give the full legal name of the employer (or other person for whom the work was prepared). You may also include the name of the employee along with the name of the employer (for example: "Elster Music Co., employer for hire of John Ferguson").

"Anonymous" or "Pseudonymous" Work: An author's contribution to a work is "anonymous" if that author is not identified on the copies or phonorecords of the work. An author's contribution to a work is "pseudonymous" if that author is identified on the copies or phonorecords under a fictitious name. If the work is "anonymous" you may: (1) leave the line blank; or (2) state "anonymous" on the line; or (3) reveal the author's identity. If the work is "pseudonymous" you may: (1) leave the line blank; or (2) give the pseudonym and identify it as such (example: "Huntley Haverstock, pseudonym"); or (3) reveal the author's name, making clear which is the real name and which is the pseudonym (for example: "Judith Barton, whose pseudonym is Madeline Elster"). However, the citizenship or domicile of the author *must* be given in all cases.

Dates of Birth and Death: If the author is dead, the statute requires that the year of death be included in the application unless the work is anonymous or pseudonymous. The author's birth date is optional, but is useful as a form of identification. Leave this space blank if the author's contribution was a "work made for hire."

Author's Nationality or Domicile: Give the country of which the author is a citizen, or the country in which the author is domiciled. Nationality or domicile *must* be given in all cases.

Nature of Authorship: Give a brief general statement of the nature of this particular author's contribution to the work. Examples: "Words"; "Coauthor of Music"; "Words and Music"; "Arrangement"; "Coauthor of Book and Lyrics"; "Dramatization"; "Screen Play"; "Compilation and English Translation"; "Editorial Revisions."

SPACE 3: Creation and Publication

General Instructions: Do not confuse "creation" with "publication." Every application for copyright registration must state "the year in which creation of the work was completed." Give the date and nation of first publication only if the work has been published.

Creation: Under the statute, a work is "created" when it is fixed in a copy or phonorecord for the first time. Where a work has been prepared over a period of time, the part of the work existing in fixed form on a particular date constitutes the created work on that date. The date you give here should be the year in which the author completed the particular version for which registration is now being sought, even if other versions exist or if further changes or additions are planned.

Publication: The statute defines "publication" as "the distribution of copies or phonorecords of a work to the public by sale or other transfer of ownership, or by rental, lease, or lending"; a work is also "published" if there has been an "offering to distribute copies or phonorecords to a group of persons for purposes of further distribution, public performance, or public display." Give the full date (month, day, year) when, and the country where, publication first occurred. If first publication took place simultaneously in the United States and other countries, it is sufficient to state "U.S.A."

SPACE 4: Claimant(s)

Name(s) and Address(es) of Copyright Claimant(s): Give the name(s) and address(es) of the copyright claimant(s) in this work even if the claimant is the same as the author. Copyright in a work belongs initially to the author of the work (including, in the case of a work made for hire, the employer or other person for whom the work was prepared). The copyright claimant is either the author of the work or a person or organization to whom the copyright initially belonging to the author has been transferred.

Transfer: The statute provides that, if the copyright claimant is not the author, the application for registration must contain "a brief statement of how the claimant obtained ownership of the copyright." If any copyright claimant named in space 4 is not an author named in space 2, give a brief statement explaining how the claimant(s) obtained ownership of the copyright. Examples: "By written contract"; "Transfer of all rights by author"; "Assignment"; "By will." Do not attach transfer documents or other attachments or riders.

SPACE 5: Previous Registration

General Instructions: The questions in space 5 are intended to show whether an earlier registration has been made for this work and, if so, whether there is any basis for a new registration. As a general rule, only one basic copyright registration can be made for the same version of a particular work.

Same Version: If this version is substantially the same as the work covered by a previous registration, a second registration is not generally possible unless: (1) the work has been registered in unpublished form and a second registration is now being sought to cover this first published edition; or (2) someone other than the author is identified as copyright claimant in the earlier registration, and the author is now seeking registration in his or her own name. If either of these two exceptions applies, check the appropriate box and give the earlier registration number and date. Otherwise, do not submit Form PA; instead, write the Copyright Office

for information about supplementary registration or recordation of transfers of copyright ownership.

Changed Version: If the work has been changed and you are now seeking registration to cover the additions or revisions, check the last box in space 5, give the earlier registration number and date, and complete both parts of space 6 in accordance with the instructions below.

Previous Registration Number and Date: If more than one previous registration has been made for the work, give the number and date of the latest registration.

SPACE 6: Derivative Work or Compilation

General Instructions: Complete space 6 if this work is a "changed version," "compilation," or "derivative work," and if it incorporates one or more earlier works that have already been published or registered for copyright or that have fallen into the public domain. A "compilation" is defined as "a work formed by the collection and assembling of preexisting materials or of data that are selected, coordinated, or arranged in such a way that the resulting work as a whole constitutes an original work of authorship." A "derivative work" is "a work based on one or more preexisting works." Examples of derivative works include musical arrangements, dramatizations, translations, abridgments, condensations, motion picture versions, or "any other form in which a work may be recast, transformed, or adapted." Derivative works also include works "consisting of editorial revisions, annotations, or other modifications" if these changes, as a whole, represent an original work of authorship.

Preexisting Material (space 6a): Complete this space *and* space 6b for derivative works. In this space identify the preexisting work that has been recast, transformed, or adapted. For example, the preexisting material might be: "French version of Hugo's 'Le Roi s'amuse'." Do not complete this space for compilations.

Material Added to This Work (space 6b): Give a brief, general statement of the *additional* new material covered by the copyright claim for which registration is sought. In the case of a derivative work, identify this new material. Examples: "Arrangement for piano and orchestra"; "Dramatization for television"; "New film version"; "Revisions throughout; Act III completely new." If the work is a compilation, give a brief, general statement describing both the material that has been compiled *and* the compilation itself. Example: "Compilation of 19th Century Military Songs."

SPACE 7, 8, 9: Fee, Correspondence, Certification, Return Address

Deposit Account: If you maintain a Deposit Account in the Copyright Office, identify it in space 7a. Otherwise, leave the space blank and send the fee with your application and deposit.

Correspondence (space 7b): Give the name, address, area code, telephone number, fax number, and email address (if available) of the person to be consulted if correspondence about this application becomes necessary.

Certification (space 8): The application cannot be accepted unless it bears the date and the **handwritten signature** of the author or other copyright claimant, or of the duly authorized agent of the author, claimant, or owner of exclusive right(s).

Address for Return of Certificate (space 9): The address box must be completed legibly since the certificate will be returned in a window envelope.

████ MORE INFORMATION ████

How to Register a Recorded Work: If the musical or dramatic work that you are registering has been recorded (as a tape, disk, or cassette), you may choose either copyright application Form PA (Performing Arts) or Form SR (Sound Recordings), depending on the purpose of the registration.

Use Form PA to register the underlying musical composition or dramatic work. Form SR has been developed specifically to register a "sound recording" as defined by the Copyright Act—a work resulting from the "fixation of a series of sounds," separate and distinct from the underlying musical or dramatic work. Form SR should be used when the copyright claim is limited to the sound recording itself. (In one instance, Form SR may also be used to file for a copyright registration for both kinds of works—see (4) below.) Therefore:

(1) File Form PA if you are seeking to register the musical or dramatic work, not the "sound recording," even though what you deposit for copyright purposes may be in the form of a phonorecord.

(2) File Form PA if you are seeking to register the audio portion of an audiovisual work, such as a motion picture soundtrack; these are considered integral parts of the audiovisual work.

(3) File Form SR if you are seeking to register the "sound recording" itself, that is, the work that results from the fixation of a series of musical, spoken, or other sounds, but not the underlying musical or dramatic work.

(4) File Form SR if you are the copyright claimant for both the underlying musical or dramatic work and the sound recording, *and* you prefer to register both on the same form.

(5) File both forms PA and SR if the copyright claimant for the underlying work and sound recording differ, or you prefer to have separate registration for them.

"Copies" and "Phonorecords": To register for copyright, you are required to deposit "copies" or "phonorecords." These are defined as follows:

Musical compositions may be embodied (fixed) in "copies," objects from which a work can be read or visually perceived, directly or with the aid of a machine or device, such as manuscripts, books, sheet music, film, and videotape. They may also be fixed in "phonorecords," objects embodying fixations of sounds, such as tapes and phonograph disks, commonly known as phonograph records. For example, a song (the work to be registered) can be reproduced in sheet music ("copies") or phonograph records ("phonorecords"), or both.

Copyright Office fees are subject to change. For current fees, check the Copyright Office website at *www.copyright.gov,* write the Copyright Office, or call (202) 707-3000.

For best results, fill in the form on-screen and then print it.

Form PA
For a Work of Performing Arts
UNITED STATES COPYRIGHT OFFICE

REGISTRATION NUMBER

PA   PAU

EFFECTIVE DATE OF REGISTRATION

Month   Day   Year

DO NOT WRITE ABOVE THIS LINE. IF YOU NEED MORE SPACE, USE A SEPARATE CONTINUATION SHEET.

1

TITLE OF THIS WORK ▼

PREVIOUS OR ALTERNATIVE TITLES ▼

NATURE OF THIS WORK ▼ See instructions

2

a

NAME OF AUTHOR ▼

DATES OF BIRTH AND DEATH
Year Born ▼   Year Died ▼

Was this contribution to the work a "work made for hire"?
☐ Yes
☐ No

AUTHOR'S NATIONALITY OR DOMICILE
Name of Country
OR { Citizen of _____
Domiciled in _____

WAS THIS AUTHOR'S CONTRIBUTION TO THE WORK
Anonymous? ☐ Yes ☐ No
Pseudonymous? ☐ Yes ☐ No

If the answer to either of these questions is "Yes," see detailed instructions.

NATURE OF AUTHORSHIP Briefly describe nature of material created by this author in which copyright is claimed. ▼

NOTE

Under the law, the "author" of a "work made for hire" is generally the employer, not the employee (see instructions). For any part of this work that was "made for hire" check "Yes" in the space provided, give the employer (or other person for whom the work was prepared) as "Author" of that part, and leave the space for dates of birth and death blank.

b

NAME OF AUTHOR ▼

DATES OF BIRTH AND DEATH
Year Born ▼   Year Died ▼

Was this contribution to the work a "work made for hire"?
☐ Yes
☐ No

AUTHOR'S NATIONALITY OR DOMICILE
Name of Country
OR { Citizen of _____
Domiciled in _____

WAS THIS AUTHOR'S CONTRIBUTION TO THE WORK
Anonymous? ☐ Yes ☐ No
Pseudonymous? ☐ Yes ☐ No

If the answer to either of these questions is "Yes," see detailed instructions.

NATURE OF AUTHORSHIP Briefly describe nature of material created by this author in which copyright is claimed. ▼

c

NAME OF AUTHOR ▼

DATES OF BIRTH AND DEATH
Year Born ▼   Year Died ▼

Was this contribution to the work a "work made for hire"?
☐ Yes
☐ No

AUTHOR'S NATIONALITY OR DOMICILE
Name of Country
OR { Citizen of _____
Domiciled in _____

WAS THIS AUTHOR'S CONTRIBUTION TO THE WORK
Anonymous? ☐ Yes ☐ No
Pseudonymous? ☐ Yes ☐ No

If the answer to either of these questions is "Yes," see detailed instructions.

NATURE OF AUTHORSHIP Briefly describe nature of material created by this author in which copyright is claimed. ▼

3

a YEAR IN WHICH CREATION OF THIS WORK WAS COMPLETED This information must be given in all cases.
_____ Year

b DATE AND NATION OF FIRST PUBLICATION OF THIS PARTICULAR WORK
Complete this information ONLY if this work has been published.
Month _____ Day _____ Year _____ Nation

4

See instructions before completing this space.

COPYRIGHT CLAIMANT(S) Name and address must be given even if the claimant is the same as the author given in space 2. ▼

TRANSFER If the claimant(s) named here in space 4 is (are) different from the author(s) named in space 2, give a brief statement of how the claimant(s) obtained ownership of the copyright. ▼

DO NOT WRITE HERE
OFFICE USE ONLY

APPLICATION RECEIVED

ONE DEPOSIT RECEIVED

TWO DEPOSITS RECEIVED

FUNDS RECEIVED

MORE ON BACK ▶
· Complete all applicable spaces (numbers 5-9) on the reverse side of this page.
· See detailed instructions.   · Sign the form at line 8.

DO NOT WRITE HERE

Page 1 of _____ pages

EXAMINED BY

FORM PA

CHECKED BY

☐ CORRESPONDENCE
   Yes

FOR
COPYRIGHT
OFFICE
USE
ONLY

DO NOT WRITE ABOVE THIS LINE. IF YOU NEED MORE SPACE, USE A SEPARATE CONTINUATION SHEET.

PREVIOUS REGISTRATION Has registration for this work, or for an earlier version of this work, already been made in the Copyright Office?
☐ **Yes** ☐ **No** If your answer is "Yes," why is another registration being sought? (Check appropriate box.) ▼ If your answer is No, do **not** check box A, B, or C.
a. ☐ This is the first published edition of a work previously registered in unpublished form.
b. ☐ This is the first application submitted by this author as copyright claimant.
c. ☐ This is a changed version of the work, as shown by space 6 on this application.
If your answer is "Yes," give: **Previous Registration Number** ▼   **Year of Registration** ▼

5

DERIVATIVE WORK OR COMPILATION Complete both space 6a and 6b for a derivative work; complete only 6b for a compilation.
Preexisting Material Identify any preexisting work or works that this work is based on or incorporates. ▼

a **6**

Material Added to This Work Give a brief, general statement of the material that has been added to this work and in which copyright is claimed. ▼

b

See instructions
before completing
this space.

DEPOSIT ACCOUNT If the registration fee is to be charged to a Deposit Account established in the Copyright Office, give name and number of Account.
Name ▼   **Account Number** ▼

a **7**

CORRESPONDENCE Give name and address to which correspondence about this application should be sent. Name/Address/Apt/City/State/Zip▼

b

Area code and daytime telephone number   (   )   Fax number   (   )
Email

CERTIFICATION* I, the undersigned, hereby certify that I am the
                                                Check only one ▶ {
                                                ☐ author
                                                ☐ other copyright claimant
                                                ☐ owner of exclusive right(s)
                                                ☐ authorized agent of _____
                                                    Name of author or other copyright claimant, or owner of exclusive right(s) ▲
of the work identified in this application and that the statements made by me in this application are correct to the best of my knowledge.

8

Typed or printed name and date ▼ If this application gives a date of publication in space 3, do not sign and submit it before that date.

                                                                    Date

Handwritten signature (X) ▼

☞   x _____

Certificate
will be
mailed in
window
envelope
to this
address:

Name ▼

Number/Street/Apt ▼

City/State/Zip ▼

YOU MUST:
• Complete all necessary spaces
• Sign your application in space 8
**SEND ALL 3 ELEMENTS
IN THE SAME PACKAGE:**
1. Application form
2. Nonrefundable filing fee in check or money
order payable to *Register of Copyrights*
3. Deposit material
MAIL TO:
Library of Congress
Copyright Office
101 Independence Avenue SE
Washington, DC 20559-6000

9

*17 *USC* §506(e): Any person who knowingly makes a false representation of a material fact in the application for copyright registration provided for by section 409, or in any written statement filed in connection
with the application, shall be fined not more than $2,500.

Form SR

Detach and read these instructions before completing this form.
Make sure all applicable spaces have been filled in before you return this form.

When to Use This Form: Use Form SR for registration of published or unpublished sound recordings. It should be used when the copyright claim is limited to the sound recording itself, and it may also be used where the same copyright claimant is seeking simultaneous registration of the underlying musical, dramatic, or literary work embodied in the phonorecord.

With one exception, "sound recordings" are works that result from the fixation of a series of musical, spoken, or other sounds. The exception is for the audio portions of audiovisual works, such as a motion picture soundtrack or an audio cassette accompanying a filmstrip. These are considered a part of the audiovisual work as a whole.

Deposit to Accompany Application: An application for copyright registration must be accompanied by a deposit consisting of phonorecords representing the entire work for which registration is to be made.

Unpublished Work: Deposit one complete phonorecord.

Published Work: Deposit two complete phonorecords of the best edition, together with "any printed or other visually perceptible material" published with the phonorecords.

Work First Published Outside the United States: Deposit one complete phonorecord of the first foreign edition.

Contribution to a Collective Work: Deposit one complete phonorecord of the best edition of the collective work.

The Copyright Notice: Before March 1, 1989, the use of copyright notice was mandatory on all published works, and any work first published before that date should have carried a notice. For works first published on and after March 1, 1989, use of the copyright notice is optional. For more information about copyright notice, see Circular 3, *Copyright Notices.*

For Further Information: To speak to a Copyright Office staff member, call (202) 707-3000 (TTY: (202) 707-6737). Recorded information is available 24 hours a day. Order forms and other publications from Library of Congress, Copyright Office, 101 Independence Avenue SE, Washington, DC 20559-6000 or call the Forms and Publications Hotline at (202) 707-9100. Access and download circulars, forms, and other information from the Copyright Office website at *www.copyright.gov.*

PRIVACY ACT ADVISORY STATEMENT Required by the Privacy Act of 1974 (P.L. 93-579)
The authority for requesting this information is title 17 *USC*, secs. 409 and 410. Furnishing the requested information is voluntary. But if the information is not furnished, it may be necessary to delay or refuse registration and you may not be entitled to certain relief, remedies, and benefits provided in chapters 4 and 5 of title 17 *USC*.
The principal uses of the requested information are the establishment and maintenance of a public record and the examination of the application for compliance with the registration requirements of the copyright code.
Other routine uses include public inspection and copying, preparation of public indexes, preparation of public catalogs of copyright registrations, and preparation of search reports upon request.
NOTE: No other advisory statement will be given in connection with this application. Please keep this statement and refer to it if we communicate with you regarding this application.

Please type or print neatly using black ink. The form is used to produce the certificate.

SPACE 1: Title

Title of This Work: Every work submitted for copyright registration must be given a title to identify that particular work. If the phonorecords or any accompanying printed material bears a title (or an identifying phrase that could serve as a title), transcribe that wording completely and exactly on the application. Indexing of the registration and future identification of the work may depend on the information you give here.

Previous, Alternative, or Contents Titles: Complete this space if there are any previous or alternative titles for the work under which someone searching for the registration might be likely to look, or under which a document pertaining to the work might be recorded. You may also give the individual contents titles, if any, in this space or you may use a Continuation Sheet. Circle the term that describes the titles given.

SPACE 2: Author(s)

General Instructions: After reading these instructions, decide who are the "authors" of this work for copyright purposes. Then, unless the work is a "collective work," give the requested information about every "author" who contributed any appreciable amount of copyrightable matter to this version of the work. If you need further space, request additional Continuation Sheets. In the case of a collective work such as a collection of previously published or registered sound recordings, give information about the author of the collective work as a whole. If you are submitting this Form SR to cover the recorded musical, dramatic, or literary work as well as the sound recording itself, it is important for space 2 to include full information about the various authors of all of the material covered by the copyright claim, making clear the nature of each author's contribution.

Name of Author: The fullest form of the author's name should be given. Unless the work was "made for hire," the individual who actually created the work is its "author." In the case of a work made for hire, the statute provides that "the employer or other person for whom the work was prepared is considered the author."

What Is a "Work Made for Hire"? A "work made for hire" is defined as: (1) "a work prepared by an employee within the scope of his or her employment"; or (2) "a work specially ordered or commissioned for use as a contribution to a collective

work, as a part of a motion picture or other audiovisual work, as a translation, as a supplementary work, as a compilation, as an instructional text, as a test, as answer material for a test, or as an atlas, if the parties expressly agree in a written instrument signed by them that the work shall be considered a work made for hire." If you have checked "Yes" to indicate that the work was "made for hire," you must give the full legal name of the employer (or other person for whom the work was prepared). You may also include the name of the employee along with the name of the employer (for example: "Elster Record Co., employer for hire of John Ferguson").

"Anonymous" or "Pseudonymous" Work: An author's contribution to a work is "anonymous" if that author is not identified on the copies or phonorecords of the work. An author's contribution to a work is "pseudonymous" if that author is identified on the copies or phonorecords under a fictitious name. If the work is "anonymous" you may: (1) leave the line blank; or (2) state "anonymous" on the line; or (3) reveal the author's identity. If the work is "pseudonymous" you may: (1) leave the line blank; or (2) give the pseudonym and identify it as such (for example: "Huntley Haverstock, pseudonym"); or (3) reveal the author's name, making clear which is the real name and which is the pseudonym (for example: "Judith Barton, whose pseudonym is Madeline Elster"). However, the citizenship or domicile of the author *must* be given in all cases.

Dates of Birth and Death: If the author is dead, the statute requires that the year of death be included in the application unless the work is anonymous or pseudonymous. The author's birth date is optional, but is useful as a form of identification. Leave this space blank if the author's contribution was a "work made for hire."

Author's Nationality or Domicile: Give the country in which the author is a citizen, or the country in which the author is domiciled. Nationality or domicile *must* be given in all cases.

Nature of Authorship: Sound recording authorship is the performance, sound production, or both, that is fixed in the recording deposited for registration. Describe this authorship in space 2 as "sound recording." If the claim also covers the underlying work(s), include the appropriate authorship terms for each author, for example, "words," "music," "arrangement of music," or "text."

Generally, for the claim to cover both the sound recording and the underlying work(s), every author should have contributed to both the sound recording *and* the underlying work(s). If the claim includes artwork or photographs, include the appropriate term in the statement of authorship.

SPACE 3: Creation and Publication

General Instructions: Do not confuse "creation" with "publication." Every application for copyright registration must state "the year in which creation of the work was completed." Give the date and nation of first publication only if the work has been published.

Creation: Under the statute, a work is "created" when it is fixed in a copy or phonorecord for the first time. Where a work has been prepared over a period of time, the part of the work existing in fixed form on a particular date constitutes the created work on that date. The date you give here should be the year in which the author completed the particular version for which registration is now being sought, even if other versions exist or if further changes or additions are planned.

Publication: The statute defines "publication" as "the distribution of copies or phonorecords of a work to the public by sale or other transfer of ownership, or by rental, lease, or lending"; a work is also "published" if there has been an "offering to distribute copies or phonorecords to a group of persons for purposes of further distribution, public performance, or public display." Give the full date (month, date, year) when, and the country where, publication first occurred. If first publication took place simultaneously in the United States and other countries, it is sufficient to state "U.S.A."

SPACE 4: Claimant(s)

Name(s) and Address(es) of Copyright Claimant(s): Give the name(s) and address(es) of the copyright claimant(s) in the work even if the claimant is the same as the author. Copyright in a work belongs initially to the author of the work (including, in the case of a work made for hire, the employer or other person for whom the work was prepared). The copyright claimant is either the author of the work or a person or organization to whom the copyright initially belonging to the author has been transferred.

Transfer: The statute provides that, if the copyright claimant is not the author, the application for registration must contain "a brief statement of how the claimant obtained ownership of the copyright." If any copyright claimant named in space 4a is not an author named in space 2, give a brief statement explaining how the claimant(s) obtained ownership of the copyright. Examples: "By written contract"; "Transfer of all rights by author"; "Assignment"; "By will." Do not attach transfer documents or other attachments or riders.

SPACE 5: Previous Registration

General Instructions: The questions in space 5 are intended to show whether an earlier registration has been made for this work and, if so, whether there is any basis for a new registration. As a rule, only one basic copyright registration can be made for the same version of a particular work.

Same Version: If this version is substantially the same as the work covered by a previous registration, a second registration is not generally possible unless: (1) the work has been registered in unpublished form and a second registration is now being sought to cover this first published edition; or (2) someone other than the author is identified as copyright claimant in the earlier registration and the author is now seeking registration in his or her own name. If either of these two exceptions applies, check the appropriate box and give the earlier registration number and date. Otherwise, do not submit Form SR. Instead, write the Copyright Office for information about supplementary registration or recordation of transfers of copyright ownership.

Changed Version: If the work has been changed and you are now seeking reg-

istration to cover the additions or revisions, check the last box in space 5, give the earlier registration number and date, and complete both parts of space 6 in accordance with the instructions below.

Previous Registration Number and Date: If more than one previous registration has been made for the work, give the number and date of the latest registration.

SPACE 6: Derivative Work or Compilation

General Instructions: Complete space 6 if this work is a "changed version," "compilation," or "derivative work," and if it incorporates one or more earlier works that have already been published or registered for copyright, or that have fallen into the public domain, or sound recordings that were fixed before February 15, 1972. A "compilation" is defined as "a work formed by the collection and assembling of preexisting materials or of data that are selected, coordinated, or arranged in such a way that the resulting work as a whole constitutes an original work of authorship." A "derivative work" is "a work based on one or more preexisting works." Examples of derivative works include recordings reissued with substantial editorial revisions or abridgments of the recorded sounds, and recordings republished with new recorded material, or "any other form in which a work may be recast, transformed, or adapted." Derivative works also include works "consisting of editorial revisions, annotations, or other modifications" if these changes, as a whole, represent an original work of authorship.

Preexisting Material (space 6a): Complete this space *and* space 6b for derivative works. In this space identify the preexisting work that has been recast, transformed, or adapted. The preexisting work may be material that has been previously published, previously registered, or that is in the public domain. For example, the preexisting material might be: "1970 recording by Sperryville Symphony of Bach Double Concerto."

Material Added to This Work (space 6b): Give a brief, general statement of the **additional** new material covered by the copyright claim for which registration is sought. In the case of a derivative work, identify this new material. Examples: "Recorded performances on bands 1 and 3"; "Remixed sounds from original multitrack sound sources"; "New words, arrangement, and additional sounds." If the work is a compilation, give a brief, general statement describing both the material that has been compiled *and* the compilation itself. Example: "Compilation of 1938 Recordings by various swing bands."

SPACE 7,8,9: Fee, Correspondence, Certification, Return Address

Deposit Account: If you maintain a Deposit Account in the Copyright Office, identify it in space 7a. Otherwise, leave the space blank and send the filing fee with your application and deposit. (See space 8 on form.) (**Note:** Copyright Office fees are subject to change. For current fees, check the Copyright Office website at *www.copyright.gov*, write the Copyright Office, or call (202) 707-3000.)

Correspondence (space 7b): Give the name, address, area code, telephone number, fax number, and email address (if available) of the person to be consulted if correspondence about this application becomes necessary.

Certification (space 8): This application cannot be accepted unless it bears the date and the *handwritten signature* of the author or other copyright claimant, or of the owner of exclusive right(s), or of the duly authorized agent of the author, claimant, or owner of exclusive right(s).

Address for Return of Certificate (space 9): The address box must be completed legibly since the certificate will be returned in a window envelope.

MORE INFORMATION

"Works": "Works" are the basic subject matter of copyright; they are what authors create and copyright protects. The statute draws a sharp distinction between the "work" and "any material object in which the work is embodied."

"Copies" and "Phonorecords": These are the two types of material objects in which "works" are embodied. In general, "copies" are objects from which a work can be read or visually perceived, directly or with the aid of a machine or device, such as manuscripts, books, sheet music, film, and videotape. "Phonorecords" are objects embodying fixations of sounds, such as audio tapes and phonograph disks. For example, a song (the "work") can be reproduced in sheet music ("copies") or phonograph disks ("phonorecords"), or both.

"Sound Recordings": These are "works," not "copies" or "phonorecords." "Sound recordings" are "works that result from the fixation of a series of musical, spoken, or other sounds, but not including the sounds accompanying a motion picture or other audiovisual work." Example: When a record company issues a new release, the release will typically involve two distinct "works": the "musical work" that has been recorded, and the "sound recording" as a separate work in itself. The material objects that the record company sends out are "phonorecords": physical reproductions of both the "musical work" and the "sound recording."

Should You File More Than One Application?
If your work consists of a recorded musical, dramatic, or literary work and if both that "work" and the sound recording as a separate "work" are eligible for registration, the application form you should file depends on the following:

File Only Form SR if: The copyright claimant is the same for both the musical, dramatic, or literary work and for the sound recording, and you are seeking a single registration to cover both of these "works."

File Only Form PA (or Form TX) if: You are seeking to register only the musical, dramatic, or literary work, not the sound recording. Form PA is appropriate for works of the performing arts; Form TX is for nondramatic literary works.

Separate Applications Should Be Filed on Form PA (or Form TX) and on Form SR if: (1) The copyright claimant for the musical, dramatic, or literary work is different from the copyright claimant for the sound recording; or (2) You prefer to have separate registrations for the musical, dramatic, or literary work and for the sound recording.

Copyright Office fees are subject to change.
For current fees, check the Copyright Office
website at *www.copyright.gov*, write the Copyright Office, or call (202) 707-3000.

For best results, fill in the form on-screen and then print it.

C **Form SR**
For a Sound Recording
UNITED STATES COPYRIGHT OFFICE

REGISTRATION NUMBER

_____

SR _____ SRU _____
EFFECTIVE DATE OF REGISTRATION

_____

Month   Day   Year

DO NOT WRITE ABOVE THIS LINE. IF YOU NEED MORE SPACE, USE A SEPARATE CONTINUATION SHEET.

1 TITLE OF THIS WORK ▼

_____

PREVIOUS, ALTERNATIVE, OR CONTENTS TITLES (CIRCLE ONE) ▼

_____

2 a NAME OF AUTHOR ▼

DATES OF BIRTH AND DEATH
Year Born ▼   Year Died ▼

Was this contribution to the work a
"work made for hire"?
❏ Yes
❏ No

AUTHOR'S NATIONALITY OR DOMICILE
Name of Country
OR { Citizen of ▶ _____
Domiciled in ▶ _____

WAS THIS AUTHOR'S CONTRIBUTION TO
THE WORK
Anonymous?   ❏ Yes ❏ No
Pseudonymous?   ❏ Yes ❏ No

If the answer to either
of these questions is
"Yes," see detailed
instructions.

NATURE OF AUTHORSHIP Briefly describe nature of material created by this author in which copyright is claimed. ▼

NOTE

Under the law,
the "author" of
a "work made
for hire" is
generally the
employer, not
the employee
(see instruc-
tions). For any
part of this
work that was
"made for
hire," check
"Yes" in the
space
provided, give
the employer
(or other
person for
whom the work
was prepared)
as "Author" of
that part, and
leave the
space for dates
of birth and
death blank.

b NAME OF AUTHOR ▼

DATES OF BIRTH AND DEATH
Year Born ▼   Year Died ▼

Was this contribution to the work a
"work made for hire"?
❏ Yes
❏ No

AUTHOR'S NATIONALITY OR DOMICILE
Name of Country
OR { Citizen of ▶ _____
Domiciled in ▶ _____

WAS THIS AUTHOR'S CONTRIBUTION TO
THE WORK
Anonymous?   ❏ Yes ❏ No
Pseudonymous?   ❏ Yes ❏ No

If the answer to either
of these questions is
"Yes," see detailed
instructions.

NATURE OF AUTHORSHIP Briefly describe nature of material created by this author in which copyright is claimed. ▼

c NAME OF AUTHOR ▼

DATES OF BIRTH AND DEATH
Year Born ▼   Year Died ▼

Was this contribution to the work a
"work made for hire"?
❏ Yes
❏ No

AUTHOR'S NATIONALITY OR DOMICILE
Name of Country
OR { Citizen of ▶ _____
Domiciled in ▶ _____

WAS THIS AUTHOR'S CONTRIBUTION TO
THE WORK
Anonymous?   ❏ Yes ❏ No
Pseudonymous?   ❏ Yes ❏ No

If the answer to either
of these questions is
"Yes," see detailed
instructions.

NATURE OF AUTHORSHIP Briefly describe nature of material created by this author in which copyright is claimed. ▼

3 a YEAR IN WHICH CREATION OF THIS
WORK WAS COMPLETED

_____ ◀ Year

This information
must be given
in all cases.

b DATE AND NATION OF FIRST PUBLICATION OF THIS PARTICULAR WORK

Complete this information
ONLY if this work
has been published.

Month ▶ _____ Day ▶ _____ Year ▶ _____ ◀ Nation

4 a COPYRIGHT CLAIMANT(S) Name and address must be given even if the claimant is the same as
the author given in space 2. ▼

See instructions
before completing
this space.

b TRANSFER If the claimant(s) named here in space 4 is (are) different from the author(s) named in
space 2, give a brief statement of how the claimant(s) obtained ownership of the copyright. ▼

DO NOT WRITE HERE
OFFICE USE ONLY

APPLICATION RECEIVED

ONE DEPOSIT RECEIVED

TWO DEPOSITS RECEIVED

FUNDS RECEIVED

MORE ON BACK ▶ • Complete all applicable spaces (numbers 5-9) on the reverse side of this page.
• See detailed instructions.   • Sign the form at line 8.

DO NOT WRITE HERE

Page 1 of _____ pages

EXAMINED BY	FORM SR
CHECKED BY	
CORRESPONDENCE ☐ Yes	FOR COPYRIGHT OFFICE USE ONLY

DO NOT WRITE ABOVE THIS LINE. IF YOU NEED MORE SPACE, USE A SEPARATE CONTINUATION SHEET.

PREVIOUS REGISTRATION Has registration for this work, or for an earlier version of this work, already been made in the Copyright Office?

☐ **Yes**   ☐ **No**   If your answer is "Yes," why is another registration being sought? (Check appropriate box) ▼

a. ☐ This work was previously registered in unpublished form and now has been published for the first time.

b. ☐ This is the first application submitted by this author as copyright claimant.

c. ☐ This is a changed version of the work, as shown by space 6 on this application.

If your answer is "Yes," give: **Previous Registration Number** ▼   **Year of Registration** ▼

5

DERIVATIVE WORK OR COMPILATION

Preexisting Material Identify any preexisting work or works that this work is based on or incorporates. ▼

a

Material Added to This Work Give a brief, general statement of the material that has been added to this work and in which copyright is claimed. ▼

b

6

See instructions before completing this space.

DEPOSIT ACCOUNT If the registration fee is to be charged to a deposit account established in the Copyright Office, give name and number of Account.

Name ▼   Account Number ▼

a

7

CORRESPONDENCE Give name and address to which correspondence about this application should be sent. Name/Address/Apt/City/State/Zip ▼

b

Area code and daytime telephone number   Fax number

Email

CERTIFICATION* I, the undersigned, hereby certify that I am the

Check only one ▼

☐ author

☐ other copyright claimant

☐ owner of exclusive right(s)

☐ authorized agent of _____

Name of author or other copyright claimant, or owner of exclusive right(s) ▲

of the work identified in this application and that the statements made by me in this application are correct to the best of my knowledge.

Typed or printed name and date ▼ If this application gives a date of publication in space 3, do not sign and submit it before that date.

_____   **Date** _____

Handwritten signature ▼

_____

8

Certificate will be mailed in window envelope to this address	Name ▼	**9**
	Number/Street/Apt ▼	
	City/State/Zip ▼	

YOU MUST:
· Complete all necessary spaces
· Sign your application in space 8

SEND ALL 3 ELEMENTS IN THE SAME PACKAGE:
1. Application form
2. Nonrefundable filing fee in check or money order payable to *Register of Copyrights*
3. Deposit material

MAIL TO:
Library of Congress
Copyright Office
101 Independence Avenue SE
Washington, DC 20559-6000

*17 *USC* §506(e): Any person who knowingly makes a false representation of a material fact in the application for copyright registration provided for by section 409, or in any written statement filed in connection with the application, shall be fined not more than $2,500.

Form SR-Full   Rev: 11/2006   Print: 11/2006—60,000   Printed on recycled paper   U.S. Government Printing Office: 2007-330-945/60,138

Form VA

Detach and read these instructions before completing this form.
Make sure all applicable spaces have been filled in before you return this form.

When to Use This Form: Use Form VA for copyright registration of published or unpublished works of the visual arts. This category consists of "pictorial, graphic, or sculptural works," including two-dimensional and three-dimensional works of fine, graphic, and applied art, photographs, prints and art reproductions, maps, globes, charts, technical drawings, diagrams, and models.

What Does Copyright Protect? Copyright in a work of the visual arts protects those pictorial, graphic, or sculptural elements that, either alone or in combination, represent an "original work of authorship." The statute declares: "In no case does copyright protection for an original work of authorship extend to any idea, procedure, process, system, method of operation, concept, principle, or discovery, regardless of the form in which it is described, explained, illustrated, or embodied in such work."

Works of Artistic Craftsmanship and Designs: "Works of artistic craftsmanship" are registrable on Form VA, but the statute makes clear that protection extends to "their form" and not to "their mechanical or utilitarian aspects." The "design of a useful article" is considered copyrightable "only if, and only to the extent that, such design incorporates pictorial, graphic, or sculptural features that can be identified separately from, and are capable of existing independently of, the utilitarian aspects of the article."

Labels and Advertisements: Works prepared for use in connection with the sale or advertisement of goods and services are registrable if they contain "original work of authorship." Use Form VA if the copyrightable material in the work you are registering is mainly pictorial or graphic; use Form TX if it consists mainly of text. **Note:** Words and short phrases such as names, titles, and slogans cannot be protected by copyright, and the same is true of standard symbols, emblems, and other commonly used graphic designs that are in the public domain. When used commercially, material of that sort can sometimes be protected under state laws of unfair competition or under the federal trademark laws. For information about trademark registration, write to the U.S. Patent and Trademark Office, PO Box 1450, Alexandria, VA 22313-1450.

Architectural Works: Copyright protection extends to the design of buildings created for the use of human beings. Architectural works created on or after December 1, 1990, or that on December 1, 1990, were unconstructed and embodied only in unpublished plans or drawings are eligible. Request Circular 41, *Copyright Claims in Architectural Works*, for more information. Architectural works and technical drawings cannot be registered on the same application.

Deposit to Accompany Application: An application for copyright registration must be accompanied by a deposit consisting of copies representing the entire work for which registration is to be made.

Unpublished Work: Deposit one complete copy.

Published Work: Deposit two complete copies of the best edition.

Work First Published Outside the United States: Deposit one complete copy of the first foreign edition.

Contribution to a Collective Work: Deposit one complete copy of the best edition of the collective work.

The Copyright Notice: Before March 1, 1989, the use of copyright notice was mandatory on all published works, and any work first published before that date should have carried a notice. For works first published on and after March 1, 1989, use of the copyright notice is optional. For more information about copyright notice, see Circular 3, *Copyright Notice*.

For Further Information: To speak to a Copyright Office staff member, call (202) 707-3000 (TTY: (202) 707-6737). Recorded information is available 24 hours a day. Order forms and other publications from the address in space 9 or call the Forms and Publications Hotline at (202) 707-9100. Access and download circulars, forms, and other information from the Copyright Office website at *www.copyright.gov*.

Please type or print using black ink. The form is used to produce the certificate.

SPACE 1: Title

Title of This Work: Every work submitted for copyright registration must be given a title to identify that particular work. If the copies of the work bear a title (or an identifying phrase that could serve as a title), transcribe that wording *completely* and *exactly* on the application. Indexing of the registration and future identification of the work will depend on the information you give here. For an architectural work that has been constructed, add the date of construction after the title; if unconstructed at this time, add "not yet constructed."

Publication as a Contribution: If the work being registered is a contribution to a periodical, serial, or collection, give the title of the contribution in the "Title of This Work" space. Then, in the line headed "Publication as a Contribution," give information about the collective work in which the contribution appeared.

Nature of This Work: Briefly describe the general nature or character of the pictorial, graphic, or sculptural work being registered for copyright. Examples: "Oil Painting"; "Charcoal Drawing"; "Etching"; "Sculpture"; "Map"; "Photograph"; "Scale Model"; "Lithographic Print"; "Jewelry Design"; "Fabric Design."

Previous or Alternative Titles: Complete this space if there are any additional titles for the work under which someone searching for the registration might be likely to look, or under which a document pertaining to the work might be recorded.

SPACE 2: Author(s)

General Instruction: After reading these instructions, decide who are the "authors" of this work for copyright purposes. Then, unless the work is a "collective work," give the requested information about every "author" who contributed any appreciable amount of copyrightable matter to this version of the work. If you need further space, request Continuation Sheets. In the case of a collective work, such as a catalog of paintings or collection of cartoons by various authors, give information about the author of the collective work as a whole.

Name of Author: The fullest form of the author's name should be given. Unless the work was "made for hire," the individual who actually created the work is its "author." In the case of a work made for hire, the statute provides that "the employer or other person for whom the work was prepared is considered the author."

What Is a "Work Made for Hire"? A "work made for hire" is defined as: (1) "a work prepared by an employee within the scope of his or her employment"; or (2) "a work specially ordered or commissioned for use as a contribution to a collective work, as a part of a motion picture or other audiovisual work, as a translation, as a supplementary work, as a compilation, as an instructional text, as a test, as answer material for a test, or as an atlas, if the parties expressly agree in a written instrument signed by them that the work shall be considered a work made for hire." If you have checked "Yes" to indicate that the work was "made for hire," you must give the full legal name of the employer (or other person for whom the work was prepared). You may also include the name of the employee along with the name of the employer (for example: "Elster Publishing Co., employer for hire of John Ferguson").

"Anonymous" or "Pseudonymous" Work: An author's contribution to a work is "anonymous" if that author is not identified on the copies or phonorecords of the work. An author's contribution to a work is "pseudonymous" if that author is identified on the copies or phonorecords under a fictitious name. If the work is "anonymous" you may: (1) leave the line blank; or (2) state "anonymous" on the line; or (3) reveal the author's identity. If the work is "pseudonymous" you may: (1) leave the line blank; or (2) give the pseudonym and identify it as such (for example: "Huntley Haverstock, pseudonym"); or (3) reveal the author's name, making clear which is the real name and which is the pseudonym (for example: "Henry Leek, whose pseudonym is Priam Farrel"). However, the citizenship or domicile of the author *must* be given in all cases.

Dates of Birth and Death: If the author is dead, the statute requires that the year of death be included in the application unless the work is anonymous or pseudonymous. The author's birth date is optional but is useful as a form of identification. Leave this space blank if the author's contribution was a "work made for hire."

a citizen or the country in which the author is domiciled. Nationality or domicile *must* be given in all cases.

Nature of Authorship: Categories of pictorial, graphic, and sculptural authorship are listed below. Check the box(es) that best describe(s) each author's contribution to the work.

3-Dimensional sculptures: fine art sculptures, toys, dolls, scale models, and sculptural designs applied to useful articles.

2-Dimensional artwork: watercolor and oil paintings; pen and ink drawings; logo illustrations; greeting cards; collages; stencils; patterns; computer graphics; graphics appearing in screen displays; artwork appearing on posters, calendars, games, commercial prints and labels, and packaging, as well as 2-dimensional artwork applied to useful articles, and designs reproduced on textiles, lace, and other fabrics; on wallpaper, carpeting, floor tile, wrapping paper, and clothing.

Reproductions of works of art: reproductions of preexisting artwork made by, for example, lithography, photoengraving, or etching.

Maps: cartographic representations of an area, such as state and county maps, atlases, marine charts, relief maps, and globes.

Photographs: pictorial photographic prints and slides and holograms.

Jewelry designs: 3-dimensional designs applied to rings, pendants, earrings, necklaces, and the like.

Technical drawings: diagrams illustrating scientific or technical information in linear form, such as architectural blueprints or mechanical drawings.

Text: textual material that accompanies pictorial, graphic, or sculptural works, such as comic strips, greeting cards, games rules, commercial prints or labels, and maps.

Architectural works: designs of buildings, including the overall form as well as the arrangement and composition of spaces and elements of the design.

NOTE: Any registration for the underlying architectural plans must be applied for on a separate Form VA, checking the box "Technical drawing."

3   SPACE 3: Creation and Publication

General Instructions: Do not confuse "creation" with "publication." Every application for copyright registration must state "the year in which creation of the work was completed." Give the date and nation of first publication only if the work has been published.

Creation: Under the statute, a work is "created" when it is fixed in a copy or phonorecord for the first time. Where a work has been prepared over a period of time, the part of the work existing in fixed form on a particular date constitutes the created work on that date. The date you give here should be the year in which the author completed the particular version for which registration is now being sought, even if other versions exist or if further changes or additions are planned.

Publication: The statute defines "publication" as "the distribution of copies or phonorecords of a work to the public by sale or other transfer of ownership, or by rental, lease, or lending"; a work is also "published" if there has been an "offering to distribute copies or phonorecords to a group of persons for purposes of further distribution, public performance, or public display." Give the full date (month, day, year) when, and the country where, publication first occurred. If first publication took place simultaneously in the United States and other countries, it is sufficient to state "U.S.A."

4   SPACE 4: Claimant(s)

Name(s) and Address(es) of Copyright Claimant(s): Give the name(s) and address(es) of the copyright claimant(s) in this work even if the claimant is the same as the author. Copyright in a work belongs initially to the author of the work (including, in the case of a work make for hire, the employer or other person for whom the work was prepared). The copyright claimant is either the author of the work or a person or organization to whom the copyright initially belonging to the author has been transferred.

Transfer: The statute provides that, if the copyright claimant is not the author, the application for registration must contain "a brief statement of how the claimant obtained ownership of the copyright." If any copyright claimant named in space 4 is not an author named in space 2, give a brief statement explaining how the claimant(s) obtained ownership of the copyright. Examples: "By written contract"; "Transfer of all rights by author"; "Assignment"; "By will." Do not attach transfer documents or other attachments or riders.

5   SPACE 5: Previous Registration

General Instructions: The questions in space 5 are intended to find out whether an earlier registration has been made for this work and, if so, whether there is any basis for a new registration. As a rule, only one basic

Same Version: If this version is substantially the same as the work covered by a previous registration, a second registration is not generally possible unless: (1) the work has been registered in unpublished form and a second registration is now being sought to cover this first published edition; or (2) someone other than the author is identified as a copyright claimant in the earlier registration, and the author is now seeking registration in his or her own name. If either of these two exceptions applies, check the appropriate box and give the earlier registration number and date. Otherwise, do not submit Form VA; instead, write the Copyright Office for information about supplementary registration or recordation of transfers of copyright ownership.

Changed Version: If the work has been changed and you are now seeking registration to cover the additions or revisions, check the last box in space 5, give the earlier registration number and date, and complete both parts of space 6 in accordance with the instruction below.

Previous Registration Number and Date: If more than one previous registration has been made for the work, give the number and date of the latest registration.

6   SPACE 6: Derivative Work or Compilation

General Instructions: Complete space 6 if this work is a "changed version," "compilation," or "derivative work," and if it incorporates one or more earlier works that have already been published or registered for copyright, or that have fallen into the public domain. A "compilation" is defined as "a work formed by the collection and assembling of preexisting materials or of data that are selected, coordinated, or arranged in such a way that the resulting work as a whole constitutes an original work of authorship." A "derivative work" is "a work based on one or more preexisting works." Examples of derivative works include reproductions of works of art, sculptures based on drawings, lithographs based on paintings, maps based on previously published sources, or "any other form in which a work may be recast, transformed, or adapted." Derivative works also include works "consisting of editorial revisions, annotations, or other modifications" if these changes, as a whole, represent an original work of authorship.

Preexisting Material (space 6a): Complete this space *and* space 6b for derivative works. In this space identify the preexisting work that has been recast, transformed, or adapted. Examples of preexisting material might be "Grunewald Altarpiece" or "19th century quilt design." Do not complete this space for compilations.

Material Added to This Work (space 6b): Give a brief, general statement of the *additional* new material covered by the copyright claim for which registration is sought. In the case of a derivative work, identify this new material. Examples: "Adaptation of design and additional artistic work"; "Reproduction of painting by photolithography"; "Additional cartographic material"; "Compilation of photographs." If the work is a compilation, give a brief, general statement describing both the material that has been compiled *and* the compilation itself. Example: "Compilation of 19th century political cartoons."

7, 8, 9   SPACE 7, 8, 9: Fee, Correspondence, Certification, Return Address

Deposit Account: If you maintain a Deposit Account in the Copyright Office, identify it in space 7a. Otherwise, leave the space blank and send the fee with your application and deposit.

Correspondence (space 7b): Give the name, address, area code, telephone number, email address, and fax number (if available) of the person to be consulted if correspondence about this application becomes necessary.

Certification (space 8): The application cannot be accepted unless it bears the date and the *handwritten signature* of the author or other copyright claimant, or of the owner of exclusive right(s), or of the duly authorized agent of the author, claimant, or owner of exclusive right(s).

Address for Return of Certificate (space 9): The address box must be completed legibly since the certificate will be returned in a window envelope.

Copyright Office fees are subject to change. For current fees, check the Copyright Office website at *www.copyright.gov*, write the Copyright Office, or call (202) 707-3000.

For best results, fill in the form on-screen and then print it.

Form VA
For a Work of the Visual Arts
UNITED STATES COPYRIGHT OFFICE

REGISTRATION NUMBER

_____

VA   VAU

EFFECTIVE DATE OF REGISTRATION

Month   Day   Year

DO NOT WRITE ABOVE THIS LINE. IF YOU NEED MORE SPACE, USE A SEPARATE CONTINUATION SHEET.

1

Title of This Work ▼   **NATURE OF THIS WORK ▼** See instructions

Previous or Alternative Titles ▼

Publication as a Contribution If this work was published as a contribution to a periodical, serial, or collection, give information about the collective work in which the contribution appeared. **Title of Collective Work ▼**

If published in a periodical or serial give: **Volume ▼**   **Number ▼**   **Issue Date ▼**   **On Pages ▼**

2
a

NOTE

Under the law, the "author" of a "work made for hire" is generally the employer, not the employee (see instructions). For any part of this work that was "made for hire" check "Yes" in the space provided, give the employer (or other person for whom the work was prepared) as "Author" of that part, and leave the space for dates of birth and death blank.

b

NAME OF AUTHOR ▼   **DATES OF BIRTH AND DEATH**
                                                        Year Born ▼   Year Died ▼

Was this contribution to the work a "work made for hire"?
☐ Yes
☐ No

Author's Nationality or Domicile
Name of Country
OR { Citizen of _____
Domiciled in _____

Was This Author's Contribution to the Work
Anonymous?   ☐ Yes ☐ No
Pseudonymous? ☐ Yes ☐ No

If the answer to either of these questions is "Yes," see detailed instructions.

Nature of Authorship Check appropriate box(es). **See instructions**
☐ 3-Dimensional sculpture   ☐ Map   ☐ Technical drawing
☐ 2-Dimensional artwork   ☐ Photograph   ☐ Text
☐ Reproduction of work of art ☐ Jewelry design ☐ Architectural work

Name of Author ▼   **Dates of Birth and Death**
                                                        Year Born ▼   Year Died ▼

Was this contribution to the work a "work made for hire"?
☐ Yes
☐ No

Author's Nationality or Domicile
Name of Country
OR { Citizen of _____
Domiciled in _____

Was This Author's Contribution to the Work
Anonymous?   ☐ Yes ☐ No
Pseudonymous? ☐ Yes ☐ No

If the answer to either of these questions is "Yes," see detailed instructions.

Nature of Authorship Check appropriate box(es). **See instructions**
☐ 3-Dimensional sculpture   ☐ Map   ☐ Technical drawing
☐ 2-Dimensional artwork   ☐ Photograph   ☐ Text
☐ Reproduction of work of art ☐ Jewelry design ☐ Architectural work

3
a   **b**

Year in Which Creation of This Work Was Completed
This information must be given
_____ Year in all cases.

Date and Nation of First Publication of This Particular Work
Complete this information ONLY if this work has been published.
Month _____ Day _____ Year _____
_____ Nation

4

See instructions before completing this space.

COPYRIGHT CLAIMANT(S) Name and address must be given even if the claimant is the same as the author given in space 2. ▼

Transfer If the claimant(s) named here in space 4 is (are) different from the author(s) named in space 2, give a brief statement of how the claimant(s) obtained ownership of the copyright. ▼

DO NOT WRITE HERE
OFFICE USE ONLY

APPLICATION RECEIVED

ONE DEPOSIT RECEIVED

TWO DEPOSITS RECEIVED

FUNDS RECEIVED

MORE ON BACK ▶ • Complete all applicable spaces (numbers 5-9) on the reverse side of this page.
                     • See detailed instructions.   • Sign the form at line 8.

DO NOT WRITE HERE

Page 1 of _____ pages

EXAMINED BY	FORM VA
CHECKED BY	

□ CORRESPONDENCE
Yes

FOR
COPYRIGHT
OFFICE
USE
ONLY

DO NOT WRITE ABOVE THIS LINE. IF YOU NEED MORE SPACE, USE A SEPARATE CONTINUATION SHEET.

PREVIOUS REGISTRATION Has registration for this work, or for an earlier version of this work, already been made in the Copyright Office?

□ **Yes** □ **No** If your answer is "Yes," why is another registration being sought? (Check appropriate box.) ▼

a. □ This is the first published edition of a work previously registered in unpublished form.

b. □ This is the first application submitted by this author as copyright claimant.

c. □ This is a changed version of the work, as shown by space 6 on this application.

If your answer is "Yes," give: **Previous Registration Number** ▼   **Year of Registration** ▼

5

DERIVATIVE WORK OR COMPILATION Complete both space 6a and 6b for a derivative work; complete only 6b for a compilation.

a. Preexisting Material Identify any preexisting work or works that this work is based on or incorporates. ▼

b. Material Added to This Work Give a brief, general statement of the material that has been added to this work and in which copyright is claimed. ▼

6
a
b

See instructions
before completing
this space.

DEPOSIT ACCOUNT If the registration fee is to be charged to a Deposit Account established in the Copyright Office, give name and number of Account.

Name ▼   **Account Number** ▼

CORRESPONDENCE Give name and address to which correspondence about this application should be sent. Name/Address/Apt/City/State/Zip ▼

7
a
b

Area code and daytime telephone number   (   )   Fax number   (   )

Email

CERTIFICATION* I, the undersigned, hereby certify that I am the

check only one ▶ {
□ author
□ other copyright claimant
□ owner of exclusive right(s)
□ authorized agent of _____
Name of author or other copyright claimant, or owner of exclusive right(s) ▲

8

of the work identified in this application and that the statements made by me in this application are correct to the best of my knowledge.

Typed or printed name and date ▼ If this application gives a date of publication in space 3, do not sign and submit it before that date.

                                                                                Date

Handwritten signature (X) ▼

X _____

Certificate will be mailed in window envelope to this address:	Name ▼	YOU MUST: • Complete all necessary spaces • Sign your application in space 8
	Number/Street/Apt ▼	SEND ALL 3 ELEMENTS IN THE SAME PACKAGE: 1. Application form 2. Nonrefundable filing fee in check or money order payable to *Register of Copyrights* 3. Deposit material
	City/State/ZIP ▼	MAIL TO: Library of Congress Copyright Office 101 Independence Avenue SE Washington, DC 20559-6000

9

Form SE

Detach and read these instructions before completing this form.
Make sure all applicable spaces have been filled in before you return this form.

BASIC INFORMATION

When to Use This Form: Use a separate Form SE for registration of each individual issue of a serial. A serial is defined as a work issued or intended to be issued in successive parts bearing numerical or chronological designations and intended to be continued indefinitely. This class includes a variety of works: periodicals; newspapers; annuals; the journals, proceedings, transactions, etc., of societies. Do not use Form SE to register an individual contribution to a serial. Request Form TX for such contributions.

Deposit to Accompany Application: An application for copyright registration must be accompanied by a deposit consisting of copies or phonorecords representing the entire work for which registration is to be made. The following are the general deposit requirements as set forth in the statute:

Unpublished Work: Deposit one complete copy (or phonorecord).

Published Work: Deposit two complete copies (or one phonorecord) of the best edition.

Work First Published Outside the United States: Deposit one complete copy (or phonorecord) of the first foreign edition.

Mailing Requirements: It is important that you send the application, the deposit copy or copies, and the registration fee together in the same envelope or package. The Copyright Office cannot process them unless they are received together. Send to: *Library of Congress, Copyright Office, 101 Independence Avenue SE, Washington DC 20559-6000.*

The Copyright Notice: Before March 1, 1989, the use of copyright notice was mandatory on all published works, and any work first published before that date should have carried a notice. For works first published on and after March 1, 1989, use of the copyright notice is optional. For more information about copyright notice, see Circular 3, *Copyright Notices.*

For Further Information: To speak to a Copyright Office staff member, call (202) 707-3000 (TTY: (202) 707-6737). Recorded information is available 24 hours a day. Order forms and other publications from the address in space 9 or call the Forms and Publications Hotline at (202) 707-9100. Access and download circulars, forms, and other information from the Copyright Office website at *www.copyright.gov.*

LINE-BY-LINE INSTRUCTIONS

Please type or print using black ink. The form is used to produce the certificate.

SPACE 1: Title

Title of This Serial: Every work submitted for copyright registration must be given a title to identify that particular work. If the copies or phonorecords of the work bear a title (or an identifying phrase that could serve as a title), copy that wording *completely* and *exactly* on the application. Give the volume and number of the periodical issue for which you are seeking registration. The "Date on Copies" in space 1 should be the date appearing on the actual copies (for example: "June 1981," "Winter 1981"). Indexing of the registration and future identification of the work will depend on the information you give here.

Previous or Alternative Titles: Complete this space only if there are any additional titles for the serial under which someone searching for the registration might be likely to look or under which a document pertaining to the work might be recorded.

SPACE 2: Author(s)

General Instructions: After reading these instructions, decide who are the "authors" of this work for copyright purposes. In the case of a serial issue, the organization that directs the creation of the serial issue as a whole is generally considered the author of the "collective work" (see "Nature of Authorship") whether it employs a staff or uses the efforts of volunteers. Where, however, an individual is independently responsible for the serial issue, name that person as author of the "collective work."

Name of Author: The fullest form of the author's name should be given. In the case of a "work made for hire," the statute provides that "the employer or other person for whom the work was prepared is considered the author." If this issue is a "work made for hire," the author's name will be the full legal name of the hiring organization, corporation, or individual. The title of the periodical should not ordinarily be listed as "author" because the title itself does not usually correspond to a legal entity capable of authorship. When an individual creates an issue of a serial independently and not as an "employee" of an organization or corporation, that individual should be listed as the "author."

Author's Nationality or Domicile: Give the country of which the author is a citizen, or the country in which the author is domiciled. Nationality or domicile *must* be given in all cases. The citizenship of an organization formed under U.S. federal or state law should be stated as "U.S.A."

What Is a "Work Made for Hire"? A "work made for hire" is defined as (1) "a work prepared by an employee within the scope of his or her employment"; or (2) "a work specially ordered or commissioned for use as a contribution to a collective work, as a part of a motion picture or other audiovisual work, as a translation, as a supplementary work, as a compilation, as an instructional text, as a test, as answer material for a test, or as an atlas, if the parties expressly agree in a written instrument signed by them that the work shall be considered a work made for hire." An organization that uses the efforts of volunteers in the creation of a "collective work" (see "Nature of Authorship") may also be considered the author of a "work made for hire" even though those volunteers were not specifically paid by the organization. In the case of a "work made for hire," give the full legal name of the employer and check "Yes" to indicate that the work was made for hire. You may also include the name of the employee along with the name of the employer (for example: "Elster Publishing Co., employer for hire of John Ferguson").

"Anonymous" or "Pseudonymous" Work: Leave this space *blank* if the serial is a "work made for hire." An author's contribution to a work is "anonymous" if that author is not identified on the copies or phonorecords of the work. An author's contribution to a work is "pseudonymous" if that author is identified on the copies or phonorecords under a fictitious name. If the work is "anonymous" you may: (1) leave the line blank; or (2) state "anonymous" on the line; or (3) reveal the author's identify. If the work is "pseudonymous" you may: (1) leave the line blank; or (2) give the pseudonym and identify it as such (for example: "Huntley Haverstock, pseudonym"); or (3) reveal the author's name, making clear which is the real name and which is the pseudonym (for example: "Judith Barton, whose pseudonym is Madeline Elster"). However, the citizenship or domicile of the author *must* be given in all cases.

Dates of Birth and Death: Leave this space blank if the author's contribution was a "work made for hire." If the author is dead, the statute requires that the year of death be included in the application unless the work is anonymous or pseudonymous. The author's birth date is optional but is useful as a form of identification.

Nature of Authorship: Give a brief statement of the nature of the particular author's contribution to the work. If an organization directed, controlled, and supervised the creation of the serial issue as a whole, check the box "collective work." The term "collective work" means that the author is responsible for compilation and editorial revision and may also be responsible for certain individual contributions to the serial issue. Further examples of "Authorship" which may apply both to organizational and to individual authors are "Entire text"; "Text and illustrations"; "Editorial revision, compilation, and additional new material."

SPACE 3: Creation and Publication

General Instructions: Do not confuse "creation" with "publication." Every application for copyright registration must state "the year in which creation of the work was completed." Give the date and nation of first publication only if the work has been published.

Creation: Under the statute, a work is "created" when it is fixed in a copy or phonorecord for the first time. Where a work has been prepared over a period of time, the part of the work existing in fixed form on a particular date constitutes the created work on that date. The date you give here should be the year in which this particular issue was completed.

Publication: The statute defines "publication" as "the distribution of copies or phonorecords of a work to the public by sale or other transfer of ownership or by rental, lease, or lending; a work is also "published" if there has been an "offering to distribute copies or phonorecords to a group of persons for purposes of further distribution, public performance, or public display." Give the full date (month, day, year) when, and the country where, publication of this particular issue first occurred. If first publication took place simultaneously in the United States and other countries, it is sufficient to state "U.S.A."

SPACE 4: Claimant(s)

Name(s) and Address(es) of Copyright Claimant(s): This space must be completed. Give the name(s) and address(es) of the copyright claimant(s) of this work even if the claimant is the same as the author named in space 2. Copyright in a work belongs initially to the author of the work (including, in the case of a work made for hire, the employer or other person for whom the work was prepared). The copyright claimant is either the author of the work or a person or organization to whom the copyright initially belonging to the author has been transferred.

Transfer: The statute provides that, if the copyright claimant is not the author, the application for registration must contain "a brief statement of how the claimant obtained ownership of the copyright." If any copyright claimant named in space 4 is not an author named in space 2, give a brief statement explaining how the claimant(s) obtained ownership of the copyright. Examples: "By written contract"; "Transfer of all rights by author"; "Assignment"; "By will." Do not attach transfer documents or other attachments or riders.

SPACE 5: Previous Registration

General Instructions: This space rarely applies to serials. Complete space 5 if this particular issue has been registered earlier or if it contains a substantial amount of material that has been previously registered. Do not complete this space if the previous registrations are simply those made for earlier issues.

Previous Registration:
a. Check this box if this issue has been registered in unpublished form and a second registration is now sought to cover the first published edition.

b. Check this box if someone other than the author is identified as copyright claimant in the earlier registration and the author is now seeking registration in his or her own name. If the work in question is a contribution to a collective work as opposed to the issue as a whole, file Form TX, not Form SE.

c. Check this box (and complete space 6) if this particular issue or a substantial portion of the material in it has been previously registered and you are now seeking registration for the additions and revisions that appear in this issue for the first time.

Previous Registration Number and Date: Complete this line if you checked one of the boxes above. If more than one previous registration has been made for the issue or for material in it, give only the number and year date for the latest registration.

SPACE 6: Derivative Work or Compilation

General Instructions: Complete space 6 if this issue is a "changed version," "compilation," or "derivative work" that incorporates one or more earlier works that have already been published or registered for copyright or that have fallen into the public domain. Do not complete space 6 for an issue consisting of entirely new material appearing for the first time such as a new issue of a continuing serial. A "compilation" is defined as "a work formed by the collection and assembling of preexisting materials or of data that are selected, coordinated, or arranged in such a way that the resulting work as a whole constitutes an original work of authorship." A "derivative work" is "a work based on one or more preexisting works." Examples of derivative works include translations, fictionalizations, abridgments, condensations, or "any other form in which a work may be recast, transformed, or adapted." Derivative works also include works "consisting of editorial revisions, annotations, or other modifications" if these changes, as a whole, represent an original work of authorship.

Preexisting Material (space 6a): For derivative works, complete this space *and* space 6b. In space 6a identify the preexisting work that has been recast, transformed, adapted, or updated. Example: "1978 Morgan Co. Sales Catalog." Do not complete space 6a for compilations.

Material Added to This Work (space 6b): Give a brief, general statement of the new material covered by the copyright claim for which registration is sought. *Derivative work* examples include: "Editorial revisions and additions to the Catalog"; "Translation"; "Additional material." If a periodical issue is a *compilation*, describe both the compilation itself and the material that has been compiled. Examples: "Compilation of previously published journal articles"; "Compilation of previously published data." An issue may be both a derivative work and a compilation, in which case a sample statement might be: "Compilation of [describe] and additional new material."

SPACE 7, 8, 9: Fee, Correspondence, Certification, Return Address

Deposit Account (Space 7a): If you maintain a deposit account in the Copyright Office, identify it in space 7a. Otherwise leave the space blank and send the fee with your application and deposit.

Correspondence (space 7b): This space should contain the name, address, area code, and telephone and fax numbers and email address of the person to be consulted if correspondence about this application becomes necessary.

Certification (space 8). The application cannot be accepted unless it bears the date and the *handwritten signature* of the author or other copyright claimant, or of the owner of exclusive right(s), or of the duly authorized agent of the author, claimant, or owner of exclusive right(s).

Address for Return of Certificate (space 9): The address box must be completed legibly since the certificate will be returned in a window envelope.

Copyright Office fees are subject to change. For current fees, check the Copyright Office website at *www.copyright.gov*, write the Copyright Office, or call (202) 707-3000.

For best results, fill in the form on-screen and then print it.

(C) **Form SE**
For a Serial
UNITED STATES COPYRIGHT OFFICE

REGISTRATION NUMBER

U

EFFECTIVE DATE OF REGISTRATION

Month   Day   Year

DO NOT WRITE ABOVE THIS LINE. IF YOU NEED MORE SPACE, USE A SEPARATE CONTINUATION SHEET.

1

TITLE OF THIS SERIAL ▼

Volume ▼   Number ▼   Date of Copies ▼   Frequency of Publication ▼

PREVIOUS OR ALTERNATIVE TITLES ▼

2 **a**

NAME OF AUTHOR ▼

DATES OF BIRTH AND DEATH
Year Born ▼   Year Died ▼

Was this contribution to the work a "work made for hire"?
☐ Yes
☐ No

AUTHOR'S NATIONALITY OR DOMICILE
Name of Country
OR { Citizen of ▶ _____
Domiciled in ▶ _____

WAS THIS AUTHOR'S CONTRIBUTION TO THE WORK
Anonymous?   ☐ Yes ☐ No
Pseudonymous?   ☐ Yes ☐ No
If the answer to either of these questions is "Yes," see detailed instructions.

NATURE OF AUTHORSHIP Briefly describe nature of material created by this author in which copyright is claimed. ▼
☐ Collective Work   Other:

NOTE

Under the law, the "author" of a "work made for hire" is generally the employer, not the employee (see instructions). For any part of this work that was "made for hire" check "Yes" in the space provided, give the employer (or other person for whom the work was prepared) as "Author" of that part, and leave the space for dates of birth and death blank.

b

NAME OF AUTHOR ▼

DATES OF BIRTH AND DEATH
Year Born ▼   Year Died ▼

Was this contribution to the work a "work made for hire"?
☐ Yes
☐ No

AUTHOR'S NATIONALITY OR DOMICILE
Name of Country
OR { Citizen of ▶ _____
Domiciled in ▶ _____

WAS THIS AUTHOR'S CONTRIBUTION TO THE WORK
Anonymous?   ☐ Yes ☐ No
Pseudonymous?   ☐ Yes ☐ No
If the answer to either of these questions is "Yes," see detailed instructions.

NATURE OF AUTHORSHIP Briefly describe nature of material created by this author in which copyright is claimed. ▼
☐ Collective Work   Other:

c

NAME OF AUTHOR ▼

DATES OF BIRTH AND DEATH
Year Born ▼   Year Died ▼

Was this contribution to the work a "work made for hire"?
☐ Yes
☐ No

AUTHOR'S NATIONALITY OR DOMICILE
Name of Country
OR { Citizen of ▶ _____
Domiciled in ▶ _____

WAS THIS AUTHOR'S CONTRIBUTION TO THE WORK
Anonymous?   ☐ Yes ☐ No
Pseudonymous?   ☐ Yes ☐ No
If the answer to either of these questions is "Yes," see detailed instructions.

NATURE OF AUTHORSHIP Briefly describe nature of material created by this author in which copyright is claimed. ▼
☐ Collective Work   Other:

3 **a**

YEAR IN WHICH CREATION OF THIS WORK WAS COMPLETED This information must be given in all cases. ◀ Year

b **DATE AND NATION OF FIRST PUBLICATION OF THIS PARTICULAR WORK**
Complete this information ONLY if this work has been published.
Month ▶ _____ Day ▶ _____ Year ▶ _____
◀ Nation

4

COPYRIGHT CLAIMANT(S) Name and address must be given even if the claimant is the same as the author given in space 2. ▼

See instructions before completing this space.

TRANSFER If the claimant(s) named here in space 4 is (are) different from the author(s) named in space 2, give a brief statement of how the claimant(s) obtained ownership of the copyright. ▼

DO NOT WRITE HERE OFFICE USE ONLY

APPLICATION RECEIVED

ONE DEPOSIT RECEIVED

TWO DEPOSITS RECEIVED

FUNDS RECEIVED

MORE ON BACK ▶ • Complete all applicable spaces (numbers 5–9) on the reverse side of this page.
• See detailed instructions.   • Sign the form at line 8.

DO NOT WRITE HERE

Page 1 of _____ pages

EXAMINED BY		FORM SE
CHECKED BY		
☐ CORRESPONDENCE Yes		FOR COPYRIGHT OFFICE USE ONLY

DO NOT WRITE ABOVE THIS LINE. IF YOU NEED MORE SPACE, USE A SEPARATE CONTINUATION SHEET.

PREVIOUS REGISTRATION Has registration for this work, or for an earlier version of this work, already been made in the Copyright Office?

☐ **Yes** ☐ **No** If your answer is "Yes," why is another registration being sought? (Check appropriate box.) ▼

a. ☐ This is the first published edition of a work previously registered in unpublished form.

b. ☐ This is the first application submitted by this author as copyright claimant.

c. ☐ This is a changed version of the work, as shown by space 6 on this application.

If your answer is "Yes," give: **Previous Registration Number** ▶   **Year of Registration** ▶

5

DERIVATIVE WORK OR COMPILATION   Complete both space 6a and 6b for a derivative work; complete only 6b for a compilation.

Preexisting Material Identify any preexisting work or works that this work is based on or incorporates. ▼

a

6

Material Added to This Work Give a brief, general statement of the material that has been added to this work and in which copyright is claimed. ▼

b

See instructions
before completing
this space.

DEPOSIT ACCOUNT If the registration fee is to be charged to a Deposit Account established in the Copyright Office, give name and number of Account.

Name ▼   **Account Number** ▼

a

7

CORRESPONDENCE Give name and address to which correspondence about this application should be sent.   Name/Address/Apt/City/State/Zip ▼

b

Area code and daytime telephone number ▶   Fax number ▶

Email ▶

CERTIFICATION* I, the undersigned, hereby certify that I am the

Check only one ▶ {
☐ author
☐ other copyright claimant
☐ owner of exclusive right(s)
☐ authorized agent of _____

Name of author or other copyright claimant, or owner of exclusive right(s) ▲

of the work identified in this application and that the statements made
by me in this application are correct to the best of my knowledge.

8

Typed or printed name and date ▼ If this application gives a date of publication in space 3, do not sign and submit it before that date.

_____   Date ▶ _____

Handwritten signature ▼

_____

Certificate will be mailed in window envelope to this address:	Name ▼	**YOU MUST:** • Complete all necessary spaces • Sign your application in space 8
	Number/Street/Apt ▼	**SEND ALL 3 ELEMENTS IN THE SAME PACKAGE:** 1. Application form 2. Nonrefundable filing fee in check or money order payable to *Register of Copyrights* 3. Deposit material
	City/State/Zip ▼	**MAIL TO:** Library of Congress Copyright Office 101 Independence Avenue SE Washington, DC 20559-6222

9

*17 *USC* §506(e): Any person who knowingly makes a false representation of a material fact in the application for copyright registration provided for by section 409, or in any written statement filed in connection with the application, shall be fined not more than $2,500.

Form SE–Full   Rev: 11/2006   Print: 11/2006   Printed on recycled paper   U.S. Government Printing Office: 2006-xxx-xxx/xx.xxx

Form RE

Detach and read these instructions before completing this form.
Make sure all applicable spaces have been filled in before you return this form.

How to Register a Renewal Claim

First: Read the information on this page and make sure you know the answers to two questions:

1 What is the renewal filing period in your case?

2 Who can claim the renewal?

Second: Read through the instructions for filling out Form RE. Before completing the form, make sure that the copyright is now eligible for renewal, that you are authorized to file a renewal claim, and that you have all needed information about the copyright.

Third: Complete all applicable spaces on Form RE, following the line-by-line instructions. Use typewriter or print in black ink.

Fourth: Detach this sheet and send your completed Form RE to: *Library of Congress, Copyright Office, 101 Independence Avenue SE, Washington, DC 20559-6000.* Unless you have a Copyright Office deposit account, your application must be accompanied by a check or money order payable to *Register of Copyrights.* Do not send copies, phonorecords, or supporting documents with your renewal application unless specifically requested to do so by the Copyright Office.

What Is Renewal of Copyright?

For works copyrighted before January 1, 1978, the copyright law provides a first term of copyright protection lasting 28 years followed by a second term of protection known as the renewal term. However, these works were required to be renewed within strict time limits to obtain a second term of copyright protection. If copyright was originally secured before January 1, 1964, and was not renewed at the proper time, copyright protection expired permanently at the end of the 28th year of the first term and could not be renewed.

  Public Law 102-307, enacted on June 26, 1992, amended the copyright law with respect to works copyrighted between January 1, 1964, and December 31, 1977, to secure *automatically* the second term of copyright and to make renewal registration optional. The renewal term automatically vests in the party entitled to claim renewal on December 31 of the 28th year of the first term.

  Public Law 105-298, enacted on October 27, 1998, extended the renewal term an additional 20 years for all works still under copyright, whether in their first term or renewal term at the time the law became effective. The 1992 and 1998 amendments do not retroactively restore copyright to U.S. works that are in the public domain. For information concerning the restoration of copyright in certain foreign works under the 1994 Uruguay Round Agreements Act, request Circular 38b, *Highlights of Copyright Amendments Contained in the Uruguay Round Agreements Act.*

Some Basic Points About Renewal

1 A work is eligible for renewal registration at the beginning of the 28th year of the first term of copyright.

2 There is no requirement to make a renewal filing ito extend the original 28-year copyright term to the full term of 95 years; however, there are benefits from making a renewal registration during the 28th year of the original term. For more information, request Circular 15, *Renewal of Copyright.*

3 Only certain persons who fall into specific categories named in the law can claim renewal.

4 For works originally copyrighted on or after January 1, 1978, the copyright law has eliminated all renewal requirements and established a single copyright term and different methods for computing the duration of a copyright. For further information, request Circular 15a, *Duration of Copyright.*

Renewal Filing Period

The amended copyright statute provides that, to register a renewal copyright, the renewal application and fee must be received in the Copyright Office within the last (28th) calendar year before the expiration of the original term of copyright or at any time during the renewed and extended term of 67 years.

  To determine the filing period for renewal in your case:

1 First, find out the date of original copyright for the work. In the case of works originally registered in unpublished form, the date of copyright is the date of registration; for published works, copyright begins on the date of first publication.

2 Then add 28 years to the year the work was originally copyrighted.

Your answer will be the calendar year during which the copyright will become eligible for renewal. Example: A work originally copyrighted on April 19, 1975, was eligible for renewal in the calendar year 2003.

  To renew a copyright during the original copyright term, the renewal application and fee *must* be received in the Copyright Office within 1 year prior to the expiration of the original copyright. All terms of the original copyright run through the end of the 28th calendar year making the period for renewal registration during the original term from December 31st of the 27th year of the copyright through December 31st of the following year.

Who May Claim Renewal

Renewal copyright may be claimed only by those persons specified in the law. Except in the case of four specific types of works, the law gives the right to claim renewal to the individual author of the work, regardless of who owned the copyright during the original term. If the author is dead, the statute gives the right to claim renewal to certain of the author's beneficiaries (widow and children, executors, or next of kin, depending on the circumstances). The present owner (proprietor) of the copyright is entitled to claim renewal only in four specified cases as explained in more detail on the reverse of this page.

For Further Information

To speak to a Copyright Office staff member, call (202) 707-3000 (TTY: (202) 707-6737). Recorded information is available 24 hours a day. Order forms and other publications from the address in space 8 or call the Forms and Publications Hotline at (202) 707-9100 24 hours a day. Access and download circulars, forms, and other information from the Copyright Office website at *www.copyright.gov.*

  Other helpful publications include 37CFR202.20, "Deposit of Copies and Phonorecords for Copyright Registration"; 37CFR202.21 "Deposit of Identifying Material Instead of Copies"; 37CFR202.17, "Renewals."

Please type or print neatly using black ink. The form is used to produce the certificate.

SPACE 1: Renewal Claimant(s)

  General Instructions: For this application to result in a valid renewal, space 1 must identify one or more of the persons who are entitled to renew the copyright under the statute. Give the full name and address of each claimant, with a statement of the basis of each claim, using the wording given in these instructions.

  For registration in the 28th year of the original copyright term, the renewal claimant is the individual(s) or entity who is entitled to claim renewal copyright on the date filed.

  For registration after the 28th year of the original copyright term, the renewal claimant is the individual(s) or entity who is entitled to claim renewal copyright on December 31st of the 28th year.

Persons Entitled to Renew:

A. The following persons may claim renewal in all types of works except those enumerated in Paragraph B below:

1 The author, if living. State the claim as: *the author*

2   The widow, widower, and/or children of the author, if the author is not living. State the claim as: *the widow (widower) of the author* (name of author) *and/or the child (children) of the deceased author* (name of author)

3   The author's executor(s), if the author left a will and if there is no surviving widow, widower, or child. State the claim as: *the executor(s) of the author* (name of author)

4   The next of kin of the author, if the author left no will and if there is no surviving widow, widower, or child. State the claim as: *the next of kin of the deceased author* (name of author) *there being no will.*

B   In the case of the following four types of works, the proprietor (owner of the copyright at the time of renewal registration) may claim renewal:

1   Posthumous work (a work published after the author's death as to which no copyright assignment or other contract for exploitation has occurred during the author's lifetime). State the claim as: *proprietor of copyright in a posthumous work.*

2   Periodical, cyclopedic, or other composite work. State the claim as: *proprietor of copyright in a composite work.*

3   "Work copyrighted by a corporate body otherwise than as assignee or licensee of the individual author." State the claim as: *proprietor of copyright in a work copyrighted by a corporate body otherwise than as assignee or licensee of the individual author.* This type of claim is considered appropriate in relatively few cases.

4   Work copyrighted by an employer for whom such work was made for hire. State the claim as: *proprietor of copyright in a work made for hire.*

SPACE 2: Work Renewed

General Instructions: This space is to identify the particular work being renewed. The information given here should agree with that appearing in the certificate of original registration.

Title: Give the full title of the work, together with any subtitles or descriptive wording included with the title in the original registration. In the case of a musical composition, give the specific instrumentation of the work.

Renewable Matter: Copyright in a new version of a previously published or copyrighted work such as an arrangement, translation, dramatization, compilation, or work republished with new matter covers only the additions, changes, or other new material appearing for the first time in that version. If this work was a new version, state in general the new matter upon which copyright was claimed.

Contribution to Periodical, Serial, or other Composite Work: Separate renewal registration is possible for a work published as a contribution to a periodical, serial, or other composite work, whether the contribution was copyrighted independently or as part of the larger work in which it appeared. Each contribution published in a separate issue ordinarily requires a separate renewal registration. However, the law provides an alternative, permitting groups of periodical contributions by the same individual author to be combined under a single renewal application and fee in certain cases.

If this renewal application covers a single contribution, give all the requested information in space 2. If you are seeking to renew a group of contributions, include a reference such as "See space 5" in space 2 and give the requested information about all the contributions in space 5.

SPACE 3: Author(s)

General Instructions: The copyright secured in a new version of a work is independent of any copyright protection in material published earlier. The only "authors" of a new version are those who contributed copyrightable matter to it. Thus, for renewal purposes, the person who wrote the original version on which the new work is based cannot be regarded as an "author" of the new version, unless that person also contributed to the new matter.

Authors of Renewable Matter: Give the full names of all living or deceased authors who contributed copyrightable matter to this particular version of the work. If any authors are deceased, give the complete date of death (month, day, and year).

SPACE 4: Facts of Original Registration

General Instructions: Each item in space 4 should agree with the information appearing in the original registration for the work. If the work being renewed is a single contribution to a periodical or composite work that was not separately registered, give information about the particular issue in which the contribution appeared. You may leave this space blank if you are completing space 5.

Original Registration Number: Give the full registration number, which appears in the upper right hand corner of the front of the certificate of registration.

Original Copyright Claimant: Give the name in which ownership of the copyright was claimed in the original registration.

Date of Publication or Registration: Give only one date. If the original registration gave a publication date, it should be transcribed here; otherwise the registration was for an unpublished work, and the date of registration should be given. See Note below.

SPACE 5: Group Renewals

General Instructions: A renewal registration using a single application and fee can be made for a group of works if *all* the following statutory conditions are met: (1) all the works were written by the same author, who is named in space 3 and who is or was an individual (not an employer for hire); (2) all the works were first published as contributions to periodicals (including newspapers) and were copyrighted on their first publication either through separate copyright notice and registration or by virtue of a general copyright notice in the periodical issue as a whole; (3) the renewal claimant or claimants and the basis of claim or claims, as stated in space 1, are the same for all the works; (4) the renewal application and fee are received not less than 27 years after the 31st day of December of the calendar year in which all the works were first published (See following note); and (5) the renewal application identifies each work separately, including the periodical containing it and the date of first publication.

Note: During the 28th year of the original term and during the extended 67-year renewal term, renewal registration may be made for a single work or a group of works without having made an original registration. This option requires filing a renewal application Form RE accompanied by a Form RE Addendum, a copy of the work as first published or appropriate identifying material in accordance with the requirements of 37 *CFR* 202.17, and the filing fee.

Time Limits for Group Renewals: To be renewed as a group, all the contributions must have been first published during the same calendar year. For example, suppose six contributions by the same author were published on April 1, 1968; July 1, 1968; November 1, 1968; February 1, 1969; July 1, 1969; and March 1, 1970. The three 1968 copyrights can be combined and renewed at any time during 1996, and the two 1969 copyrights can be renewed as a group during 1997, but the 1970 copyright must be renewed by itself in 1998.

Identification of Each Work: Give all the requested information for each contribution. The registration number should be that for the contribution itself if it was separately registered, and the registration number for the periodical issue if it was not.

SPACES 6, 7, 8: Deposit Account (Fee), Correspondence, Return Address

Deposit Account (Fee): If you maintain a deposit account in the Copyright Office, identify it in space 6. Otherwise, leave the space blank and send the fee for Form RE *and* the fee for Form RE Addendum with your application and deposit.

Correspondence: Include the name, address, area code, telephone number, fax number, and email address of the person to be consulted if correspondence about this application becomes necessary.

Certification (Space 7): The renewal application is not acceptable unless it bears the date and the handwritten signature of the renewal claimant or the duly authorized agent of the renewal claimant.

Address for Return of Certificate (Space 8): The address box must be completed legibly since the certificate will be returned in a window envelope.

Copyright Office fees are subject to change. For current fees, check the Copyright Office website at *www.copyright.gov*, write the Copyright Office, or call (202) 707-3000.

Form RE
For Renewal of a Work
UNITED STATES COPYRIGHT OFFICE

REGISTRATION NUMBER

EFFECTIVE DATE OF RENEWAL REGISTRATION

| Month | Day | Year |

For best results, fill in the form on-screen and then print it.

DO NOT WRITE ABOVE THIS LINE. IF YOU NEED MORE SPACE, USE A SEPARATE CONTINUATION SHEET (FORM RE/CON).

1 **RENEWAL CLAIMANT(S), ADDRESS(ES), AND STATEMENT OF CLAIM ▼** (See Instructions)

a
Name ....
Address ....
Claiming as ....
(Use appropriate statement from instructions)

b
Name ....
Address ....
Claiming as ....

c
Name ....
Address ....
Claiming as ....

2 **TITLE OF WORK IN WHICH RENEWAL IS CLAIMED ▼**

RENEWABLE MATTER ▼ If any author is deceased, give the complete date of death (month, day, and year).

PUBLICATION AS A CONTRIBUTION If this work was published as a contribution to a periodical, serial, or other composite work, give information about the collective work in which the contribution appeared.   **Title of Collective Work ▼**

If published in a periodical or serial, give: **Volume ▼**   **Number ▼**   **Issue Date ▼**

3 **AUTHOR(S) OF RENEWABLE MATTER ▼** (If any author is deceased, give month, day, and year of death.)

Name: _____   Date of death: _____
Name: _____   Date of death: _____
Name: _____   Date of death: _____

4 **ORIGINAL REGISTRATION NUMBER ▼**   **ORIGINAL COPYRIGHT CLAIMANT ▼**

ORIGINAL DATE OF COPYRIGHT

If the original registration for this work was made in published form, give:
DATE OF PUBLICATION: _____
(Month)   (Day)   (Year)

OR

If the original registration for this work was made in unpublished form, give:
DATE OF REGISTRATION: _____
(Month)   (Day)   (Year)

MORE ON BACK ➤ • Complete all applicable spaces (numbers 5–8) on the reverse side of this page.
• See detailed instructions.   • Sign the form at space 7.

DO NOT WRITE HERE

Page 1 of _____ pages

RENEWAL APPLICATION RECEIVED	FORM RE
CORRESPONDENCE ❑ YES	
EXAMINED BY	FOR
CHECKED BY	COPYRIGHT OFFICE
FUNDS RECEIVED	USE ONLY

DO NOT WRITE ABOVE THIS LINE. IF YOU NEED MORE SPACE, USE A SEPARATE CONTINUATION SHEET (FORM RE/CON).

RENEWAL FOR GROUP OF WORKS BY SAME AUTHOR: To make a single registration for a group of works by the same individual author published as contributions to periodicals (see instructions), give full information about each contribution. If more space is needed, request continuation sheet (Form RE/CON).

5

a
Title of Contribution: ....
Title of Periodical: .... Vol: .... No: .... Issue Date:.........
Date of Publication: .... Registration Number: ....
(Month)   (Day)   (Year)

b
Title of Contribution: ....
Title of Periodical: .... Vol: .... No: .... Issue Date:.........
Date of Publication: .... Registration Number: ....
(Month)   (Day)   (Year)

c
Title of Contribution: ....
Title of Periodical: .... Vol: .... No: .... Issue Date:.........
Date of Publication: .... Registration Number: ....
(Month)   (Day)   (Year)

d
Title of Contribution: ....
Title of Periodical: .... Vol: .... No: .... Issue Date:.........
Date of Publication: .... Registration Number: ....
(Month)   (Day)   (Year)

DEPOSIT ACCOUNT: If the registration fee is to be charged to a deposit account established in the Copyright Office, give name and number of account.

Name _____

_____

Account Number _____

Area code and daytime telephone number ▶ _____   Fax number ▶ _____

6

CORRESPONDENCE: Give name and address to which correspondence about this application should be sent.

Name _____

Address _____
(Apt)

_____
(City)   (State)   (ZIP)

Email address ▶ _____

CERTIFICATION* I, the undersigned, hereby certify that I am the: (Check one)
❑ renewal claimant   ❑ duly authorized agent of _____
(Name of renewal claimant)
of the work identified in this application and that the statements made by me in this application are correct to the best of my knowledge.

Typed or printed name ▼   Date ▼

_____   _____

Handwritten signature (X) ▼

7

Certificate will be mailed in window envelope to this address:

Name ▼

Number/Street/Apt ▼

City/State/Zip ▼

YOU MUST:
• Complete all necessary spaces
• Sign your application in space 7
SEND ALL ELEMENTS IN THE SAME PACKAGE:
1. Application form
2. Nonrefundable filing fee in check or money order payable to *Register of Copyrights*
MAIL TO:
Library of Congress
Copyright Office
101 Independence Avenue SE
Washington, DC 20559-6000

8

*17 *USC* §506(e): Any person who knowingly makes a false representation of a material fact in the application for copyright registration provided for by section 409, or in any written statement filed in connection with the application, shall be fined not more than $2,500.

Form RE-Full   Rev: 07/2006   Print: 07/2006—xx.xxx   Printed on recycled paper   U.S. Government Printing Office: 2006-xx-xxx/xx.xxx

For best results, fill in the form on-screen and then print it.

Continuation Sheet
for Application Forms

 Form _____ /CON
UNITED STATES COPYRIGHT OFFICE

REGISTRATION NUMBER

PA	PAU	SE	SEG	SEU	SR	SRU	TX	TXU	VA	VAU

EFFECTIVE DATE OF REGISTRATION

_____

(Month)   (Day)   (Year)

CONTINUATION SHEET RECEIVED

_____

Page _____ of _____ pages

- This Continuation Sheet is used in conjunction with Forms CA, PA, SE, SR, TX, and VA only. Indicate which basic form you are continuing in the space in the upper right-hand corner.
- Try to fit the information called for into the spaces provided on the basic form.
- If you do not have enough space on the basic form, use this Continuation Sheet, and submit it with the basic form.
- If you submit this Continuation Sheet, clip (do not tape or staple) it to the basic form and fold the two together before submitting them.
- Space A of this sheet is intended to identify the basic application.
  Space B is a continuation of space 2 on the basic application.
  Space B is not applicable to Short Forms.
  Space C (on the reverse side of this sheet) is for the continuation of Spaces 1, 4, or 6 on the basic application or for the continuation of Space 1 on any of the three Short Forms PA, TX, or VA.

DO NOT WRITE ABOVE THIS LINE. FOR COPYRIGHT OFFICE USE ONLY

A
Identification
of
Application

IDENTIFICATION OF CONTINUATION SHEET: This sheet is a continuation of the application for copyright registration on the basic form submitted for the following work:
- TITLE: Give the title as given under the heading "Title of this Work" in space 1 of the basic form.

....

- NAME(S) AND ADDRESS(ES) OF COPYRIGHT CLAIMANT(S) : Give the name and address of at least one copyright claimant as given in space 4 of the basic form or space 2 of any of the Short Forms PA, TX, or VA.

B
Continuation
of Space 2

d

NAME OF AUTHOR ▼

DATES OF BIRTH AND DEATH
Year Born▼   Year Died▼

Was this contribution to the work a "work made for hire"?
❑ Yes
❑ No

AUTHOR'S NATIONALITY OR DOMICILE
Name of Country
OR { Citizen of ▶ _____
{ Domiciled in ▶ _____

WAS THIS AUTHOR'S CONTRIBUTION TO THE WORK
Anonymous? ❑ Yes ❑ No
Pseudonymous? ❑ Yes ❑ No

If the answer to either of these questions is "Yes," see detailed instructions.

NATURE OF AUTHORSHIP Briefly describe nature of the material created by the author in which copyright is claimed. ▼

e

NAME OF AUTHOR ▼

DATES OF BIRTH AND DEATH
Year Born▼   Year Died▼

Was this contribution to the work a "work made for hire"?
❑ Yes
❑ No

AUTHOR'S NATIONALITY OR DOMICILE
Name of Country
OR { Citizen of ▶ _____
{ Domiciled in ▶ _____

WAS THIS AUTHOR'S CONTRIBUTION TO THE WORK
Anonymous? ❑ Yes ❑ No
Pseudonymous? ❑ Yes ❑ No

If the answer to either of these questions is "Yes," see detailed instructions.

NATURE OF AUTHORSHIP Briefly describe nature of the material created by the author in which copyright is claimed. ▼

f

NAME OF AUTHOR ▼

DATES OF BIRTH AND DEATH
Year Born▼   Year Died▼

Was this contribution to the work a "work made for hire"?
❑ Yes
❑ No

AUTHOR'S NATIONALITY OR DOMICILE
Name of Country
OR { Citizen of ▶ _____
{ Domiciled in ▶ _____

WAS THIS AUTHOR'S CONTRIBUTION TO THE WORK
Anonymous? ❑ Yes ❑ No
Pseudonymous? ❑ Yes ❑ No

If the answer to either of these questions is "Yes," see detailed instructions.

NATURE OF AUTHORSHIP Briefly describe nature of the material created by the author in which copyright is claimed. ▼

Use the reverse side of this sheet if you need more space for continuation of spaces 1, 4, or 6 of the basic form or for the

CONTINUATION OF (Check which):   ❏ **Space 1**   ❏ **Space 4**   ❏ **Space 6**

C

**Continuation
of other
Spaces**

Certificate will be mailed in window envelope to this address:	Name ▼	YOU MUST:

Certificate will be mailed in window envelope to this address:

Name ▼

Number/Street/Apt ▼

City/State/Zip ▼

YOU MUST:
· Complete all necessary spaces
· Sign your application

**SEND ALL 3 ELEMENTS
IN THE SAME PACKAGE:**
1. Application form
2. Nonrefundable fee in check or
   money order payable to Register
   of Copyrights
3. Deposit Material

MAIL TO:
Library of Congress, Copyright Office
101 Independence Avenue SE
Washington, DC 20559-6000

D

Form CON   Rev: 07/2006   Print: 07/2007 — xx,000   Printed on recycled paper

U.S. Government Printing Office: 2006-xxx-xxx/60,xxx

Recommended Reading

Photographic Theory for the Motion Picture Cameraman
Russell Campbell, A.S. Barnes 1974

Film Directing Shot by Shot
Steven D. Katz, Michael Wiese Productions 1991

Practical Motion Picture Photography
Russell Campbell, A.S. Barnes, 1970

American Cinematographer Manual
Fred Detmers, ASC, 1986

The Technique of Special Effects Cinematography
Raymond Fielding, Focal Press, 1985

Motion Picture Camera and Lighting Equipment
David W. Samuelson, Focal Press, 1986

The Hollywood Guide to Film Budgeting and Script Breakdown
Danford Chamness, S.J. Brooks Co., 1986

Script Supervising and Film Continuity
Pat P. Miller, Focal Press, 1990

The Technique of Film Production
Steven Bernstein, Focal Press, 1988

Film Sense
Sergei Eisenstein, Harcourt Brace Jovanovich, 1942

Lessons with Eisenstein
Vladimir Nizhny, DeCapo Press Inc., 1979

On Film Editing
Edward Dmytryk, Focal Press, 1988

The Technique of Film Editing
Karel Reisz and Gavin Miller, Focal Press 1982

What's on the DVD?

When you put the DVD that came with this book in a standalone player, you will see a typical video DVD with multiple menus, options, and extra features. When you insert the DVD into your computer, you will have the option of navigating your way through the extra features using your web browser. Just click on index.html and you're good to go.

The Forms Library

Available from the browser interface, the forms in Appendix C are all replicated in Adobe PDF format. If you don't have Adobe Reader, just surf to www.adobe.com and install it.

Animated Backgrounds

These are royalty-free animated backgrounds created in particleIllusion 2.0 SE and rendered at 720x480. They range from 6-10 seconds in length and are in both MSAVI (.AVI) and QuickTime (.MOV) format. Compatible with Windows and OS X.

Free and Trial Software

With the help of some great software manufacturers, I've been able to put some cool tools in your hands. The DVD contains trial or free software that will help you do a variety of video and web tasks.

PARTICLEILLUSION 3.0

Thanks to Alan Lorence at wondertouch™ you can play with the latest release of particleIllusion! You can create explosions, starbursts, lens flares, smoke, water, and hundreds of other particle-based effects very quickly. There are few programs out there that you can have more fun with in the first five minutes after loading. It won't take you long to see what you can do to your video with this tool. Windows and OS X versions included.

I have also included a viewer for the particleIllusion emitter libraries. Trial versions of the new release 3.05 are on the accompanying DVD in both Mac and Windows format.

BRYCE 5.5 FULL VERSION

Special thanks go to Steve Gregerson at DAZ3D for permitting me to share the full version of Bryce 5.5 for both Mac and Windows users. Bryce is a great tool for creating some of the motion backgrounds that you will find on the DVD and our lip-sync video. You need waves, clouds, or outer space? This is the app for you! Be sure to surf over to the website for more 3D models and environments. DAZ3D has built one of the largest online 3D communities in the world. To make things sweeter still: If you surf to http://www. daz3d.com/i.x/shop/catmain/-/?cat=326 and type in discount code B6TENOFFMUSIC, you'll get 10 percent off upgrading to the full 6.0 version!

COFFEECUP WEB SUITE

I have been singing the praises of this company since my last book and nothing has changed. It is hard to find better value from a web software company. As an example, I bought their HTML editor back around version 2.0. It is now in version 9.0 and every time an upgrade was available, they would send me a notification and a link to the free upgrade. Once you buy one of their very reasonably priced products, upgrades are free forever. I would also like to note that I have paid for every product I've bought from them and there is no enticement from CoffeeCup for this glowing praise. (Sorry Mac users, this software is Windows only.)

CoffeeCup is also offering a discount to purchasers of this book! If you surf to coffeecup.com and purchase any product or suite of products, you will receive 20 percent off by entering the discount code of 226STS. Heartfelt thanks to the folks at CoffeeCup for making their web tools so accessible and affordable.

When I contacted software vendors to include trial versions, not all were responsive to the idea and some were downright snooty. To contrast, here's what CoffeeCup would like to share with you on this DVD:

Free HTML Editor 8.0
I like to call this the "Little Big Editor." The application's small footprint on your hard drive belies the power within. There are a number of great widgets and Java scriptlets to play with. It integrates with CoffeeCup's Free FTP nicely too. For the price, and even more, there is nothing close.

Trial HTML Editor 9.0
This is a trial version of the new 9.0 release with a number of significant updates and features.

Free FTP 3.0
This is a full-featured drag-and-drop FTP client You get a nag screen at the end but it's a great and easy-to-use web tool.

Trial Flash Photo Gallery 5.0
One of the most common ways to protect your web photos is by creating a Flash animation, because visitors can't just right-click

and download the image. The Photo Gallery will allow you to set transitions, insert comments for each image and add your own sound track. Quick previews of your work without having to save the project is a handy feature too.

Trial Web Video Player 4.6

This application is similar to the Photo Gallery but encodes a Flash video that is displayed in nice web TV screen. You can experiment easily trying different video screen sizes with a quick preview.

Flash Firestarter 6.7

Flash Firestarter is an easy-to-use entry level program for creating your own Flash animations with animated titles and a great degree of image control. This software is a good introduction to Flash animation.

Free ZIP Wizard 2.5

Although the price of admission is again a nag screen when closing the program, this .ZIP compatible will let you compress and decompress files of varying formats. You can also archive your .ZIP as an executable (.exe) when compressing which is a real handy feature. It could also serve as a "poor man's" application installer.

MP3 Ripper and Burner 3.0

With a name like that, what more is to say?

TIP

Don't forget to drop by musicoffice.com for more trial software, animated backgrounds, and access to the book's user group with more tips, tricks, and feedback.

INDEX